The Saltwater Angler's Guide to Tampa Bay
and Southwest Florida

WILD FLORIDA

UNIVERSITY PRESS OF FLORIDA

Florida A&M University, Tallahassee
Florida Atlantic University, Boca Raton
Florida Gulf Coast University, Ft. Myers
Florida International University, Miami
Florida State University, Tallahassee
New College of Florida, Sarasota
University of Central Florida, Orlando
University of Florida, Gainesville
University of North Florida, Jacksonville
University of South Florida, Tampa
University of West Florida, Pensacola

The Saltwater Angler's Guide to Tampa Bay and Southwest Florida

TOMMY L. THOMPSON

University Press of Florida

Gainesville · Tallahassee · Tampa · Boca Raton

Pensacola · Orlando · Miami · Jacksonville · Ft. Myers · Sarasota

17 16 15 14 13 12   6 5 4 3 2 1

Library of Congress Cataloging-in-Publication Data
Thompson, Tommy L.
The saltwater angler's guide to Tampa Bay and Southwest Florida /
Tommy L. Thompson
p. cm.—(Wild Florida)
Includes bibliographical references and index.
ISBN 978-0-8130-4208-4 (alk. paper)—ISBN 0-8130-4208-9 (alk. paper)
    1. Saltwater fishing—Florida—Tampa Bay. 2. Saltwater fishing—Florida.
3. Tampa Bay (Fla.)—Guidebooks. 4. Florida—Guidebooks. I. O'Keefe, M.
Timothy. II. Title. III. Series: Wild Florida.
SH457.T55 2012
799.16—dc23   2012018878

The University Press of Florida is the scholarly publishing agency for the
State University System of Florida, comprising Florida A&M University,
Florida Atlantic University, Florida Gulf Coast University, Florida
International University, Florida State University, New College of Florida,
University of Central Florida, University of Florida, University of North
Florida, University of South Florida, and University of West Florida.

University Press of Florida
15 Northwest 15th Street
Gainesville, FL 32611-2079
http://www.upf.com

CONTENTS

Introduction

This book follows *The Saltwater Angler's Guide to Florida's Big Bend and Emerald Coast*, published in 2009. That volume covered Florida's Gulf Coast from Citrus County to the Florida-Alabama border, and this one details angler-friendly information from Hernando County south to the northern edges of the Everglades. I considered titling it *Chassahowitzka to Chokoloskee*, but spelling those place names would have made Internet searches for the book a chore. The current title is long enough. I hope you'll enjoy reading the entire book and not just the chapter that deals with your destination. As there are no real physical boundaries between the locations I've chosen to describe, a certain overlap of information is inevitable. Besides that, I've tried to make each location-chapter different from the others and not so cookbook-like. On our Gulf Coast, the fish are the same, only the tactics for catching them change. There are also two chapters dealing with universal fishing and boating knowledge that I hope you'll enjoy. In the first book, I made no promises that spouses or children with interests other than fishing would find its recommendations interesting and suggested the reader consult more general travel guides for non-fishing possibilities. No angler complained about the lack of tourist-trap listings, so I'm happy to follow the same model for this book. That explained, if you're a visitor, or just a resident needing some practical fishing information, please read on.

Anglers have special needs. We eat, we sleep, and we fish. If you're like me, fishing comes first, but after a "hard" day on the water, it's nice to come back to a good meal and a nice bed. It's also nice to start the day in strange or seldom-fished territory with good advance information as to where to launch your boat, where to buy fuel and supplies, and where and how to start fishing. This book is about those details, but unlike the first book, this one covers a much more populated area and much more shoreline. Therefore I've not listed all the amenities in some locations—just the ones recommended to me by trusted sources, usually anglers or local guides, or personally visited by me.

A brief explanation of the conventions used in the book will be helpful. First, I use "Gulf" to simplify any reference to the Gulf of Mexico. There are plenty of bays, harbors, and inlets located within the geographic scope of this guide—but only one Gulf. There is no "ocean" on the west side of Florida. Second, I assume that everyone can navigate Florida's west coast by car. A basic knowledge of US19, US41, and I-75 will help. Authoritative map resources exist, and a visit to your local American Automobile Association office or bookstore will provide you the necessary tools to get to a jumping-off spot from the big roads. Don't overlook owning a copy of DeLorme's *Florida Atlas & Gazetteer*, a terrific resource showing roads and trails in very fine detail. Third, although this is a fishing guide and GPS coordinates are listed for some fishing spots (in latitude/longitude format), space for elaborate, detailed fishing maps is limited. I have checked my GPS coordinates and they are reasonably "right," but I don't guarantee that they are absolutely accurate. Use them with some care, as you would any navigational directions. U.S. Government NOAA charts, available from most marine suppliers, are essential. Even if you carry a sophisticated GPS unit loaded with digital charts, you'll still need paper charts to plan your trip. Good commercial interpretations of NOAA charts are also available and take accurate navigation a step further. I highly recommend the charts created by Waterproof Charts, Inc. (www.waterproofcharts.com) and those sold by *Florida Sportsman* magazine (www.floridasportsman.com). These excellent selections of charts are produced at various levels of coverage and detail. Waterproof Charts kindly furnished the chart illustrations in this guide. If you're really interested in very fine detail and bottom relief, you'll want to take a look at the Aegis Topographic Maps of Tampa Bay and Charlotte Harbor (www.aegismarine.com). Maptech's *Chartkit* books are complete sets of enhanced NOAA charts. They offer a wealth of information to anglers and boaters not found on the basic NOAA charts, such as GPS grids and a companion CD that allows viewing your charts on a computer. Their Region 8 set, *Florida West Coast and the Keys*, is a great investment for any Gulf angler, particularly if you plan to fish from a boat. Another good, albeit slightly outdated, reference is the series of Boater's Guides, produced by the Florida Department of Environmental Protection's Marine Research Institute. These valuable (and free) guides are available for many areas of the Gulf Coast at many tackle shops and visitors' bureaus.

I don't aim to go into tremendous detail about each species of fish found in the Gulf, but I will mention some species-specific information and mention their food value. While many sport fishermen, including myself, practice catch-and-release fishing, those planning to keep and eat seafood should be aware of safe storage practices. The basic rule is to ice your catch quickly and always use more ice than you think you need.

Finally, I will make references to fishing tackle and fishing-related gear. I recommend things I've personally used or that come highly recommended by guides and serious anglers I know, and, if it's an obscure or hard-to-get item, I'll mention where it can be found. Part 2 of this guide, Practical Matters, will help you understand certain general terms and techniques mentioned in first nine chapters.

Though this guidebook is based on my knowledge of and

visits to all the locations covered, time can be a factor. Hurricanes, unusually cold winters, pollution, and real-estate developers have, in recent years, affected Florida and the fishing here. Not only do marinas and boat ramps disappear in the wake of "progress," but entire navigable channels may be redirected and grass flats scrubbed clean by Mother Nature. Local, state, and federal authorities frequently update rules and regulations, too. This guide's information is regularly updated at its award-winning companion website, www.saltwater anglersguide.com. Please check it before you head out, just to be sure. I'd love your input, too. Let me know if you've had a good or bad experience, noticed a change in a location, or simply discovered the "best lure ever made." My contact information is on the website.

I've fished Florida's Gulf Coast all my life, and despite the proclamation, "It's called fishing, not catching," by many anglers after a slow day on the water, I'm still disappointed coming home after catching nothing. Certainly, factors like equipment failure and weather are insurmountable and make for some forgettable days. It is hoped this guide will provide enough local knowledge to get you started fishing a new location—and make catching a reality.

PART 1

The Destinations

1

Tampa Bay and Southwest Florida

It's hard to imagine that, not long ago, Hillsborough and Pinellas counties were perceived as separated geographically by Tampa Bay—and even then, the Gulf communities of Pinellas and many west-facing Tampa Bay towns in Hillsborough were separated by some amount of raw, rural land. Now, a vast urban megalopolis, it's all called the Tampa Bay Area, its growth northward and eastward slowed only by economics, and its sprawl to the south and west contained by the waters of the Gulf of Mexico and Tampa Bay. That urban growth, fueled by an influx of neo-pioneers seeking favorable tax rates, freedom from cold weather, and the prospect of 99-cent breakfasts, has now moved across the bay and is steadily closing the rural gaps between communities such as Sarasota, Punta Gorda, Fort Myers, and Naples. Soon there may be no identifiable places along our Gulf Coast with names like Weeki Wachee, Ozona, Gulfport, Safety Harbor, Ruskin, Palmetto, Osprey, Cortez, Placida, Pineland, Estero, or Chokoloskee. It will all be just "one big place."

What seems to distinguish the area covered by this book is the fact that, with the exception of the lonely upper Hernando County coastline and Collier County's Ten Thousand Islands, the entire area is protected by barrier islands with white, sandy beaches. Those islands, the bays, harbors, and inlets behind them, and the passes between them are what make the fishing so good here. Also, "dredge and fill" development did, in fact, build homes where there once was water. Everyone's desire to have a waterfront home produced thousands of miles of residential canals with sea walls and lighted docks—every one a potential fishing "hot spot." And not only inshore fishing possibilities should get the attention of anglers; offshore fish species in this shallower end of the Gulf of Mexico are plentiful and easy to reach for the casual angler, while the depths of the Florida Middle Grounds are slightly more than 100 miles away.

Fishing options vary all along this coastline. Offshore anglers don't really have as many options as their inshore and near shore brethren, but there's still plenty to keep them busy. If you fish offshore, you will need to go aboard a boat—your craft, or a chartered or "head" boat. A boat's not necessary for successful inshore angling. Excellent bridge fishing, pier fishing, and wade-fishing opportunities abound all up and down the Gulf.

The "locations" chapters that follow address things of interest to anglers in particular. If you have a boat, there's information on marinas, launching, fueling, and basic navigation. If you need bait, food, or lodging, you'll find information about where to find those too. If you don't know where to go to catch a few fish, I pass along some inshore and offshore suggestions with GPS coordinates. And, if you want to fish a location with no "overhead," a list of eager, professional fishing guides is included.

2

The Upper Suncoast—
Hernando and Pasco Counties

Upper Suncoast, or lower Big Bend? This area's a tough one to categorize. Structurally, the stretch of Pasco and Hernando County Gulf coastline north of the Anclote River at Tarpon Springs is much like that found up along Florida's Big Bend. But hindsight being 20/20, I for some reason ended my Big Bend and Emerald Coast fishing book at the Citrus/Hernando county line. So, I'll start this book there, where the other left off—and I'll also offer no explanation as to why one book starts mid-peninsula and heads north—and the other south. Just bear with me.

Many visitors to this area say that "civilization" either begins or ends in Hernando and Pasco counties. That depends on whether you're heading north or south. The sunny Gulf beaches and barrier islands to the south have, for the last century, attracted tourists and the infrastructure (cities, big hotels, deepwater marinas) that follows them. To the north, there are lonesome rivers with names like Pithlachascotee, Weeki Wachee, and Chassahowitzka. Each of these, with its adjacent creeks and rock and shell bars, are places that make this region of the state special to anglers.

With no barrier islands along this shallow stretch of coast, expect to find rock piles well offshore, and some inshore too. Geologically, islands may form in this area someday in the distant future, but only if the unlikely happens and sea levels fall.

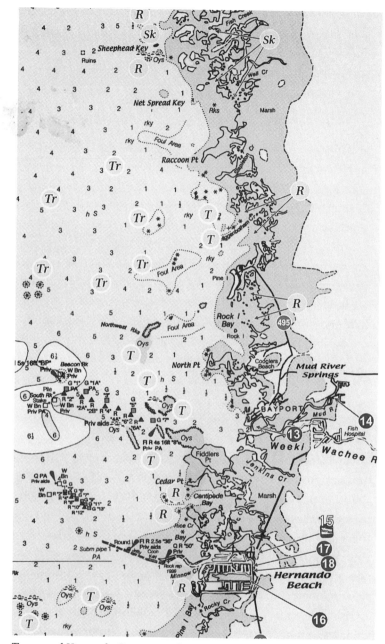

The rugged Hernando County coastline is shallow, providing excellent inshore angling for seatrout, redfish, snook, and tarpon. (Map courtesy of Waterproof Charts, Inc.)

There are two small rivers along this coastline, the Weeki Wachee and the Pithlachascotee (known locally as the "Cootie"). The Weeki Wachee River is spring fed and flows from a major spring well upriver. (Its headwater spring is the site of a major tourist attraction where, I'm proud to say, my cousin Bonnie was once a "mermaid"!) The Weeki Wachee River joins the Mud River, and a marked channel runs offshore from the settlement at Bayport, emptying into relatively shallow depths. The "Cootie" River is tidal and short, beginning quietly in "downtown" Port Richey; like the Weeki Wachee River, it does not have a deepwater channel to the Gulf. There are also several other channels leading ashore along this stretch of Gulf coast. Many are privately maintained and lead to residential developments and fishing villages at Hernando Beach, Aripeka, Hudson, and Gulf Harbor. When boating here, pay particular attention to areas on your charts marked, "scattered rocks"—they're not kidding.

Inshore and Near Shore Fishing

Anglers should understand the concept of "flats" and "flats fishing" and what it means at different locations in Florida. From southern Pasco County north into the Big Bend, the term "flats" means the one big stretch of lush grass beds extending from the shore into the depths of the Gulf of Mexico. In other parts of the state, flats can mean shallow sandy bars, some smaller than basketball courts and scattered throughout bays and sounds. But here, sandy patches are the exception to that rule, and not usually called "flats," but "potholes." There are a few exceptions, such as the Oklahoma Flats, the name given to a sandy area north of Bayport by Keys tarpon anglers visiting the area. It looked like (and fished like) a Keys "flat" to them. Confused? Simply remember that if you're going "flats fishing" on the Upper Suncoast, you'll likely be over miles of grass rather than sand.

If you're not going fishing on the inshore "flats," you're probably going fishing in the backwaters. Here, that means you'll be a stone's throw from a shoreline—in a creek mouth, over a pile of shallow limestone rocks, or next to an oyster bar. While it has miles of grass flats, the Upper Suncoast also has miles of ragged coastline.

The inshore species you're most likely to encounter (and hopefully catch) along the Hernando and Pasco county coastlines are spotted seatrout and redfish. Tactics for these fish change seasonally, but both species can be caught year-round. Snook are also found in the backwaters, but this stretch of coast has always been considered the northern Gulf range of that species. The extremely cold winter of 2010 did significant damage to the snook population statewide, and it's likely their numbers have decreased here. In addition to trout, reds, and snook, you'll find some flounder around creek mouths and Spanish mackerel over deeper grass. Tarpon and cobia roam here too, and are species for which any inshore angler should be prepared by keeping a big spinning rod handy—just in case. Finally, one of the most unique features of this area is the great number of big rocks in water as shallow as 8 feet. These rocks are just like those found far offshore in other parts of the Gulf, yet well within sight of land. Not only are these rocks hazards to boaters, they're also excellent places for inshore anglers to catch fish that are usually considered offshore species.

As an example of this area's coastal structure, launching your boat from the ramp at the County Park in Bayport and heading out the Bayport Channel toward the Gulf doesn't necessarily mean that you're going to end up in deep water. Don't let yourself be fooled by thinking that marker #1 is in water that's necessarily "safe," even though it's more than 3 miles offshore. The marked channel here, like those at other Upper Suncoast ports, is simply a convenience to get you outside most of the really bad stuff. Much of the inshore water in Hernando and Pasco counties is treacherous and shallow, and 5- or 6-foot depths are considered "deep."

Regarding spotted seatrout, you don't have to be a rocket scientist to catch them, but you do need to learn a few basic things about this popular species. First, trout are ambush feeders, attacking their prey from hiding places such as rocks, bars, and the edges of small white sand holes on the flats. Second, when the water's warm they seek cooler depths (on deep grass flats), and conversely, when the water's cold they seek warmer depths (in river channels, canals, and creek holes). They just want to be comfy. And finally, trout are omnivorous, eating just about anything that looks tasty, including their own young (MirrOlure's "TT" lure designation means "tiny trout"!).

Finding trout on the flats here is a simple matter of finding the depth at which they're holding on a particular day. Expect the best flats fishing in this "deeper" water to begin in March and end in November. Drifting an area like that north of the Bayport Channel marker #5 and offering your favorite trout bait is a good way to prospect for them. Similar areas that hold trout can also be found south of Hernando Beach (near N28 29.086 W82 43.807), southwest of Aripeka (near N28 25.159 W82 46.342), and other 3- to 6-foot-deep flats between the Hudson Channel and the "Cootie" River Channel. When you find a few trout, assume you've found their comfort zone and throw out a marker buoy or hit the "Man Overboard" button on your GPS. I prefer a buoy so I do not have to run back and forth, front of boat to back, to look at my GPS. Visual bearings are much easier. As the tide rises or falls, you'll notice that the fish move along with whatever depth they feel comfortable. While live shrimp, fished under popping corks at grasstop depths, are certainly the most popular trout bait on these flats, anglers have excellent results with soft jerk baits (D.O.A. C.A.L.s) and hard-bodied plugs (MirrOlure Catch 2000s). In water less than about 3 feet deep, hungry trout will also readily attack topwater lures like my favorite, Heddon's Super Spook, Jr. With artificials, use lighter colors in clear water and darker colors if the water's muddy or stained.

At Bayport, in addition to the flat mentioned above (near N28 33.668 W82 41.419), you'll find some excellent trout fishing all the way to the mouth of the Chassahowitzka River, about 8 miles north. Along this stretch of water, you will see rocks, and I encourage you to fish near them, especially if you see pods of bait nearby. Despite the shallow depths, in the spring and summer there are likely to be cobia, Spanish mackerel, and even grouper around the bigger rocks. Another good area for seatrout here is the grassy bank between the Bayport Channel and the mouth of the Hernando Beach Channel, just a mile or so to the south.

Cold weather and cold water push seatrout toward shore and into the relative comfort and safety of creeks and rivers. Leaving from Bayport, head to the backwaters behind Saddle Key (N28 39.029 W82 39.895) or Higgenbotham Creek (N28 34.897 W82 38.792) or to the shallow bay behind Pine Island (approx. N28 33.938 W82 39.067). You may have to wait out a tide cycle to get out and get back to the boat ramp, but expect to find trout in the deeper holes on extremely low winter tides. If you have a boat with a deeper draft, you'll find any number of deep holes in the Mud, Weeki Wachee, or Pithlachascotee rivers that hold trout, sometimes in brackish or fresh water. The residential canals at Hudson and Gulf harbors are also good wintertime trout hot spots. Be sure to fish near dock pilings too, as they tend to warm up in the sunlight and attract fish. In any of these spots, slow-moving MirrOlures (Paul Brown Corkys or TTs), live shrimp, and cut mullet are good choices of bait. Patience and a thermos of hot coffee help too!

If the weather's making a transition from warm to cool, or vice versa, as in spring and fall, expect trout to be close to creek and river mouths, and not necessarily in them. Look for rocky bars and shoreline points that heat up with the sun's radiation

The backwaters near Bayport are home to spring and fall redfish.

during a morning low tide and attract baitfish and trout as the tide rises in the afternoon. It's likely that you'll catch your "personal best" seatrout under these conditions.

Slot-sized redfish, another popular inshore species, normally don't wander quite as far off the shoreline as trout. This species attains sexual maturity when it reaches lengths greater than 30 inches, when it moves offshore to spawn. Large "bull" reds are often caught by offshore anglers in the spring and fall as these big fish school up.

Inshore, reds are less likely to be found over grass, unless they're traveling from one rocky or structured area to another. Along the Pasco and Hernando coastline, look for oyster bars or other areas of rough bottom that hold crustaceans like shrimp and crabs, the favorite foods of redfish. That's where the reds, with their downward-oriented mouths, will be, searching every nook and cranny for something to eat.

Your opportunities for catching redfish are dependent on both tide and water temperature. Like other cold-blooded species, redfish enjoy temperate water, but they are more tolerant of heat and cold than trout and tend to stay "closer to home" throughout the year. They also like moving water. If there's no bait washing by, they will move on. Keep your eyes peeled for mullet and you'll likely find redfish, not necessarily eating the mullet, but foraging under them for churned-up crabs and shrimp.

The shoreline at Pasco and Hernando counties is an excellent example of redfish habitat. Tidal creeks, bays, and even dredged-out residential canals offer the structure that reds enjoy. And the fact that the coastline here is not totally developed by humans means that angler pressure on fish is light. You'll find more development to the south, near the "big cities" of Hudson and New Port Richey, and for the most part this is a pretty lonesome place.

There are literally hundreds of places to look for redfish here—*look* being the operative word. While some anglers drift and fish the shallow flats for seatrout, others enjoy the "hunt" for redfish. Of course, there are times, usually short periods in the spring and fall, when you'll find those big schools of reds on the move, but for the most part, and for most of the year, expect to find them hanging out and feeding, in twos or threes, over or near structure. The habits of redfish make them excellent targets for anglers who appreciate and enjoy stalking fish and sight fishing with light tackle or flies.

It's safe to say that if you enter the Gulf from any "civilized" place on the Upper Suncoast and travel a mile or two to the north or south, you'll find yourself somewhere redfish are likely to be.

At Bayport, fish around North Point (N28 33.003 W82 39.935) or farther north along the shoreline between Higgenbotham Creek (N28 34.993 W82 39.160) and Raccoon Point (approx. N28 35.453 W82 39.781). Another area to try is across the mouth of Centipede Bay (N28 30.879 W82 40.139) between Bayport and Hernando Beach.

From Hernando Beach, you might consider exploring the coastline south from the mouth of Rocky Creek (N28 29.209 W82 40.139) to the rocks north of Dinner Point (N28 27.923 W82 41.061).

If you leave the Aripeka area, your best bet for reds is to head south toward the mouth of Fillman Bayou (approx. N28 24.520 W82 42.110) and fish the rocky areas there. And if your boat's draft allows, head into Fillman Bayou and look there.

The stretch of coastline between Hudson and New Port Richey has several excellent creek mouths and bays that deserve attention. Exploring the entire shore between Bayonet Point (N28 19.524 W82 43.951) and the rocks outside Green Key (N28 15.266 W82 45.601) is not a one-day exercise, but it might make an interesting week of fishing for an ambitious inshore angler.

To the south of New Port Richey and Gulf Harbors, the shoreline smooths a bit as it, along with Anclote Key, creates

Try wading creek mouths for a change of pace.

the funnel that forms the upper part of St. Joseph Sound. If you're looking for reds, don't neglect the Sand Bay area (approx. N28 12.733 W82 46.179) just north of Baileys Bluff.

* * *

While spotted seatrout and redfish are certainly the most sought-after fish on the Upper Suncoast, I'd be remiss to leave out some of the other species you're likely to encounter. I'm a firm believer in catch-and-release (or catch, photograph, and release) but there are three species found here that almost always end up on my dinner table: flounder, Spanish mackerel, and pompano. All three are abundant here and often taken while fishing for trout and reds. Flounder usually stay close to shore, sometimes in bays or creeks, and eat slow-moving baits that wash over their heads. Spanish mackerel travel mostly in schools during the fall, mostly over deep grass flats (except when they come to very shallow water to eat anglers' topwater plugs!). Pompano, usually found skipping along beaches elsewhere in the state, are still caught along deep, sandy patches, mostly by anglers tossing jigs sweetened with a piece of cut shrimp.

From a sport-fishing point of view, it's hard to dismiss the importance of snook, cobia, and tarpon here. Snook are likely found in some of the same places you find redfish, but count on them to be hiding under snags or mangrove outcroppings. They are the ultimate ambush feeders and will attack almost any baits; however, the lush grass flats off the coast here provide them plenty of "white bait," and many won't move from cover to eat anything else. Snook are also more sensitive to cold than redfish and move to protected waters (up creeks and rivers and into bays) as soon as they begin to feel a chill in the water. In cold water, they can be sluggish and often turn their noses up at most baits, but if the water's warm, there's nothing quite like a big snook hitting a topwater plug off a rocky shore or mangrove-covered point.

Cobia are often mistaken for sharks by anglers who sight them swimming along the flats. There's no comparison of the two species at the dinner table. Known as "crab eaters" by many anglers, this hard-fighting species can be found cruising open areas, or hiding near channel markers and the large rocks found along the Upper Suncoast. Spring and fall bring cobia migrations, and I urge anglers to always keep a big spinning outfit "locked and loaded" with a brightly colored jig or Hogy eel imitation should one swim by the boat.

As tarpon migrate north in the spring, they typically pass between Anclote Key and the mainland, heading to what many anglers consider their spawning grounds off Chassahowitzka and Homosassa. There's plenty of bait available on the flats, however, and these migrating fish don't stop eating just because they're traveling. Expect to see large schools of big tarpon all along the Upper Suncoast, many willing to eat a live pinfish, a realistic plug, or a fly.

Consider yourself lucky if you have a chance to fish the Upper Suncoast. Despite the busy inland areas of Hernando and Pasco counties, the coastal areas are not so crowded and almost desolate compared with the waters all the way to Marco Island, well more than 100 miles south. "Progress" is likely on the way, so enjoy this area—while you can!

Offshore Fishing

In spite of the fact that it's a long run to deep water from the Upper Suncoast, there's some productive fishing for offshore species here. If you travel 15 miles west from Bayport, Hernando Beach, or Hudson, you're still likely to be in water that's not quite 20 feet deep. But considering that there are lots of pretty big rocks in these coastal shallows, don't think you won't come home with a grouper or king mackerel, even if you don't go too far offshore.

Some of the most productive shallow rocks on Florida's west coast are found between 10 and 15 miles west-northwest of Bayport and Hernando Beach. In many cases, these are not necessarily groups of rocks, but single structures. There's a good "garden" of rock piles at about N28 34.935 W82 58.473 and another at about N28 37.553 W82 48.805. Fair warning, though—don't just head offshore and run to these numbers, as there are likely more rocky spots on your course, and many have engine-eating tops just below the surface. Another area of deeper structure is about 35 miles to the northwest of Bayport in about 50 feet of water. Several rocky outcrops here hold large numbers of grouper throughout the year and act as attractants for bait and pelagic species like mackerel in the summer and fall. Head toward N28 47.016 W83 20.692, and when you get there, work your way east, trolling deep plugs until you find active bottom. And don't complain that you're closer to Cedar Key than home. That's why you bought that big, fast boat!

Getting Around

The Florida Gulf coastline known as the "Upper Suncoast" is oriented north/south and paralleled by US19, SR589 (the Suncoast Parkway), and I-75. At the north end of Hernando County, US98 runs east from the settlement at Chassahowitzka. Farther down, in the middle of Hernando County and into Pasco County, the main east/west connectors are SR50, 52, and 54. Any of these roads will get you toward or away from the coast. None are "country roads" but busy commercial highways. Knowing a few connectors like County Roads 550, 597, and 595 at Bayport, Hernando Beach, and Aripeka will keep you away from civilization—for a while. And Strauber Highway and Baileys Bluff Road will get you a good look at the Pasco County Gulf coast.

Where to Stay

The simple truth is that you'll never be very far from a hotel or motel on a major highway when you're fishing in this area. A broad range of lodging options is available here. Visitors should remember that lodging rates are often based on whether it's summer or winter. "Tourist season" means greater demand and higher prices. Here I list a few choices that might be of interest to visiting anglers.

BAYPORT

Bayport Inn, (352) 596-1088. Located at the intersection of Pine Island Dr and CR550. A small motel is adjacent to the restaurant.

Fish camps, like Mary's on the Mud River at Bayport, are a rarity in these days of chain motels.

HERNANDO BEACH

Hernando Beach Motel and Condos, (352) 596-2527, 4291 Shoal Line Blvd.

Where to Eat

Personally, I shy away from fast-food restaurants and have listed some places I think have a bit more character. Some are likely to serve the Fisherman's Four—the basic food groups of sugar, salt, grease, and alcohol. Enjoy these places, but if you get a hankerin' for a donut or a quiche, you'll likely find one up on Highway 19, just a mile or so from the Gulf.

BAYPORT

Bayport Inn, (352) 596-1088. Located at intersection of Pine Island Dr. and CR550. Excellent food, outside deck.

WEEKI WACHEE

Weekend at Bernie's, (352) 596-3300. CR597 at Weeki Wachee River, adjacent to Rogers Park.

HERNANDO BEACH

Tropical Storm Beach Bar and Grill, (352) 592-2420, Calienta Street.

Bare Bones Fish & Steakhouse, (352) 597-9403, 3192 Shoal Line Blvd.

PORT RICHEY

Seaside Inn, (727) 846-1112, 5330 Treadway Dr.

Crab Shack, (727) 847-6300. North shore of Pithlachascotee River. Tiki bar, kayak rentals, bait and tackle

Marinas, Marine Supplies and Service, Bait and Tackle Shops, and Launching Ramps

BAYPORT

Bayport ramp, end of CR550 (Cortez Blvd). Excellent paved ramp with plenty of parking and good access to the Gulf and backwaters. There's a fishing pier, too.

Dixie Lee Bait & Tackle, (352) 596-5151, CR550, Bayport.

Bait and Tackle

Precision Tackle, (352) 686-9520, 3284 US19, Spring Hill. Excellent selection of inshore and offshore tackle, kayak and Gheenoe rigging and sales, tackle repairs.

Rogers Park boat ramp, on Weeki Wachee River at CR597 (Shoal Line Blvd).

Weeki Wachee Marina, (352) 596-2852. Weeki Wachee River at CR597, supplies, tackle, canoe and kayak rentals. Friendly folks, deserving of your business.

HERNANDO BEACH

Jenkins Creek Park, between the Weeki Wachee River and Hernando Beach on CR597. Single paved ramp (free), good parking, fishing pier.

Sterling Marina, (352) 596-4010, 4211 Shoal Line Blvd. Fuel, wet slips, boat lift, pontoon boat rentals.

Hernando Beach Bait & Tackle, adjacent to Sterling Marina. Live and frozen bait, tackle, ice.

HUDSON

Port Hudson Marina, (727) 869-1840, Crabtrap Court. Full-service marina, fuel, tackle, restaurant, dockage, marine service, easy access to Gulf of Mexico. www.porthudson.com

Cooper's Shrimp Shack, (727) 868-8736, 14633 Old Dixie Hwy. Live and frozen bait, tackle, ice. Open 7 days.

Sully's Beach and Bait Store, (727) 697-3923, Clark Street, Hudson Beach. Ice, tackle, live and frozen bait.

Hudson Beach Marina, (727) 863-9093, Clark Street, Hudson Beach, next to Strickland Park boat ramp. Fuel, bait, ice, wet and dry boat storage.

Strickland Park boat ramp, Clark Street, Hudson Beach. Single paved ramp (free), good parking.

Skeleton Key Marina, (727) 868-3411, Clark Street, Hudson Beach. Fuel, wet and dry boat storage, pump-out station.

Florida Fisherman, (727) 868-6405, 12052 US19, Hudson. Live and frozen bait, tackle, rod and reel repair.

ARIPEKA

Norfleet Fish Camp, (352) 666-2900, 221 Osowaw Blvd.

PORT RICHEY

Sunset Landing Marina, (727) 849-5092, 5115 Sunset Blvd on the Pithlachascotee River. Full services, fuel, bait and tackle, boat rentals, storage, repairs. www.sunsetlandingmarinas.com

American Marina, (727) 842-4065, 4800 Ebbtide Lane. Full services.

Nick's Park boat ramp, on north side of Pithlachascotee River. Free single ramp with bad drop-off, next door to Hooter's Restaurant.

Cotee River Bait and Tackle, (727) 841-7664, on north side of Pithlachascotee River. Tackle, boat and kayak rentals, frozen bait.

Salonika Bait & Tackle, (727) 849-6377, 6211 Ridge Rd. Tackle, live and frozen bait, rod and reel repair, snacks, ice.

ANCLOTE/HOLIDAY

West Marine, (727) 846-1903, 3346 US19, Holiday. Marine supplies and tackle.

Fisherman's World, (727) 942-8944, 1500 US19, Holiday. Excellent selection of inshore and offshore tackle, known far and wide for excellent fishing reel repairs. www.fishingtacklegiant.com

Anclote River Park boat ramp, 1119 Baileys Bluff Road, in county park. Watch out for the crosscurrent at this boat ramp!

Hart's 1-Stop, (727) 938-5364, 1234 Baileys Bluff Road. Bait, tackle, gas, food, ice.

One Stop Bait and Tackle, (727) 842-5610, 4726 Trouble Creek Rd. Bait, tackle, ice, boat storage.

Local Fishing Guides

Capt. Rick Rodriguez, Hernando Beach, (727) 992-9494. Offshore and inshore. www.gulfgrouper.com

Capt. Curt Romanowski, New Port Richey, (727) 919-1221. Inshore. www.flbwc.com

Capt. Sam Medigovich, Hernando Beach, (352) 303-2718. Offshore. www.rock-boss.com

S & I Fishing Charters, Inc. (coastal booking service), (813) 973-7132. www.reelfishy.com

Capts. Mark and Luke Magnuson, Hernando Beach, (352) 596-5151. Inshore.

Capt. Joe Meadows, Paladin Fishing Charters, Port Richey, (888) 227-8563. Offshore.

Capt. Dan Malzone, Hudson, (813) 833-0312. Inshore light tackle and fly-fishing, tarpon specialist.

Capt. Frank Bourgeois, Hernando and Pasco counties, (352) 666-6234. Inshore.

Capt. Rick Burns, Hernando Beach and Bayport, (352) 201-6111. Inshore. www.reelburns.com

*   *   *

Many inshore guides from the coastal communities here are familiar with the waters in both Hernando and Pasco counties, and most offshore waters here are familiar places to guides and charter captains from Tarpon Springs and the Pinellas peninsula. Please consult the listings for those areas, if necessary. Also the website of the Florida Guides Association (www.florida-guides.com) has a complete listing of USCG licensed and insured fishing guides.

Before You Leave Home

Be sure to check this guide's companion website, www.saltwateranglersguide.com, for updates to local information.

3

Tarpon Springs and North Pinellas County

The busy Anclote River is the de facto boundary along Florida's Gulf Coast marking the beginning of the long stretches of barrier islands and beaches that reach southward to the Ten Thousand Islands. It's also the first full-service port south of Steinhatchee, 80-plus miles north on the Big Bend, and the location where the Intracoastal Waterway (ICW) ends its offshore transit from Carrabelle.

The Anclote River begins well above US19 at Tarpon Springs and flows slowly toward the Gulf. The river is mostly tidal, but there are several minor springs that feed the upper river. Spring Bayou, in the middle of town, no longer has an active spring but is connected to Lake Tarpon, and at times of heavy rain a slight boil can be seen. Two other major bayous, Kreamer and Whitcomb, are mostly surrounded by residential development. The river is navigable for larger boats upstream to the Sponge Exchange, a historic site with some excellent eateries, many the result of the city's Greek heritage. There are several full-service marinas located along the river.

Located about two miles offshore of the river's mouth, Anclote Key is uninhabited, a rare state for a Gulf island these days, and provides shelter toward shore for anglers and boaters plying St. Joseph Sound. In dramatic contrast, just a few miles to the south, there's Clearwater Beach and adjacent Sand Key, both highly developed. Three Rooker Bar (now an island),

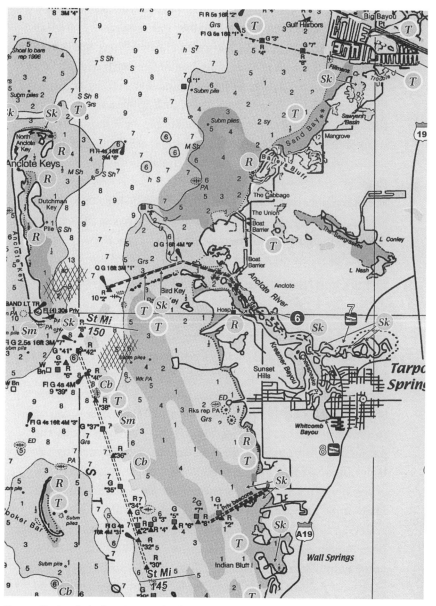

Tarpon Springs's Anclote Key marks the northern end of Gulf beaches in Pinellas County. (Map courtesy of Waterproof Charts, Inc.)

Honeymoon Island, and Caladesi Island form the middle of this range of Gulf-front barriers. To the south of Tarpon Springs, boat ramps and marinas at Palm Harbor, Ozona, Dunedin, and Clearwater all offer excellent access and services for anglers to St. Joseph Sound and Clearwater Harbor. There are passes between all the Gulf islands here, but anglers with larger boats should be aware that the Anclote channel is shallow and subject to shoaling and consider a direct Gulf approach to the ICW through Clearwater Pass. Smaller boats can easily navigate the sound but should be aware of changing shallows in the minor passes, like Hurricane Pass, and of the spoil lumps alongside the ICW.

If it's civilization you need as part of your fishing trip, this is where it really begins. Expect to find anything your little heart desires—including some outstanding angling action.

Inshore and Near Shore Fishing

The inshore fishery here is a three-part story. There's St. Joseph Sound, the body of water lying inside the barrier islands, the beaches, and the Anclote River. Expect to find the three most popular species of sport fish, spotted seatrout, snook, and redfish, in the sound or near the shore. Depending on water temperatures, the inland bayous and Anclote River can be productive for those species too. On the "outside" or in the passes, you'll probably have a better chance of catching pelagics (like Spanish mackerel and bluefish), snook, and cobia, especially when the water's temperate. Tarpon and cobia are likely to be anywhere in the area, tripletail will hang around crab trap floats and channel markers, and sheepshead can be found under docks and over structure. I'm not saying that fish will pay any attention to my "rules," but I encourage you to plan your fishing outing accordingly. Of course, there are no real boundaries, but there's a decided difference in these waters: in the sound and river, the water's clean, but not clear; outside, on the beachfronts, it's usually as clear as gin.

In warmer months, you're going to find seatrout over and along the edges of grass flats. Large stretches of grass reach from Baileys Bluff, just north of the Anclote River, to Clearwater Pass. Above Hurricane Pass, the grassy areas are mostly on the east side of St. Joseph Sound. Between Hurricane Pass and Clearwater Pass, they're mostly on the west side. Expect the good trout "bite" on the flats to begin in March and last until the water temperatures get into the high 80s, usually in August. Then, expect the fish to search out deeper, cooler areas along channels, in passes, and along the deep edges of ICW spoil islands.

If you launch your boat near Tarpon Springs, you've several flats to choose from for some good trout fishing.

My first choice, especially on early summer mornings, is along the east side of Anclote Key. A nice shallow grass flat runs from the north end of Dutchman Key (N28 12.107 W82 50.842), behind the island (between it and Anclote Key) to marker #7X, also called the "Blind Stake" (N28 10.168 W82 50.179) at the southern end of Anclote Key. It's known to hold some nice trout and can be a fun destination if you enjoy fishing topwater lures. Popping corks rigged above light hooks, baited with live shrimp, white bait, or pinfish work well here, too. This flat is very shallow, so plan your trip there on a rising tide, then fish until the high water and let the tide take you toward the east to the point where the flats drop off into deep water. As the tide washes bait off that "ledge," expect seatrout (and other species, including redfish, flounder, tarpon, snook, and cobia) to be waiting—and ready to eat your jig or slow-sinking lure.

Another good trout flat is northeast of the Anclote River mouth, off Baileys Bluff (N28 12.526 W82 46.898) and Sand Bay (N28 12.984 W82 46.114). Learning to navigate the swash

The edges of the Klosterman Channel provide good cover for snook, redfish, and seatrout.

channel that runs northwest from marker #9 will make this an easy trip from the main Anclote River channel. And while here, don't be tempted to get too close to the mouth of the power plant's hot water discharge (N28 11.512 W82 47.325) in warmer months. It's only when the temperature gradient between the ambient Gulf water and the discharge water is greater than about 15 degrees that the discharge area attracts fish (other than catfish and ladyfish!).

My third trout flat of choice when fishing from Tarpon Springs (or from the Sutherland Bayou ramp at Palm Harbor) runs from the few remaining "dredge lumps" on the south side of the Anclote River channel, to the Honeymoon Island Causeway (CR586). This 8-mile stretch is a good bet, but pay special attention to the areas in front of Fred Howard Park (approx. N28 09.221 W82 48.551), the edges of the Klosterman Channel (intersecting the ICW at marker #31), and the back sides of the ICW spoil islands and bars. On lower tides, fish channelside and toss topwater lures parallel to the drop-offs.

As you travel farther south, or depart from Dunedin or Clearwater, you'll find that the southern end of St. Joseph Sound is narrower and a bit more protected than the northern part. That's good—and bad. There's less impact from weather here, but boat traffic and wakes can be constant, especially in the ICW and on weekends. The eastern shoreline here has some grassy areas that almost reach shore, and these hold trout, especially on higher tides. On the west side, the big grass flat along the back side of Caladesi Island and the smaller ones aside the Pope Channel (which begins just near ICW marker #16 and runs north toward what used to be Dunedin Pass, now closed up by shoaling) are worth checking out and fishing with either free-lined white bait or shrimp.

In colder months, seatrout spend a good bit of their time in deep water, usually in river channels, up creeks, or in residential canals where they are protected from cold. The most successful technique I've found for catching a limit of cold-water trout is to use a lure, like Paul Brown's Corky Mullet, that sinks

Bridges like this one in Clearwater attract many fish species.

Tarpon Springs's Spring Bayou is scenic and protected from bad weather.

slowly. Don't make "summertime" retrieves—these fish don't want to work that hard. In the case of the St. Joseph Sound area, where low temperatures are not that extreme, trout will head to deeper water at night or on cloudy days, only to return to the relative warmth of the deeper flats when the sun comes out. There, a quicker retrieve will work, but usually for just a few hours in the afternoon. Other places to look for trout when it's cold are around residential docks (where the pilings warm up) and bridges, and near some of the small constant-temperature springs in the area. You'll find plenty of docks up canals on either side of the Sound, especially at Clearwater and Palm Harbor. Here, try fishing a free-lined 3-inch D.O.A. shrimp (light colored if the water's clear; dark if it's stained or muddy). Springs are sometimes more difficult to find and their flow can vary. A good example is "the spring" at Spring Bayou, in downtown Tarpon Springs. What seems to be a spring here may only be an underground connection to freshwater Lake Tarpon, miles to the east. It seems to "boil" only when there's been lots of rain over the lake, unlike artesian springs that pump constantly. No matter its status as a working spring, Spring Bayou gets warmish in winter and attracts good numbers of trout on winter days.

Other areas at which you may find a bit of warmer water on cold days are the stretch of Anclote River in front of Port Tarpon Marina and the flats at Indian Bluff (approx. N28 06.453 W82 47.167), near Wall Springs. And finally, don't forget the "Holy Grail" of wintertime fishing holes—the hot water discharge at Progress Energy's Anclote Power Plant, just north of the river mouth. The trout fishing's great here when it's nasty outside, but expect a crowd!

Wading the hot-water discharge at the Anclote Power Plant is a good bet on a winter day.

I was born in Tarpon Springs (into two non-Greek families who lived on Spring Bayou) and remember the times before a net ban on inshore fishing in the area increased redfish populations. Everyone in my Mom's and Dad's families always told tales of great catches of redfish (and other species) that obviously disappeared before I arrived on the scene. Of course, we did catch some reds, but nothing like now. My brother's "big childhood catch" was a 5-pounder, and I remember my cousins catching lots of what we now call "rat reds" off their dock in Kreamer Bayou. Now, things have changed, and the reds here are plentiful, healthy, and eager to eat just about any bait you put in front of them. They eat topwater lures, shallow-running plugs, jigs, D.O.A. shrimp, live shrimp, and fiddler crabs, and they never seem to be able to resist a chunk of cut mullet or ladyfish.

Redfish are around this area all year, but for the most part they don't really school up except in the late spring and throughout the fall. Most of that "schooling" is based on the fact that sexually mature reds (usually 30–32 inches in length) gather up to swim offshore to spawn. The rest of the year, expect to find small groups of reds hanging around structure close to shore like oyster bars, docks, and mangrove bushes.

In temperate water, from about 60 degrees upward, look for reds along the northeastern shore of Anclote Key, between Dutchman Key and North Key. Other good spots near the mouth of the Anclote River are the mangrove shorelines of the many islands on the south side of the channel, including Brady Island and Rabbit Key. Don't forget the islands in the river either. All these shorelines offer excellent access for wade or paddlecraft anglers. From the river's mouth back to Chesapeake Point, there are a number of mangrove islands on the south side of the river. Fish the sloughs between them or over the oyster bars along their shores.

To the south of Tarpon Springs, you'll likely find reds (and snook and trout) on the Sound side of Honeymoon Island and

Caladesi Island. Both of these areas are fed fresh Gulf water and bait—Caladesi by Hurricane Pass, Honeymoon by the deep slough between it and Three Rooker Bar.

In winter, expect reds to head for the same protected waters that attract trout. Deep river holes, creek channels, and dredged residential canals attract them. The colder it is, the deeper they'll go. Any of the residential canals along the eastern shore of St. Joseph Sound have potential, as do the docks. Remember that dock pilings get warmer than the water when the sun's shining—something that attracts fish. Also, when the oyster bars and dark bottoms in the bays and rivers warm up, they attract bait—and reds soon follow, usually on winter afternoons. Kreamer Bayou, mentioned above, is still a good winter redfish spot, and its oyster bars and mangrove islands are healthier than ever. It can be a hard place to navigate, so take it slow entering the bayou from Chesapeake Point. Cool weather reds can also be found in the hot water discharge of the Anclote Power Plant, but it's usually a circus there. For some not-too-crowded wintertime redfishing, I recommend you head up the Anclote River beyond the Sponge Exchange and fish near the mangrove islands between Alt. US19 and US19, to the east. That's where my brother caught his 5-pound whopper—in 1956!

Snook and tarpon are the two species of inshore fish that really get my juices flowing. They are great fighters, exquisite jumpers, and finicky eaters. Snook are likely more plentiful here, as they don't migrate, but both species deserve as much time as you can devote to catching them. They're at the "top of the sport."

You're likely to find snook almost anywhere along this stretch of coast, but there are a few spots that attract local anglers. The north tip of Anclote Key (N28 12.779 W82 50.615) has probably produced more snook than any other local spot, and to many, it marks the "serious" northern latitude where snook are safe from extremely cold winters (except during the

Snook—and anglers—are attracted to the northern end of Anclote Key.

freeze of 2010, when many died here and far to the south). Throughout most of their range, snook attack all sorts of bait, live or artificial, but here, the snook have an almost Pavlovian response to live white bait, turning their noses up at anything else. If you go snookin' at the north end of Anclote Key (which has a nice beach suited to wade-fishing), be sure to stop and cast-net some scaled sardines on the way. (The flat to the north of marker #7X, the Blind Stake, is a good place to look for white bait schools.) Snook are also found in some of the other local passes, especially along the edges of Hurricane Pass, and along the front of Anclote Key, Honeymoon Island, and Three Rooker Bar. Less picky snook, willing to eat topwater lures or D.O.A. shrimp and C.A.L. jigs, are to be had all over St. Joseph

Sound around creek mouths, small bays, and, of course, along any mangrove-lined shore. They're also found in the power plant's hot-water discharge on cold days and, like redfish, are likely to search comfort up the Anclote River, above the Alt. US19 bridge, or along the south shore of Whitcomb Bayou.

On their spring migration, usually from April through June, tarpon do something interesting as they head up the Gulf beaches here. They make a turn into St. Joseph Sound and circle the area before making their final run north toward Chassahowitzka and Homosassa. This looping movement makes for pretty good possibilities that you'll find tarpon either in the Sound or along the beaches. The eastern sides of any of the islands, especially Honeymoon and Caladesi, have excellent potential. And don't neglect the flat south of Anclote River marker #4 that stretches all the way past Fred Howard Park. This is a special place, where Harold LeMaster, the inventor of the MirrOlure, spent many hours testing his lures on tarpon. Lots of Florida anglers wish we'd had the opportunity to go with Mr. LeMaster on some of those trips, and many of us still fish MirrOlure 52M18 plugs for the "Silver King."

Trout, reds, snook, and tarpon aren't the only species of fish to be found along the northern Pinellas County Gulf coast. If you fish for reds or trout and let your bait—whether plug, live shrimp, or jig—get too close to the bottom, you'll probably catch a flounder. The same thing goes for pompano, found mostly near passes or in the surf off beaches. Target them with one of Doc's Goofy Jigs—or just be glad you got one "as a bonus." On any day, spring to fall, you'll likely see schools of Spanish mackerel crashing into schools of white bait, with gulls wheeling overhead, in passes or along the beaches. Troll the edges of these bait pods with Flowering Floreos, or simply toss a Clark Caster spoon into the melee. If you have the patience to throw a live or artificial shrimp at each and every crab trap float and channel marker you pass, you're likely to take a nice tripletail home for the dinner table.

Big Pier 60 on Clearwater Beach is an excellent place to spend the day fishing—or sightseeing.

Then there are the sheepshead, found here around docks and oyster bars. They are notorious bait-stealers, difficult to clean, but wonderful to eat. And at just about any place you fish here, whether inside the Sound or on the beaches, you're likely to have a cobia swim up to your boat. If you're not targeting the species specifically in passes or along deep cuts in the flats south of the Anclote River, be sure to have a big spinning outfit rigged with an eel imitation—just in case one shows up.

Finally, a quick word about fishing piers. There's a small one at the Anclote Park near the power plant hot-water discharge and a big one on Clearwater Beach. Fish the power plant pier when the weather's cold, and plan a trip to Pier 60, on the beach at the western end of SR60 (Gulf-to-Bay Blvd), in warmer weather. All species of game fish are caught here, usually attracted by the structure and its lights.

Needless to say, there are enough inshore fishing opportunities here that you might stay busy catching fish for a lifetime. And many have!

Offshore Fishing

As the wide and shallow shelf of inshore waters that starts well north of here narrows toward Pinellas County's Gulf shoreline, the deeper water comes closer to shore. A 40-mile run to 60 feet of water from Hudson becomes a 25-mile run from Tarpon Springs, giving offshore anglers an easier trip to the depths that offer more productive searches for reef fish like grouper and amberjack. And the depths of 100-plus feet that are popular with snapper anglers are closer to shore too—at least in relative terms.

I suspect that if you asked 100 offshore anglers from this area their favorite offshore species, the answer from 90 of them would be "grouper." This species is certainly the most prevalent reef species, either in the "gag" or "red" subset. Grouper are not only good to eat, but also relatively easy to find and to catch off the Pinellas County coastline.

Finding grouper is a matter of understanding where a grouper lives and eats. Gags, for the most part, like structure. In fact, they have an uncanny ability to back themselves into a crack between two rocks that looks entirely too small for them, and wait for a passing meal. Structure of interest to gags doesn't have to be big, either. Two rocks the size of wastebaskets can easily hide a 10-pound fish. Gags will move away from structure to feed, especially when smaller baitfish can't hold place in the current and wash downtide. Finding gags away from rock piles will increase your chances of getting the fish to the surface before it has a chance to "rock you up." Red grouper also like rocks but seem just as happy out on the big prairies of "live bottom" made up of crunchy bottom, sea fans, and sponges. If you befriend a sponge diver in Tarpon Springs, he might give you some really good red grouper numbers!

There are many ways to find rocks or live bottom that hold grouper. My Dad's generation used a sounding lead packed with Octagon soap to explore the bottom. The process was to toss out the lead and see what came up stuck to the soap. We've come a long way in the last 50 years, and now most serious anglers have sonar units capable of seeing very fine detail (and fish) in depths well below 100 feet. They also have Global Positioning Satellite (GPS) units that allow them to return to a specific location with uncanny accuracy. Plenty of public GPS coordinates are available (please see the list in the back of this book), but consider them a starting point. When running to what you think might be a good reef, be sure to slow down in the general area and use your sonar bottom finder to look for what might become your own "secret honey-hole." While lots of manmade reefs are solitary, naturally occurring ones are likely part of a set.

Grouper, like many other offshore species, feed when they want to, and they seem to have "lockjaw" when the tide's extreme, either slack or running very hard. They are more likely to eat live baits (pinfish and white bait are good choices, and readily available) than cut bait (squid, cut mullet, frozen Boston mackerel, or sardines). Many anglers believe that "starting the bite" with cut bait helps, but I've seen no proof, and I think that live bait is always better, if rigged properly. A simple slip-sinker rig—made up of 80–100-pound-test fluorocarbon leader material, an egg sinker, and a big circle hook—is hard to beat. Use a sinker that's appropriate for the depth you're fishing, and don't be afraid to pack a good supply of 4-, 6-, and 8-ouncers for the trip. Re-rig as needed, depending on current and depth. If your bait doesn't stay where the fish are, you won't do much catching. Grouper also eat artificial baits. Vertical deep jigging with heavy feathers or shiny jigs is a good method, provided the fish are in an eating frame of mind. But trolling big-lipped plugs just above the bottom will sometimes get even the most stubborn grouper to eat. Pull those at 4–5 knots and always pull two or more at a time. If you get a hit on one rod, let one of your crew land that fish while another "jigs" the second rod. The bigger, slower grouper that couldn't get to the first bait may catch up to the second.

If you have the ability to fish in water that's really, really deep, like that in the Florida Middle Grounds, you're likely to come home with some grouper that are scarcer (and much better table fare) than those found closer to shore. These long boat rides, many times aboard "head" or "party" boats, often produce scamp, speckled hind (Kitty Mitchells), and snowy grouper.

If you're grouper or snapper fishing in the Gulf, you're more than likely going to find your fair share of amberjack. AJs, or "reef donkeys," so named for their steady pulling ability, usually hover above structure and are masters at intercepting live baits or shiny jigs headed down toward grouper. They're not bad to eat but can often be annoying if you're trying to catch other species. If anyone of your crew complains about a lack of action, simply put him onto a big AJ and watch the whining end.

Snapper fishing usually means getting to deeper water, but you also have a good chance of catching big grouper while you're in those depths of more than 100 feet. You're more likely to catch red or vermillion snapper (beeliners) if you head due west or northwest of Pinellas County. Big gray (mangrove or "mango") or lane snappers are more common in the deep waters to the southwest. Finding a ledge with your sonar unit seems the best method of finding most varieties of snappers. While there may be grouper under the ledge, snapper will hold above, sometimes well into the water column. All these species are easy to catch, especially if you use either live or frozen cigar minnows or live shrimp. D.O.A. Lures' 6-inch "nite glow" shrimp is an excellent artificial alternative to live bait. Reds and beeliners will bite during daylight hours, but mangos are best targeted at night.

King mackerel (kingfish) often migrate during spring and fall, often well within sight of land. But they're considered "offshore" species by some anglers based on the simple fact that it takes big tackle to land them. When they're close to shore, they can be trolled using big shiny spoons, brightly colored feathers, or live blue runners (hardtails). In deeper water, many are caught by anglers targeting grouper who set out free-lined live pinfish or blue runners over rock piles. And if you're offshore, in deep blue water more than 100 feet deep, you may want to speed up your trolling and hope to attract a wahoo, a relative of the kingfish that fights harder and is much tastier at the table.

Going offshore fishing on the Pinellas Gulf coast doesn't always mean you're going to come home with a limit of grouper, snapper, or king mackerel. Some days are just slow, and if the big fish aren't biting, you can usually lighten your tackle and catch some smaller but just-as-good-to-eat fish. Black sea bass, white snapper (red porgies), white grunts (Key West grunts or Florida snapper), and triggerfish are all smallish but have the ability to "save the day" on an offshore outing.

Getting Around

The Pinellas County coastline is oriented north/south and is paralleled by US19, SR589 (The Suncoast Parkway), and Interstate Highway 75. Just north of Tarpon Springs, Alternate US19 breaks away from US19 and heads southwest, becoming the closest highway to St. Joseph Sound and the Gulf of Mexico. County Road 76 runs west from Alt. US19, above the Anclote River, to the Anclote boat ramp and power plant discharge. Just south of the river, you'll find the small municipal marina on the edge of the historic Sponge Docks. In downtown Tarpon Springs, the main east/west street is Tarpon Avenue. Important east/west arteries that cross Alt. US19 to the south are 584A (to Palm Harbor), 584 (to Ozona), 586 (to Honeymoon Island State Park), 580 (to Dunedin), and 60 (to Clearwater Beach). Any of these roads will get you toward or away from the coast. None are "country roads"; these are busy commercial highways. Having a copy of DeLorme's *Florida Atlas & Gazetteer* in the car's not a bad thing—if you get into a traffic jam!

Where to Stay

There's no shortage of hotels and motels here; however, many are stuck on small pieces of valuable real estate, offering limited parking space for trailer rigs. Be sure to call ahead for reservations, especially during wintertime tourist season.

TARPON SPRINGS

Day's Inn, (800) 321-4062, 40050 US19 N. Not the best around, but the price is right.

Hampton Inn & Suites, (727) 945-7755, 39284 US19 N. A leading brand of quality, value-priced motels.

Holiday Inn Hotel & Suites, (877) 786-9480, 38724 US19 N. Convenient to Sutherland Bayou ramp and another safe bet.

Hickory Point RV Park, (727) 937-7357, 1181 Anclote Rd. On Anclote River, with dockage. Close to Anclote Park boat ramp. www.hickorypointmhp.com

CLEARWATER

Silver Sands Motel, (727) 442-9550, 415 Hamden Dr, Clearwater Beach Call ahead about trailer parking.

Hi-Seas Motel, (727) 446-6003, 455 S. Gulfview Blvd, Clearwater Beach. Comfortable and clean, with reasonable parking and rates.

Bay Queen Motel, (727) 441-3295, 1925 Edgewater Dr, Clearwater. Efficiencies available.

Beso Del Sol, (800) 331-2548, 1420 Bayshore Dr, Dunedin. Efficiencies and condo rentals. www.besodelsolresort.com

Holiday Inn Express, (727) 797-6300, 2580 Gulf-to-Bay Blvd (at US19), Clearwater. Predictable lodging at reasonable prices.

Belleview Biltmore Resort—just pulling your leg!

Where to Eat

The two meals that are usually of interest to anglers are breakfast and dinner. Take-aboard lunches are easily put together with a trip to the local Publix supermarket. Here, make a special effort to eat Greek cuisine at any of Tarpon Springs's excellent restaurants, and you'll find plenty of diners and fast-food joints along the roadside, many with early hours and breakfast specials.

*   *   *

Mr. Souvlaki, (727) 937-2795, 802 N. Pinellas Ave, Tarpon Springs. Excellent Greek fare. Don't miss my favorite, the Greek chow mein!

Mama Maria's, (727) 934-5678, 503 N. Pinellas Ave, Tarpon Springs. Authentic Greek food. Try the pastitso, the mousaka, or the keftedes—or all three.

Mykonos Restaurant, (727) 934-4306, 628 Dodecanese Blvd, Tarpon Springs. Authentic Greek food at the historic Sponge Docks.

Note: When in Greece, eat what the Greeks eat. In Tarpon Springs, do the same and "go Greek" at least once during your stay.

Rodie's Restaurant & Pancake House, (727) 937-9279, 1097 S. Pinellas Ave (Alt. US19), Tarpon Springs. Good breakfast and diner-style food.

Molly Goodhead's Raw Bar, (727) 786-6255, 400 Orange St, Ozona.

J.C. Cravers Bar and Grill, (727) 216-6423, 191 Orange St, Ozona. Good food and music.

Ozona Blue Grilling Company, (727) 789-4540, 125 Orange St, Palm Harbor. At Home Port Marina.

CLEARWATER

Lenny's Restaurant, (727) 799-0402, 21220 US19 N, Clearwater. Not Denny's, but Lenny's—and better! Breakfast and lunch only.

Marinas, Marine Supplies and Service, Bait and Tackle Shops, Fishing Piers, and Launching Ramps

TARPON SPRINGS

Port Tarpon Marina, (727) 937-2200, 531 Anclote Rd. Full service marina, fuel, dockage, bait and tackle, restaurant, wet slips, dry storage. www.porttarponmarina.com

Anclote Harbors Marina, (727) 934-7616, 523 Anclote Rd. Wet and dry storage, fuel, service.

Port Tarpon Marina is a full-service deepwater marina upriver in the Anclote River.

Anclote Village Marina, (727) 937-9737, 1029 Baileys Bluff Rd. Fuel, bait and tackle, boat storage, restaurant. www.anclote villagemarina.com

Belle Harbor Marina, (727) 943-8489, 307 Anclote Rd. Fuel, bait and tackle, boat rentals. Owned by Pinellas County Parks and Recreation.

Island Harbor Marina, (727) 784-3014, 123 Orange St, Palm Harbor. Dockage, easy access to St. Joseph Sound.

Home Port Marina, (727) 784-1443, 605 Orange St S, Palm Harbor. Dockage, boat storage, fuel, restaurant, tackle, frozen bait.

Sutherland Bayou boat ramp (Crystal Beach, south of Tarpon Springs). Single ramp, restrooms, $5 charge, good parking, shallow access to St. Joseph Sound.

The Anclote River boat ramp is well maintained, but watch out for the crosscurrent.

Anclote River Park boat ramp, 1119 Baileys Bluff Rd, in county park. 6 paved ramps, $5 fee, rest rooms, good parking. Watch out for the crosscurrent at this boat ramp!

Fisherman's World, (727) 942-8944, 1500 US19, Holiday, Excellent selection of inshore and offshore tackle, known far and wide for excellent fishing reel repairs. www.fishingtacklegiant.com

West Marine, (727) 846-1903, 3346 US19, Holiday. Marine supplies and tackle.

The Bait Bucket, (727) 937-1488, Alt. US19, at Anclote Road. Live and frozen bait, tackle, ice, open 7 days.

Masters Bait and Tackle, (727) 945-7191, 1810-C S. Pinellas Ave (Alt. US19). Live and frozen bait, tackle, repairs.

Speckled Trout Marina and Bait Shop, (727) 786-9566, 339 Bayshore Dr, Ozona. Bait, tackle, wet and dry boat storage, boat ramp ($10–$15).

One Stop Bait and Tackle, (727) 842-5610, 4726 Trouble Creek Rd, New Port Richey (just north of Tarpon Springs). Bait, tackle, ice, boat storage.

Anclote Gulf Park (at Progress Energy Anclote Power Plant), Baileys Bluff Rd. Fishing pier and kayak launch. Wade-fishing in discharge channel permitted.

CLEARWATER

The Complete Angler (main location), (727) 441-2248, 705 N. Ft. Harrison Ave (Alt. US19), Clearwater. Near downtown.

The Complete Angler-Express, (727) 239-7646, 290 Causeway Blvd, Dunedin. On causeway to Honeymoon Island. Bait and tackle, ice.

Tom's Tackle Shop, (727) 447-5247, 1625 N. Ft. Harrison Ave (Alt. US19), Clearwater. Complete line of tackle plus rod and reel parts and service.

Bonnie's Bait & Tackle, (727) 581-2292, 1754 Clearwater-Largo Rd. Good selection of tackle, live and frozen bait.

Big Pier 60, western terminus of SR60, Clearwater Beach. City-owned fishing pier with full bait and tackle shop. Rental equipment available.

Dunedin Fishing Center, (727) 738-5628, 2436 Bayshore Blvd (Alt. US19), Dunedin. At Curlew Creek, with good access to St. Joseph Sound.

West Marine, (727) 447-5320, 1721 Gulf-to-Bay Blvd. One of the bigger West Marine stores in the area.

Dunedin Municipal boat ramp, paved ramp with good parking at SR580 and Alt. US19. Easy access to Clearwater Harbor and southern St. Joseph Sound.

Seminole boat ramp, 198 Seminole St. 6 paved ramps, $6 launch fee (monthly and yearly rates, too), open 24 hours, in downtown Clearwater.

Belleair Causeway boat ramp, at eastern end of Belleair Causeway (CR686). 10 paved ramps, excellent parking, $6 fee, small fishing pier, good access to Clearwater Pass.

Local Fishing Guides

Viking Fleet, (727) 938-5300. Party boat fleet offering day and long-range trips, www.vikingfleet.com

Capt. David Rieumont, (727) 204-9723. Inshore. www.seascrapcharters.com

Capt. Wade Osborne, (813) 286-3474. Inshore. www.afishionado.com

Capt. Ellen White, (727) 389-5099. Inshore.

Capt. Brian Hart, (727) 224-2932. Inshore. www.floridatarponcharters.com

Capt. Dennis Wilson, (727) 940-5174. Offshore. www.cdwfishingcharters.com

Capt. Jay Masters, (727) 522-4301. Inshore and offshore. www.fatcatfishingcharters.net

Capt. Stewart Ames, (727) 421-5291. Inshore. www.tampa -fishing-charter.com

*   *   *

Most inshore guides from the coastal communities here, as well as some from Tampa, are familiar with all the waters in northern Pinellas County. And most offshore waters here are familiar places to guides and charter captains from all over the Pinellas peninsula. Please consult the listings for those areas, if necessary. Also, the website of the Florida Guides Association (www.florida-guides.com) has a complete listing of USCG licensed and insured fishing guides.

Before You Leave Home

Be sure to check this guide's companion website, www.salt wateranglersguide.com, for updates to local information.

4

St. Petersburg and the Pinellas Peninsula

If you're traveling southbound by boat, and on the outside of Pinellas County's Gulf beaches, the first thing you'll notice when you cross Clearwater Pass is that deeper water comes closer to shore the farther south you travel—and as an angler, you know that even though the bottom may be generally sandy and smooth, many offshore species are likely to wander closer to shore and to whatever structure, natural or artificial, is there. Where 30-foot depths are as many as 10 miles offshore of Tarpon Springs, expect to find deeper waters much closer off Johns Pass and even well into the mouth of Tampa Bay.

The Intracoastal Waterway (ICW) runs between the barrier islands and the mainland here, with only two navigable passes between Clearwater and the mouth of Tampa Bay. Johns Pass provides the major deepwater entry to upper Boca Ciega Bay, and Pass-A-Grille Channel allows entry about 6 miles to the south. Blind Pass, just south of Johns Pass, has a reputation for bad shoals and is sometimes dry. The deeper water of Bunces Pass, just north of Mullet Key (part of Ft. Desoto State Park), does not run through to the Gulf, but smaller boats can sometimes navigate its shallow mouth. If you're navigating south using the ICW, you'll be behind the beaches in protected waters until you're well into Tampa Bay, off Point Pinellas, the southernmost tip of St. Petersburg.

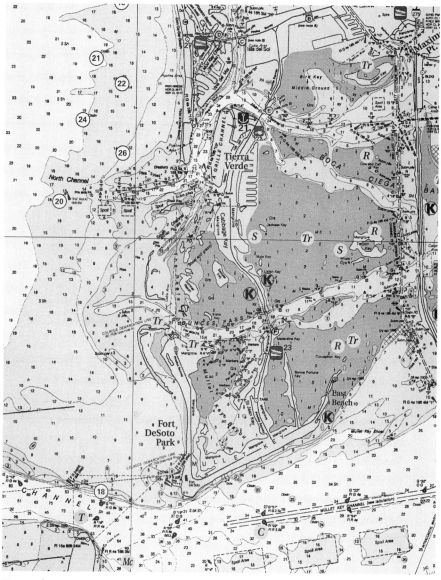

The southwesternmost tip of the Pinellas peninsula forms the northern edge of the mouth of Tampa Bay. (Map courtesy of Waterproof Charts, Inc.)

The new Sunshine Skyway spans the mouth of Tampa Bay. The remains of the old bridge attract many inshore and offshore fish species.

As you transit into Tampa Bay, whether through the ICW or via the Tampa Bay Ship Channel (under the center span of the Sunshine Skyway Bridge), you're entering one of Florida's largest bodies of protected water. While there's some great fishing on the outside of the Pinellas Gulf islands, don't neglect the bayside waters and those near the mouth of Tampa Bay. Mangrove-lined backwaters, small bays, coves, and flats abound, many with potential for incredible inshore catches. And expect some excellent fishing for reef species and even some pelagics in the bay's many deep shipping channels or at some inshore artificial reefs.

I spent my formative fishing years fishing near Point Pinellas. Then, in the 1950s and 1960s, water quality in and near Tampa Bay was not nearly as clean as it is today, and our understanding of marine conservation was sketchy, at best. The concept of "catch and release" was in its infancy. "Filet and fry in grease" was the name of the game. Since then, with efforts like those of groups like the Coastal Conservation Association (www.ccaflorida.org) and Tampa Bay Watch (www.tampabaywatch.org), the area has become one of central Florida's most popular fishing destinations.

Inshore and Near Shore Fishing

When discussing inshore fishing and popular fish in some areas of Florida, it's usually not difficult to pinpoint a single most important local species. The fishing grounds near many locations often have a specific type of coastline, bottom, or structure that gives one species the edge in terms of popularity. The Pinellas peninsula, however, from Belleair on the west side to the St. Petersburg side of the Gandy Bridge on the east, is such a diverse fishery that it's difficult to rank one species over another. Here, there's water deep enough to allow the transit of cruise ships as well as give deepwater reef-fish "diggers" a successful day of fishing well within sight of shore. In other places, and not that far away, anglers fishing from kayaks often find so little water that they must portage their craft from deep hole to deep hole in the backwaters.

With that bit of confusion taken into consideration, I'm going to explain the Pinellas peninsula's inshore fishing on a place-by-place basis, beginning at the southern end of Clearwater Harbor and then heading south to Egmont Key at the mouth of Tampa Bay. From there, I'll discuss fishing up the southern and eastern shorelines of St. Petersburg. In a discussion of available inshore fish in a habitat as diverse as the one here, there will certainly be some overlap with species that are sometimes considered "offshore." I'll mention them here—and in the next section, "Offshore Fishing."

There's just over 15 miles of Intracoastal Waterway from the Belleair Causeway to the end of St. Pete Beach and the Pass-a-Grille channel. Some of it, a stretch commonly known as "The Narrows," runs behind Indian Shores, and to the novice angler, seems an unlikely place to catch fish; however, understand that this constricted waterway, with its residential docks and oyster bars, can be an exceptional place to fish for trout, redfish, and snook. And several "no wake" zones make it attractive to anglers, especially those who enjoy kayaking and wading. In warmer weather you'll find trout under docks and along channel edges. Redfish will cruise over bars along the eastern shore. On very cool days, both species will stay in deeper holes and channels until the sun warms the shallows. And don't neglect the waters at either end of the narrow, where residential developments are larger, canals deeper, and docks more numerous. The residential canals at the southern end of Clearwater Harbor, near Belleair Bluffs and Sand Key, offer refuge to many species, including snook, when cool weather arrives. This 5-mile stretch of inland water can make a great day of fishing, especially in spring or fall. You can access the Narrows by launching at the Park Boulevard boat ramp, the Belleair Causeway (SR686) ramp to the north, or the Madeira Beach Municipal Marina ramp to the south. On the beach side, anglers on foot can also find some good action at the 1200-foot Redington Long Pier. It's open 24 hours a day and can provide good action from many species of fish, some usually considered "offshore."

Inshore anglers might also consider fishing over the stretch of artificial inshore reefs just off Sand Key. Located in about 15 feet of water and just a few hundred yards from shore, these shallow structures attract numerous species of fish throughout the year. Complete information can be found in the Pinellas

County Utilities' *Reef Guide*, available at tackle and dive shops, or online at www.pinellascounty.org/utilities/reef/.

If you launch at either the Bay Pines (War Veterans Memorial) or the Jungle Prada ramps on the mainland, you'll have good access to Long Bayou, Cross Bayou, and Johns Pass. Long Bayou and Cross Bayou drain some of the peninsula's interior land, as well as Lake Seminole; however, it's the constant tidal flushing of Johns Pass that keeps saltwater pushed a good ways upstream, especially in the less-rainy wintertime months. Expect to find trout, reds, and snook up in these well-protected backwaters all year. Closer to Johns Pass and across the ICW from the mouth of Long Bayou, you'll find some grassy flats, spoils and residential canals all the way south past Blind Pass and into Boca Ciega Bay. These areas are all good summer habitat for snook and tarpon. In cooler months, you're likely to find a mackerel, Spanish or king, or a cobia that's wandered into the pass.

Upper Boca Ciega Bay is the fairly large body of protected deeper water behind St. Pete Beach and south of the city of Gulfport. In the late 1950s, it was separated from the lower bay by the dredging-up of several large residential islands. Here, docks provide good trout and snook action on summer nights, while the dredged residential canals hold redfish and sheepshead in cooler weather. Upper Boca Ciega Bay flushes and floods mainly through the navigable and deep Pass-a-Grille channel to the southwest, creating an excellent fishery for tarpon, snook, trout, and sheepshead along the eastern shore of the island that makes up Pass-a-Grille Beach and the Vina Del Mar residential development. There's also a good pompano fishery on the south side of the Pass-a-Grille channel as it enters the Gulf, and some good snook action can be had on summer nights near the rock jetties on the north shore. If you don't have a boat, consider fishing the edge of the channel from Pass-a-Grille's historic Merry Pier, or from the adjacent seawall. Access to the upper part of the Boca Ciega Bay is easy for boaters, with an excellent ramp at the full-service Gulfport Marina in its northeast corner, at the mouth of Clam Bayou. Two other convenient boat launches are at O'Neill's Marina and Maximo Park, near the north end of the Sunshine Skyway on Maximo Point.

The Pinellas Bayway road system opened in 1962. While connecting the lower Pinellas peninsula to the beaches, it also provided a road south to Mullet Key and Tierra Verde Island. At that time, anglers no longer had to reach the southernmost inshore waters of Tampa Bay only by boat, but they could launch boats at the big county boat ramp at what is now Ft. DeSoto State Park for easy access to the entire fishery near Mullet Key, Bunces Pass, and the Sunshine Skyway causeways. They also could wade-fish from mangrove-lined shorelines, launch canoes and kayaks along roadsides, or fish from piers jutting into the Gulf or Tampa Bay. And considering that about half the water entering or leaving Tampa Bay washes over this area, inshore fishing opportunities improved.

Several things that make the fishing around the Pinellas Bayway and Ft. DeSoto Park so good, besides the excellent water quality and proximity to the Gulf, are restrictions on motorboats and carefully enforced speed zones. From the Skyway Channel (which runs parallel to and alongside the Sunshine Skyway causeways and bridges) to the Gulf front of Mullet Key and the bars that extend north toward Pass-a-Grille, you'll find a number of restricted speed zones. Some areas, like the majority of Mullet Key Bayou, are restricted to slow speeds, while others are restricted to use by nonmotorized craft only. And some, like the vast flats to the east of Tierra Verde and Mullet Key, are just plain too shallow to maneuver by any means other than an electric motor, a push pole, or a paddle. For a close and informative look at these restrictions (and those at other Tampa Bay locations), see a copy of the Florida Marine Research Institute's free *Boating and Angling Guide to Tampa Bay*, available at many tackle shops and outdoor stores.

On days with moderate air and water temperatures, anglers will find excellent opportunities for catching seatrout, snook, and redfish almost anywhere on this area's flats or mangrove shorelines. All species will most likely be in shallow water, traveling or setting up to ambush baits in potholes, or along channel edges. I'm partial to the shallows south of the east-west run of the Pass-a-Grille channel, between Indian Key (Bird Key) and Tarpon Key. Here, if the weather gets either too hot or too cold for comfort, the fish have some close-by deeper water into which they can retreat. Likewise, the flats on the edges of Bunces Pass to the west of the Ft. DeSoto boat ramp are productive in warmer months for trout, reds, and snook. If the weather's cold, try fishing near the residential docks on the east side of Tierra Verde or up in the deep backwater holes east of the boat ramp.

Anglers without boats shouldn't worry about missing opportunities to fish the southern tip of Pinellas County and the Bayway. For waders, the Bayway's roadside just north of the Bunces Pass Bridge and the Sunshine Skyway causeway rest areas offer excellent access to the Tierra Verde flats. There's also some excellent surf fishing on the northern Gulf end of Mullet Key, where snook, reds, and trout roam the western end of the Bunces Pass Channel. There are also several excellent fishing piers, including the 500-foot Ft. DeSoto Bay Pier and the 1000-foot Ft. DeSoto Gulf Pier. Both piers are free and provide lots of angling action, especially on warm summer nights. Another option for pier enthusiasts is the Sunshine Skyway North Pier, salvaged from the remains of the original main span approach. This pier, also operated by the State of Florida, extends almost to the main span of the Skyway over bottom littered with remains of the original bridge. This is certainly one of the best piers in the area, and well worth the trip. Bridges also provide good angling opportunities in lower Pinellas County. One that's particularly good, and busy day and night, is the Bayway's Tierra Verde Bridge over the Pass-a-Grille Channel. Here,

Fishing from the seawall along the Pass-a-Grille Channel is good at most times during the year.

an excellent flow of Gulf water combined with some structure more than 50 years old makes for some great angling.

"Modern" things like dredged channels, causeways, and bridge abutments have a way of cutting ancient seabeds into what seem at first glance to be separate fish habitats. For example, looking at Waterproof Charts' chart #22F, you'll see that the Sunshine Skyway's northern causeways and bridges cut through the eastern part of the Boca Ciega Bay grass flats. Anglers should avoid any confusion by thinking that the flats that lie to the east of the Skyway and wrap around Pinellas Point toward downtown St. Pete are different from those near Mullet Key and the Bayway. They are the same depth, with the same grass, and are positioned in such a way as to get the full effect of Tampa Bay's tidal movements. Of course, water can enter and exit only through either the Skyway's Pass-a-Grille (ICW) Channel Bridge or Bunces Pass Bridge, but that's a good thing to know if you plan to fish "the point" and the southeast coastline of the Pinellas peninsula. Incoming tides push bait through these channels, and falling tides pull bait toward them, and while this effect makes fishing close to either side of the causeway good, it also affects the entire area. Trout, reds, cobia, and tarpon are all attracted to the shallow "clam bars" (approx. N27 40.777 W82 40.182) just east of the Skyway. Another flat, to the north, and stretching to the old ferry landing, is closer to shore. Fish this flat for trout, but don't forget to fish its deeper north edge and the residential docks along the shore for snook and reds. The same goes for the old channel into the ferry landing (at N27 42.286 W82 38.370, the most southeastern point of the peninsula).

This channel runs out to deeper water near the ICW and is likely to hold cobia and even a grouper or two. What was once the ferry dock is now the Bay Vista Park boat ramp. (Ferry service to the other side of Tampa Bay was discontinued when the Sunshine Skyway Bridge was opened.)

To the immediate north of Bay Vista Park and along shore, you'll find some good oyster bars. Try this short stretch for reds on cold days when the bars are flooded, or fish near the adjacent docks on summer evenings. The big grass flats continue north past the entrance to Little Bayou (N27 43.177 W82 37.809), Coquina Key (Lewis Island, before dredging and development), and the entrance to Big Bayou (N27 44.660 W82 37.278). Here, the flats are fed a bit less from the overall tidal surge from Tampa Bay, but from water flowing in and out of Big and Little Bayous. In either bayou, concentrate on residential docks and mangrove shorelines for snook and reds, especially in cooler weather. There's an excellent boat ramp at Grandview Park that provides quick access to Big Bayou.

St. Petersburg has one "working" harbor, Bayboro, and another that serves mostly recreational boaters. At one time, Bayboro Harbor had a small power plant that emptied warm water into the mouth of Salt Creek, attracting snook and tarpon. Now, since the harbor has been mostly redeveloped into University of South Florida facilities, fishing here isn't the same. The harbor is also home to a U.S. Coast Guard station,

The small pier near the old ferry landing on Point Pinellas is a relaxing place to spend the day.

meaning that access is limited because of security regulations. Shorebound anglers might also consider fishing from St. Petersburg's "Million-Dollar" pier. There, pilings built on pilings over a number of reconstruction and revitalization efforts spanning decades attract all species of fish, including snook and sheepshead. Within walking distance of downtown, "The Pier" is a popular fishing spot for visitors to the city. St. Pete's Yacht Basin is pretty snazzy, but it does have one nice boat ramp at Demens Landing used by anglers heading north toward the flats between Coffee Pot Bayou and Grande Bayou. There's good trout action on these flats most of the year, but when the weather's really cold, consider launching smaller boats at either the Coffee Pot Bayou ramp or the Crisp Park ramp up in the residential backwaters and trying your luck around docks, along shorelines, and in deep holes for reds. Both these ramps also offer good access for paddlers in canoes or kayaks. Grande Bayou leads up into Riviera Bay and the backwaters of the Weedon Island Preserve, just south of the Gandy Bridge causeway. Like the fishing grounds at Ft. DeSoto Park, this area offers exceptional access to anglers using small boats, canoes, and kayaks. Much of these waters are protected, with restrictions on speed and motors. Certain areas of Riviera Bay are very shallow, and according to local fishing guide Capt. Woody Gore, special care should be taken, even by paddle anglers, to avoid being stranded there on low tides. Depth-restricted anglers might concentrate on the flats and Tampa Bay shoreline, or, in winter, on the warm water discharge from the island's Paul Bartow power plant. Pay careful attention to signs about security restrictions on boaters near the power plant. Shallow-water enthusiasts might also use the South Gandy Channel to enter Masters Bayou, behind the plant. There, they'll find an excellent snook fishery in the protected waters, as well as some deeper water well up into Snug Harbor. Visiting anglers will find an excellent inshore fishing pier and kayak launch within the Weedon Island Preserve, and larger boats can be launched from public ramps situated on both ends of the Gandy Bridge causeway.

Despite its population of about one million persons, each wanting a waterfront view, Pinellas County offers a surprising variety of inshore fishing opportunities. From pristine backwaters to deep seawalled residential canals to Gulf beaches, there's some angling here for just about everyone.

Offshore Fishing

Offshore fishing near and around the Pinellas peninsula doesn't necessarily mean you're really offshore. Tampa Bay is

Florida's largest protected bay and, as such, boasts some close-in deepwater channels, deep harbors, and a fair number of artificial reefs that attract species of fish usually considered "offshore." And, with easy access to the truly offshore waters of the Gulf of Mexico, anglers wishing to fish deep reefs, blue water, or even Florida's Middle Grounds find the Pinellas peninsula a good point of departure.

Most of the 30-foot depths in Tampa Bay relate to ship channels. The Tampa Bay Ship Channel (also called the Mullet Key Channel) actually begins east of Egmont Key, at the mouth of the bay, where the natural Egmont and Southwest channels meet. The Egmont Channel, the main navigational fairway for ships heading into the Gulf, is more than 75 feet deep as it passes close to Egmont Key. The Southwest Channel is a bit shallower, with depths in the 20-foot range. The Ship Channel is marked and takes a relatively straight course into the middle of the bay, under the main span of the Sunshine Skyway Bridge. It is joined southeast of Pinellas Point by the north-south Intracoastal Waterway (at approx. N27 39.284 W82 36.424), a straight, deep channel leading to and from St. Petersburg's downtown harbors. Several more miles up into the bay, the ship channel splits in two. The westerly leg provides ship and barge access to Weedon Island's power plant and the eastern half of Tampa's Interbay Peninsula. The easterly leg leads into Hillsborough Bay, with tributaries leading to the Big Bend power plant, the Alafia River, and the port facilities in downtown Tampa.

Many of the deep (and some of the small) channels in Tampa Bay are adjacent to areas marked "spoils" on charts. In an effort to keep them deep and straight, many channels have been dredged to specific depths, and the dredge waste pumped alongside them. In shallow inshore waters, these are sometimes visible at lower tides, but in the middle of Tampa Bay, they may be as deep as 20 feet. These deep spoils are sometimes worn down by tides and currents, but they often provide just enough relief to attract grouper, cobia, snappers, and the schools of white bait that attract pelagic species like king and Spanish mackerel. And some, usually near recent dredging activities, offer clumps of exposed rock—the perfect habitat for offshore species. By trolling big plugs along the well-defined edges of channels or spoils, you'll likely find bottom dwellers. The spoils near the intersection of the Ship Channel with the Port Manatee Channel (N27 39.619 W82 36.144) is a good spot to fish, as are some areas closer to the main span of the Sunshine Skyway; however, in each of these places, you must take special care to avoid any commercial shipping and to obey any security restrictions. In some areas near the Sunshine Skyway, restrictions against anchoring or stopping are in force. And it's important to remember that it takes a loaded oil tanker at least 10 miles to slow down. They don't get out of your way—you must get out of theirs.

There are even a few places on the peninsula that offer access to "offshore" species close to shore. Take, for instance, any of the docks, bridges, or piers along or over deep channels. The Gulf Pier at Ft. DeSoto attracts a surprising number of deep-water species, as do the old Skyway Bridge remains, just off the North Skyway Fishing Pier. And don't ever miss a chance to drop a line around bridge fenders.

Boats pass in and out of Tampa Bay through the bay's mouth, through Pass-a-Grille or through Johns Pass. The ship channel (Mullet Key, Egmont, or Tampa Bay Ship Channel—the name depends on whom you talk to or to which section you're referring!) that crosses north of Egmont Key at the mouth of Tampa Bay will get you quickly to deep water. However, for those needing to launch a trailer boat, there really are no convenient ramps, so you'll have to run a bit to get to Egmont. The Ft. DeSoto ramp is the closest, and if you want to take a chance traversing the Bunces Pass breaker bars, you're pretty close. Getting offshore is much easier if you head west via Pass-a-Grille Channel or Johns Pass, where there are better public facilities like marinas and boat ramps. The run from O'Neill's Marina or Maximo Park, at the northern base of the Sunshine Skyway causeway, to the Gulf through Pass-a-Grille is easily half the distance from the Ft. DeSoto ramp to Egmont Key. And with several marinas and launch sites in upper Boca Ciega Bay, it's a quick trip for most offshore anglers to get to deep Gulf waters through Johns Pass. Maybe that's why Hubbard's Pier has been operating successful party-boat trips out of Johns Pass for all these years. More time fishing with less time riding is always a good thing.

Pinellas County has an impressive number of artificial reefs and wreck sites. One probable reason is that there is little natural structure at the bottom. Yes, there are holes and a few natural rock piles, but many deepwater structures offshore of, or inside, Tampa Bay are manmade. And fish don't care why the structure's there, or who built it—they just enjoy the bait that's attracted to it and the places from which to ambush.

On the St. Petersburg side of the bay, three areas are worth a try for mangrove snapper, cobia, and sheepshead. One, at about N27 43.888 W82 36.666, is just east of Coquina Key. Another is at N27 45.248 W82 35.270, just to the north, east of the downtown Albert Whitted Airport. And a third, the St. Pete Reef (N27 47.111 W82 35.362), is in about 20 feet of water just northeast of downtown. Nearer the mouth of the bay, there are several piles of rubble scattered to the southwest of the main span of the Sunshine Skyway that attract bait and are worth fishing for offshore species as well as for tarpon.

Outside Tampa Bay, reef and wreck choices are numerous, and picking just one or two for a day of fishing can be complicated. Depending on your departure port, find an area with several reefs and load those coordinates into your GPS unit. (The night before the trip is a better time to do this than while the boat's running!) By "sorting out" the reefs in the general area you want to fish, you'll cover ground more economically. Try the area that's about 14 miles west of Pass-a-Grille at about N27 41.511 W82 59.203, or look at numbers closer to the beach, along the 3-fathom curve on your charts, between Pass-a-Grille and Johns Pass.

Depending on time of year, water quality, and water temperatures, the offshore fishing will vary from "hot spot" to "hot spot"—close to far, and shallow to deep. Structures closer to the beaches will hold smaller grouper and cobia in spring and summer. King mackerel will stop their migration long enough to attack pods of bait attracted to shallow structures in spring and fall. And offshore structure in depths of 40-plus feet will produce grouper and other reef fish during the warmer months. Expect these reef-dwellers to move out to 60 or 80 feet in the cold of winter.

Finally, just a few words about the Florida Middle Grounds. It's a place where rock piles, ledges, canyons, and small "mountains" attract all sorts of offshore fish species. It's where you'll catch limits of rare and tasty grouper like scamp and Kitty Mitchells, as well as giant mangrove and red snapper. It's also where you'll be more than 100 miles west of the Pinellas peninsula, in water that's measured in fathoms rather than in feet, and where you're likely to be pressing the "retrieve" button on an electric fishing reel rather than cranking to bring up your catch. These trips are best made by experienced anglers, in big boats, with several days of time on their hands. My advice is to make your first Middle Grounds trip on a "head" or party boat. Then, should you wish to take your own boat, buddy up with some friends and head westward, convoy-style.

Getting Around

Navigating the Pinellas peninsula is pretty simple. US19 forms the north-south spine, eventually crossing Tampa Bay's Sunshine Skyway Bridge, merged with Interstate 275, from Maximo Point. Interstate 275 splits off from Interstate 75 in

Tampa, heads south through Pinellas County, feeding most of downtown St. Petersburg. It eventually merges with Interstate 75, south of the bay. Alternate US19 runs parallel to US19 and is a bit closer to the Gulf of Mexico but no less busy. Gulf Boulevard, the beach road, connects the barrier islands from Clearwater to Pass-a-Grille. St. Petersburg and its suburbs (Gulfport, Seminole, and Largo) are divided into a grid: north/south roads are usually "streets"; east/west roads are "avenues." Central Avenue runs east and west from downtown to the beaches, and 4th, 9th, and 34th streets are the main north/south roads. Taking 4th Street north will get you to the Gandy Bridge and downtown Tampa. 9th Street leads north to Interstate 275 and Tampa International Airport. 34th Street is US19 and a good route north to Clearwater, Tarpon Springs, and Florida's Big Bend.

Where to Stay

Don't worry about finding a convenient place to stay in this area; however, *do* pay attention to the fact that rates (and occupancies) go up during the winter months.

*   *   *

Snug Harbor Inn, (727) 395-9256, 13655 Gulf Blvd, Madeira Beach. Efficiencies, dockage.

The Bungalows Island Retreat, (727) 542-1496, 12321 Gulf Blvd, Treasure Island. Fun—and comfortable!

Changing Tides Cottages, (727) 744-4114, 225 Boca Ciega Dr, Madeira Beach. Near Johns Pass, dockage available, pet friendly.

Bayside Inn and Docks, (800) 992-4023, 11365 Gulf Blvd, Treasure Island. Efficiencies.

Bayway Inn, (727) 866-2471, 4400 34th St S, St. Petersburg. Small motel, convenient to the Pinellas Bayway and the Sunshine Skyway.

Where to Eat

Skyway Jack's Restaurant, 2795 34th St S, St. Petersburg. A great place for a diner-style breakfast or lunch. There's a "more classy" version now open at 11140 4th St N.

Tick-Tock Restaurant, (727) 498-8563, 8123 4th St N, St. Petersburg. Breakfast and lunch diner owned by three Greek brothers. What more can I say regarding their good food?

Ted Peter's Famous Smoked Fish, (727) 381-7931, 1350 S. Pasadena Ave, Pasadena. Don't miss this place for some great smoked mullet or Spanish mackerel. A St. Pete institution for more than 50 years!

Billy's Stone Crab Restaurant, (727) 866-2115, 1 Collany Rd, Tierra Verde. Be sure to call for reservations at this popular restaurant, especially when stone crabs are in season (November to May).

Munch's Restaurant, (727) 896-5972, 3920 6th St S, St. Petersburg. I ate my first hamburger from Munch's in 1956, just a few years after the place opened. It's still there, and the basic diner-style food and sandwiches are still very good. You can even call ahead for a burger to go, dock your boat at the Grandview boat ramp just around the corner, and run in to pick it up for lunch!

Marinas, Marine Supplies and Service, Bait and Tackle Shops, and Launching Ramps

Belleair Causeway ramps, at the eastern side of the Belleair Causeway. 10 ramps, plenty of parking, $6 fee. On the Intracoastal Waterway.

Park Boulevard ramps, 18651 Gulf Blvd, Indian Shores. 6 ramps, open 24 hours, restrooms, good parking. On the Intracoastal Waterway.

Lighthouse Point Marina, (727) 384-DOCK, 8610 Bay Pines Blvd, St. Petersburg. Fuel, bait, and tackle.

Madeira Beach Municipal Marina, (727) 399-2631. $10 boat ramps, fuel, live and frozen bait, tackle. www.madbeach marina.com

Bill Jackson's Shop for Adventure, (727) 576-4169, 9501 US19 N, Pinellas Park. Even if you don't need anything from its excellent selection of tackle or kayaking gear, this great outdoor store is well worth a visit! www.billjacksons.com

Bett's Fishing Center, (727) 518-7637, 8926 126 Ave N, Largo. An excellent selection of inshore and offshore tackle, a knowledgeable staff, rod and reel repairs. Trolling motor sales and service too!

Holy Mackerel! Tackle, (727) 547-9889, 8629 49th St N, St. Petersburg. Inshore and offshore tackle, repairs, frozen bait and chum.

Mako Bait & Tackle, (727) 391-6274, 6100 Seminole Blvd, Seminole.

Dogfish Tackle, (727) 393-2102, 8750 Park Blvd, Seminole. A fishing "superstore," inshore and offshore tackle.

Redington Long Pier, (727) 391-9398, 17490 Gulf Blvd, Redington Shores. An excellent pier for night fishing adventures. www.tampabayfishingpier.com

Redington Beach Hardware & Marine, (727) 397-8031, 77 170th Ave, N. Redington Beach. Bait, tackle, marine hardware, rod and reel rentals.

Jungle Prada ramp, Park St N at Elbow Lane. Double ramp with good access to Boca Ciega Bay.

Bay Pines ramp, at War Veterans Memorial Park, Bay Pines Blvd, Seminole. Paved ramp, parking, access to Boca Ciega Bay.

Don's Dock, Johns Pass at Hubbards Pier. Gas, diesel, ice, bait and tackle.

Treasure Island boat ramps, on the ICW at 100th and 123rd avenues. Limited parking available.

Gulf-to-Bay Bait & Tackle, (727) 367-4756, 6920 Gulf Blvd, St. Pete Beach. Live and frozen bait, tackle, rod and reel repairs.

The Bait Bucket, (727) 864-2108, 108 Pinellas Bayway, Tierra Verde (on the way to Ft. DeSoto Park). Bait and tackle. Open 7 days.

Ft. DeSoto Fishing Piers (500-foot Bay and 1000-foot Gulf). On Mullet Key, at the south end of the Pinellas Bayway. Bait, tackle, and food available. Open daily, 24 hours.

Merry Pier Ship's Store, 801 Pass-a-Grille Way, Pass-a-Grille. Live and frozen bait, tackle, ice, rod and reel rentals.

Tierra Verde Marina, (727) 866-0255, on Pass-a-Grille Channel at the Pinellas Bayway bridge.

Gulfport Municipal Marina, (727) 893-1071, 4630 29th Ave S. Fuel, live and frozen bait, boat ramp, ice, tackle. www. ci.gulfport.fl.us

O'Neill's Marina, (727) 867-2585, 6701 34th St S, St. Petersburg, on Maximo Point. Full-service marina with $5 boat ramp, bait and tackle, ice, fuel, dockage. Excellent access to Boca Ciega Bay and the Sunshine Skyway. www.oneillsmarina.com

Maximo Marina, (727) 867-1102, 4801 37th St S, St. Petersburg. Fuel, bait and tackle, ice. Access to Boca Ciega Bay and the Sunshine Skyway.

Maximo Park ramp, off US19/I-275/34th St at 62nd Ave S, St. Petersburg. Public park with 2 boat ramps on Frenchman's Creek with good access to Boca Ciega Bay.

Sunshine Skyway North Fishing Pier. Not quite as long as the 8860-foot South Pier, this is one of the best fishing piers anywhere. Open 24 hours, 7 days a week. There's a bait shop, and the modest admission fee lets you drive onto the pier. "Sightseeing" passes are also available.

Bay Vista Park boat ramp, at the southern end of 4th St S, St. Petersburg. 2 ramps, restrooms, good parking.

Grandview Park boat ramp, 6th St S, St. Petersburg. 2 ramps, good parking, on Big Bayou. Within walking distance of Munch's Restaurant!

The St. Petersburg Municipal Marina is convenient to downtown hotels and restaurants.

Mastry's Bait and Tackle, (727) 896-8889, 1700 4th St S, St. Petersburg. Live and frozen bait, fresh-eating seafood, rod and reel repair, inshore and offshore tackle. Good conversations and fishing advice. The shop's motto, "by fishermen . . . for fishermen," tells the story of one of St. Petersburg's most established tackle shops.

Captain K's Bait and Tackle, (727) 343-4181, 6576 Central Ave, St. Petersburg. Bait, tackle, and fishing supplies.

Canoe Country Outfitters, (727) 545-4554, 6493 54th Ave N, St. Petersburg. Kayak, canoe, and Gheenoe sales. Rental boats available.

St. Petersburg Municipal Marina, (727) 893-7329, 300 2nd Ave S. Dockage, fuel. www.stpete.org

Demens Landing ramp, 1st Ave S, St. Petersburg. At the Municipal Marina. 2 paved ramps, limited parking.

Coffee Pot Bayou ramp, 30th Ave NE at Coffee Pot Blvd, St. Petersburg. Single paved ramp, good parking.

Crisp Park ramp, 35th Ave NE at Poplar St, St. Petersburg. On the west end of Smacks Bayou.

Discount Marine Bait & Tackle, (727) 521-4065, 401 83rd Ave N, St. Petersburg. Live bait, tackle, marine repairs and parts.

Sweetwater Kayaks, (727) 570-4844, at Weedon Island Preserve. Canoe and kayak rentals.

I.C. Sharks Bait Shop & Marina, (727) 578-5117, 13060 Gandy Blvd, St. Petersburg. Boat ramp, boat rentals, live and frozen bait, tackle. Live or steamed blue crabs too!

Riviera Bay and the backwaters of Weedon Island are excellent shallow-water fisheries.

Local Fishing Guides

Capt. Woody Gore, (813) 477-3814. Inshore and near shore. www.captainwoodygore.com

Capt. Mark Gore, (813) 434-5504. Inshore and near shore. www.captainmarkgore.com

Capt. Mike Gore, (813) 390-6600. Inshore and near shore. www.captainmikegore.com

Capt. Rick Frazier, (727) 510-4376. Inshore. www.luckydawg.com

Capt. David Zalewski, (727) 460-9893. Inshore and offshore.

Capt. Randy Rochelle, (727) 365-3218. Near shore and offshore fishing.

Capt. Sam Maisano, (727) 480-6408. Inshore, offshore, and blue water fishing.

Capt. Brent Gaskill, (727) 343-1765. Inshore fishing.

Capt. Little Jim Fesperman, (727) 515-3689. Inshore, night snook charters. www.hooksettingcharters.com

Capt. Tommy Ziesmann, (727) 432-0355. Inshore and near shore. www.action-charters.com

Capt. Chad Calhoun, (727) 432-1390. Inshore and near shore.

Capt. Larry Blue, (727) 871-1058. Inshore and offshore. www.captainlarrybluecharters.com

Capt. Jay Masters, (727) 522-4301. Inshore and offshore. www.fatcatfishingcharters.com

*　*　*

Most inshore guides from the coastal communities here, as well as some from Tampa, are familiar with all the waters around the Pinellas peninsula. Please consult the listings at the end of chapter 5, if necessary. Also, the website of the Florida Guides Association (www.florida-guides.com) has a complete listing of USCG licensed and insured fishing guides.

Before You Leave Home

Be sure to check this guide's companion website, www.salt wateranglersguide.com, for updates to local information.

5

Old Tampa Bay, Tampa Bay, and the Bay's Eastern Shore

Growing up and fishing around the southern tip of St. Petersburg at Pinellas Point, my fishing buddies and I pretty much stayed in the southwest corner of Tampa Bay. There, we fished for inshore species from the beach at Pass-A-Grille to Egmont Key and back to downtown St. Pete, mostly in small skiffs. Had we wanted to fish in Tampa waters, in Old Tampa Bay, Hillsborough County, or even south across the bay in Manatee County, we'd have needed bigger boats and longer fishing days. From the Sunshine Skyway's main span to Pinellas Point, usually a day trip for us, is only about 5 miles; however, from Pinellas Point to the mouth of the Alafia River, on the upper eastern edge of the bay, near Tampa, it's about 15 miles. And to Safety Harbor, at the top of Old Tampa Bay, the distance is more than 20 miles. Tampa Bay is a huge chunk of busy and deep water and not one to be taken casually.

There's no real boundary between Old Tampa Bay and Tampa Bay "proper," but I think most locals consider the dividing line to be Gandy Bridge and its causeway. Before I-275 and its Howard Frankland Bridge, Gandy Bridge was the main connection between Tampa and St. Pete. It is also above Port Tampa, the power plant complex on the St. Pete side and any really deep water. You're not likely to encounter any seagoing merchant ships or barges in Old Tampa Bay.

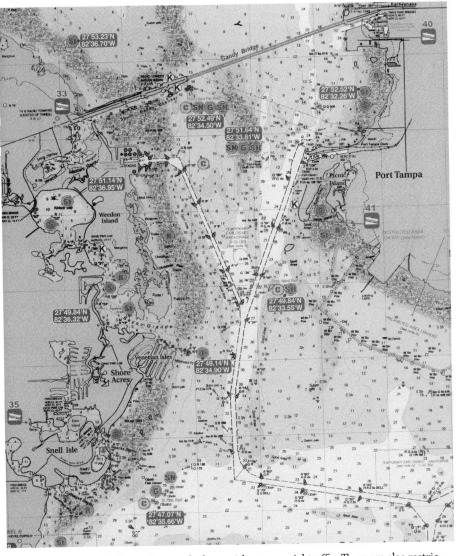

The narrowest point in Tampa Bay can be busy with commercial traffic. There are also restrictions regarding the shoreline of MacDill AFB. (Map courtesy of Waterproof Charts, Inc.)

The Pinellas County side of Old Tampa Bay has remained less developed than the eastern Hillsborough County side. At least, it looks that way from the water. From Gandy Bridge north, you'll find lots of mangrove shoreline and some impressive flats well past the St. Petersburg-Clearwater International Airport and into Mobbly Bay, east of Safety Harbor. Inshore anglers should have no trouble catching seatrout, redfish, snook, or tarpon here, depending on the season.

East and south of Mobbly Bay you'll begin to see more civilization, including many waterfront homes (with fishable docks!), some residential and commercial canals, and a few privately maintained channels. Fishing is good on this side of Old Tampa Bay, but my personal belief is that it's not as good as the other side because there's less development there and also because of a regular sea breeze that sometimes pounds the Tampa side each day. There are some good flats here, as well as some deeper cuts that extend north into Old Tampa Bay near the eastern end of the Gandy Bridge.

I often marvel at the changes that have taken place in Old Tampa Bay since I was a kid. The water's cleaner, the sea grasses are healthier, and on any given day the area's busy with successful anglers.

Hillsborough Bay is the most northeastern part of Tampa Bay and is bounded by the Interbay Peninsula to the west and the Hillsborough County mainland to the east. It includes the waterfront of downtown Tampa, the mouths of the Hillsborough and Palm rivers, as well as some huge dredge spoils and deep shipping channels. Fishing can be good along the southeastern and southwestern shorelines, but busy commercial traffic and security restrictions in the upper part of the small bay can sometimes make fishing here impractical or just plain not fun.

In spite of some large "industrial outposts" south of Riverview and the mouth of the Alafia River, the eastern Tampa Bay shoreline provides some excellent angling opportunities. Even with a large power plant and busy Port Manatee, places like the mouth of the Little Manatee River and Cockroach Bay attract droves of anglers. There are no beaches here—just miles and miles of healthy mangrove shoreline.

Inshore and Near Shore Fishing

Despite the fact that I've seen Old Tampa Bay and Hillsborough Bay on charts for years, in my mind's eye I've always considered them much smaller than the lower bay. One single day of exploring changed my mind. Just the run alongside Gandy Bridge from the Salty Sol Fleischman ramp in Tampa to the flats north of Weedon Island on the St. Pete side is almost 5 miles, and that's one of the narrowest parts of Old Tampa Bay. Similar distances apply for Hillsborough Bay, where a wintertime fishing trip from the Ballast Point ramp on the Interbay Peninsula to Gibsonton's Alafia River mouth is 6 miles. These are not small bodies of water and don't "fish" like small bays or backwaters.

The west shoreline of Old Tampa Bay, from Gandy Bridge past the end of the I-275/Howard Frankland Bridge, well past the St. Pete airport and into Safety Harbor, features grass flats extending almost 2 miles into the bay. On cooler days, especially when the sun's shining, expect to find spotted seatrout and reds moving onto the outer edges of the bars from the deeper bay. Both species are excellent targets for anglers tossing noisy topwater plugs like MirrOlure Top Dogs or Top Pups. Your ability to make long casts will increase your chances of a strike, as fish in these shallows tend to be spooky and not very tolerant of boat noises or wakes. Consider wading some of this area, too. As the weather warms, spring to summer, trout will fall off into holes and 4–6-foot depths, where lures like D.O.A. Bait Busters or 3-inch D.O.A. shrimp, rigged under popping corks, attract them. Live bait enthusiasts should be able to find plenty of white bait to net by early spring and into fall. Those live baits, rigged using small circle hooks tied to 20-pound-test fluorocarbon leader and cast toward potholes and deeper edges, will also provoke strikes. This area (and the entire shoreline of Tampa Bay) is the perfect environment in which to use your light spinning tackle, spooled with 8- or 10-pound-test Power Pro line—or your 8-weight fly gear.

Redfish and snook will appear and get active along this shoreline too, usually beginning in March. Topwater lures also work well for these species, but casting around mangrove roots can be tricky. Sometimes the worst part isn't losing a lure to the bushes, but it's spooking a nice snook or red trying to shake a plug loose. The mangrove islands behind Cedar Point (N27 54.632 W82 38.621), near the end of the Howard Frankland causeway, are popular places for kayak and canoe anglers. Paddlers and wade-anglers have good access from the bridge approaches. To the northwest of Courtney Campbell Parkway (SR60), the flats and shoreline between Cooper Bayou and Safety Harbor Marina are also active snook, trout, and redfish fisheries. Look for mullet jumping or white bait schooling and you'll likely find something to catch here. Tarpon roam the deeper channel edges all over this side of the bay throughout the summer and can be caught near the structures of the Gandy, Frankland, and Bayside bridges. On falling tides, check out the point of the bar at N27 54.232 W82 35.174, north of the Gandy Bridge, or the south end of the Howard Frankland Bridge structure for feeding tarpon. Or to the north, look in the deep water north of the Courtney Campbell Causeway at about N27 58.279 W82 39.290 or in the "neck" of Safety Harbor, off the Indian Mounds at Phillippe Point. Finally, don't forget that there are species of fish in the bay that are still fun to catch and good to eat but lack the panache of snook, seatrout, redfish, and tarpon. Any structure, like bridge and dock pilings, in Old Tampa Bay is likely to provide some year-round action from sheepshead and mangrove snappers, while creek bottoms and oyster bars provide habitat and hiding places for

Redfish are one of the most popular fish species found in Tampa Bay.

some nice flounder. A bag limit of any of these "lesser" species is always something to be proud of.

The stretch of shoreline from Booth Point (N27 59.911 W82 39.489) east across Mobbly Bay and into the residential canals northeast of the Courtney Campbell Causeway offers some of the best fishing in Old Tampa Bay. The flats here are fed by drainage from Double Branch Bay, Double Bayou, and Rocky Creek, making them excellent habitat for seatrout, snook, and redfish. In times of temperate water, they'll roam the flats all

The Salty Sol Fleischman boat ramp is convenient to almost all of upper Tampa Bay.

the way to the channel edges, especially south of Rocky Creek. As the water warms to summertime highs or dips during infrequent winter lows, reds and trout will drop off into the channels, none of which are very deep here. Snook are more likely to head into the creeks or bayous, making them excellent targets for paddling anglers. This shore is particularly suited to fishing from kayaks, canoes, or shallow-draft boats, as tides make it very shallow at times. There's good kayak and canoe launching at either Olds Park or Upper Tampa Bay Park in Oldsmar. Expect good snook and redfish action in these mangrove-lined backwaters in any season, but be aware that this can be a "buggy" place during the late spring and summer. There are many residential canals, most with docks, to the east above the causeway. If the wind's blowing, or it's cold, try fishing these structures by tossing free-lined live or 3-inch D.O.A. shrimp near the sun-warmed pilings or into deeper holes dredged by moored boats.

Rocky Point (N27 57.737 W82 34.563) juts into Old Tampa Bay south of the Courtney Campbell Causeway and marks the northern end of Tampa's western urban shoreline. From here to Port Tampa, at the southwest tip of the Interbay Peninsula, expect to find some good flats for trout, as well as numerous canals and channels. The Culbreath Bayou backwater is a good place to start, especially if you need protection from the wind. The same goes for the canals just above the Gandy Bridge eastern terminus, at the old Georgetown Apartments. This is an excellent year-round snook fishery. There's also some excellent summertime fishing for Spanish mackerel in the area between the Port Tampa and Weedon Island channels, especially when the Chief Reef (N27 51.649 W82 33.787) is holding schools of baitfish. The best access to this area for trailer-boaters is the Salty Sol Fleischman ramp on the Gandy Bridge causeway or the Picnic Island ramp south of Port Tampa.

The southern third of Tampa's Interbay Peninsula is occupied by MacDill Air Force Base, and some of that shoreline is off-limits to anglers because of security restrictions. The "MacDill flats" and waters close to shore toward Gadsden Point (N27 49.275 W82 28.364) hold trout, snook, and reds year-round. Tarpon and Spanish mackerel cruise the edges of the flats as summertime tides fall, washing baits to deeper waters. Before you head toward this area, I advise you ask at one of the local tackle shops about current restrictions to the peninsula's southern shoreline. The folks at Gandy Bait & Tackle or T. A. Mahoney will know.

Hillsborough Bay encompasses the waters from Gadsden Point on the west to Apollo Beach on the east. It's cut in half by a big north-south ship channel that splits just south of downtown Tampa into the Seddon Channel and the East Bay Channel. The Seddon Channel leads to the mouth of the Hillsborough River and the downtown cruise ship terminals. The East Bay Channel connects to the more industrialized McKay Bay and the mouth of the Palm River. The Alafia River Channel and the Big Bend Power Plant Channel run east from the ship channel. There are spoil banks on the south side of the Alafia and Big Bend channels and two huge spoils to the east of the channel. I mention all these details as a bit of a warning to boaters unfamiliar with Hillsborough Bay. Like most major U.S. ports, it's busy here, and certain Department of Homeland Security restrictions are always in force and subject to change. But it's fishy too, and generally worth the hassles.

If you plan to fish along the western shore of Hillsborough Bay, my advice is to launch at either the Ballast Point or Davis Island ramp. Ballast Point is at the eastern end of Gandy Boulevard (which leads west to Upper Tampa Bay and on to St. Petersburg), and the Davis Island ramp is reached through a more urban area of downtown Tampa. Oyster bars, docks, and small grassy areas are excellent places to fish for seatrout, redfish, and flounder all around the eastern side of the bay, most of the year. This side of the bay is also a good tarpon fishery in the summer months, especially along the edges of Long Shoal (N27 52.205 W82 27.998), southeast of Ballast Point, and off the western shore of Davis Islands. And for shorebound anglers, there's some seawall fishing along Bayshore Boulevard or from the fishing pier at Ballast Point Park.

Fishing in the downtown area of most port cities like Tampa is generally more trouble than it's worth. Security restrictions limit access to many docks and structures that traditionally hold fish. Tampa's McKay Bay still holds some fish, and snook and tarpon hang out in the city's commercial channels and near docks; however, if you're just visiting Tampa, I'd advise you to fish away from these busy areas. It's probably better to hire a local guide who's aware of the day-to-day changes in restrictions and rules.

Heading down the eastern shore of Hillsborough Bay, you'll pass the mouth of the Alafia River and Apollo Beach. Both these areas offer much better inshore fishing opportunities than the more urban areas to the north. Of course, there are still a fair number of industrial outposts, but for the most part, this shoreline is pretty "fishy." There are several good access points, including the ramps at Williams Park in Riverview, on the Alafia River, and at Apollo Beach. Anglers leaving the Alafia River should concentrate on fishing the grass flats to the south for trout, reds, and snook, especially in the area near the mouth of Bullfrog Creek (approx. N27 50.383 W82 23.793). There are also good oyster bars along the shoreline just north of the Big Bend Power Plant (north of Green Key and Whiskey Key) and some pretty good summertime tarpon hunting along the 6-foot curve, just off the flats. Tackle and bait choices for these areas are the same as those for other inshore areas in the bay. Live bait, mainly shrimp and white bait, are favored by many local anglers, but artificial lures are making their way into the repertoire of many sport anglers in this area. Some even own fly rods!

The hot-water discharge at the Big Bend Power Plant is a huge attraction for fish, and anglers, in the winter. There's good access for shorebound anglers from the north end of Surfside Boulevard, and boaters can get fairly close to the warm water entering from the bay. Here, you're likely to catch snook, pompano, cobia, redfish, Spanish mackerel, sheepshead, or even a resident wintertime tarpon. Shore anglers seem to do best by drifting live shrimp under corks along the edge of the channel, while many anglers in boats prefer artificial lures. Deep-running D.O.A. Bait Busters are a good choice for all species, except pompano, mackerel, and sheepshead. They seem to prefer Flowering Floreos, D.O.A. CALs, or Doc's Goofy Jigs tipped with a small piece of fresh or frozen shrimp.

The residential canals at Apollo Beach offer some excellent fishing during the cooler months, but the best overall fishing action near here, year-round, seems to be at the flats and rugged mangrove shoreline to the south, past Mangrove Point (N27 44.862 W82 28.631) and into the mouth of the Little Manatee River. The ramp at Simmons Park, north of that river, offers access to the flats and the backwaters, making it an excellent departure point for both motor and paddle craft. Paddlers should consider heading north toward the backwaters of Double Bayou Pass (N27 45.223 W82 27.392) or Wolf Branch (N27 45.427 W82 26.810) to hunt for trout, reds, and snook. Anglers with deeper draft boats should launch at Simmons Park, follow the shoreline channel, and head into Tampa bay at Mangrove Point. Or, they can also fish the docks, residential canals, bars, and island shores within the mouth of the Little Manatee River.

The flats and backwaters to the north and south of Cockroach Bay are popular, but sometimes crowded. Here, kayakers ply the backwaters searching for redfish and snook, while flats fishers in motorboats drift the extensive flats that reach from the southern shore of the Little Manatee River well south past Port Manatee. With the exception of times of very cold weather, snook will be active most of the year in these backwaters. Extreme cold will drive them deep, but a few days of sunshine will warm these shallow waters and get them hungry again. This area, including some of the Little Manatee River shoreline, is within the Cockroach Bay Aquatic Preserve, 4500 acres of pristine Tampa Bay real estate owned by the Hillsborough Port Authority. The area's maze of mangrove islands serves as a nursery for snook, redfish, and seatrout, and its restricted speed zones help protect and preserve the shoreline.

Offshore Fishing

It's about 10 miles from the boat ramp at the mouth of Cockroach Bay to the main span of the Sunshine Skyway Bridge, where many folks consider "offshore" fishing begins. However, as I explained in chapter 4, "The Pinellas Peninsula," there are some pretty good spots to catch "offshore" fish well within the confines of Tampa Bay, and many are within easy reach of the bay's upper and eastern shores. The piles of rubble from the construction of the Courtney Campbell and Howard Frankland bridges are good examples of reefs or "fish havens" placed in less than 20 feet of water in Old Tampa Bay. The Campbell site is at N27 57.813 W82 36.861, and the Frankland site is at N27 54.697 W82 33.251, both within easy reach of shore and each likely to hold sheepshead, mangrove snapper, and even a keeper grouper. In Hillsborough Bay, many anglers troll for grouper along the deep edges of the big spoil islands to the east of the main channel, or the channels leading into the Alafia River or Big Bend Power Plant. Even anglers departing Cockroach Bay have some nearby "offshore" choices at the Bahia Beach Reef (N27 44.887 W82 30.918) and the Port Manatee Reef (N27 39.789 W82 34.740). These examples are just more reminders that you don't necessarily have to travel "offshore" to catch offshore fish in Tampa Bay.

Getting Around

Interstate 275 (I-275) breaks away from Interstate 75 (I-75) just north of Tampa, crosses Old Tampa Bay, and reconnects to I-75 south of the Sunshine Skyway Bridge in Manatee County. It runs through the middle of both the St. Petersburg and Tampa metropolitan areas. I-4 begins in Tampa and extends to I-95, Florida's east coast and the Atlantic Ocean. I-75 runs along the east side of Tampa, on its way south to Naples.

There are four east-west routes connecting the sides of Old Tampa Bay. The southernmost, from St. Petersburg, is the Gandy Bridge, its causeway and boulevard, which hit the middle of Tampa's Interbay Peninsula, eventually dead-ending into Bayshore Boulevard near Ballast Point on Hillsborough Bay. Just to its north, the Howard Frankland Bridge is part of I-275. The Courtney Campbell Causeway is SR60 and connects the Clearwater area with Tampa, near the International Airport.

And SR584, Hillsborough Avenue, runs eastward across the top of Old Tampa Bay from Safety Harbor, eventually intersecting I-275 in downtown Tampa.

Tampa's two main north-south routes are US41 and Dale Mabry Highway (SR597). US41 parallels I-75 into southwest Florida and Dale Mabry splits the Interbay Peninsula.

Where to Stay

Hampton Inn, 4050 Ulmerton Rd, Clearwater.

Days Inn, 3910 Ulmerton Rd, Clearwater.

Sleep Inn, 3939 Ulmerton Rd, Clearwater

Holiday Inn, 3535 Ulmerton Rd, Clearwater

These hotels are near St. Pete/Clearwater International Airport, on the west side of Old Tampa Bay. If you're trailering a boat, consider the fact that this side of the bay has less traffic than the east side.

Mar Bay Suites, (727) 723-3808, 3110 Phillippe Pkwy, Safety Harbor. Efficiencies and apartment suites, geared toward extended stays. www.marbaysuites.com

Howard Johnson Express Inn and Suites, (813) 832-4656, 3314 S. Dale Mabry, Tampa. Close to Gandy Bridge and the Salty Sol Fleischman boat ramp, with adequate trailer parking.

Ramada Bayside Inn, (813) 641-2700, 6414 Surfside Blvd, Apollo Beach. Basic lodging, convenient to the boat ramp at Apollo Beach Marina.

Pirate's Point Resort, (813) 641-2052, 1800 Kofresi Court,

Ruskin. "Resort" may be a stretch, but still a good place to stay near the mouth of the Little Manatee River. www.piratespointe resort.com

Where to Eat

Personally, I shy away from fast-food restaurants and have listed some places I think have a bit more character. If you need a "McJolt" of fast food, it's not far away. Tampa's Hispanic roots show at small groceries and restaurants offering Cuban and Spanish specialties. Cuban sandwiches (made of pork, Swiss cheese, ham, salami, and pickles layered on crusty Cuban bread) should be an essential part of every angler's lunch.

*　*　*

Alessi Bakery, 2909 W. Cypress St, Tampa. Excellent sandwiches and baked goods.

The Floridian, 4424 W. Kennedy Blvd, Tampa. Home of "The Finest Cuban Sandwiches on the Planet." They serve breakfast too!

Brocato's, 5021 E. Columbus Dr, Tampa. Stuffed potatoes, black beans and rice, deviled crabs, and more Cuban sandwiches. The $10 Cuban sandwich will feed two normal humans.

La Teresita Restaurant, 3248 W. Columbus Dr, Tampa. Cuban and Spanish dishes at reasonable prices.

Roberts' Meats, 3335 S. Westshore Blvd, Tampa. Excellent burgers, fish, BBQ. Try the smoked tenderloin or have Roberts' fry up your catch.

Green Iguana Bar and Grill, 4029 S. Westshore Blvd, Tampa.

Bar food, sandwiches, and drinks. Nightlife, if you aren't too tired from fishing.

Pipo's Original Cuban Café, 411 S. MacDill Ave, Tampa. Traditional Cuban dishes, daily specials, breakfast, and sandwiches.

Marinas, Marine Supplies and Service, Bait and Tackle Shops, and Launching Ramps

Gandy Wayside Ramp, St. Petersburg, west end of Gandy Bridge.

Safety Harbor Marina, Bayshore Dr, Safety Harbor. Single paved ramp, restrooms, fishing pier.

Phillipe Park ramp, Safety Harbor. Single paved $5 ramp. Good parking, close to some excellent mangrove shorelines.

R. E. Olds Park, 107 Shore Dr W, at end of Bayview Blvd, Oldsmar. 400-foot fishing pier and kayak launch.

Upper Tampa Bay Park, Oldsmar. South end of Double Branch Road, off SR580 (Hillsborough Ave). Kayak and canoe launch, about a mile to Old Tampa Bay.

Courtney Campbell Causeway boat ramp, Tampa. East end of causeway.

Pay attention to specific rules and regulations at public boat ramps.

Salty Sol Fleischman ramp, Tampa. East end of Gandy Bridge causeway.

Picnic Island boat ramp and fishing pier, Tampa. End of Commerce St, off Interbay Blvd. 300-foot pier on Old Tampa Bay.

Ballast Point ramp and fishing pier, Tampa. Interbay Blvd, at Ballast Point, on Hillsborough Bay.

Davis Islands ramp, Tampa. Severn Ave at Seaplane Basin, on Hillsborough Bay.

Williams Park ramp, Riverview. US41 on north side of Alafia River. 2 paved ramps, good parking, boat wash area, fishing pier.

Apollo Beach Marina, Surfside Blvd, Apollo Beach. On Tampa Bay.

You'll find several small fishing piers near river mouths along Tampa Bay's eastern shore.

Simmons Park, Ruskin. End of 19th Ave NW. 2 paved ramps, $2 park fee plus $5 launch fee, boat wash area, camping available.

Cockroach Bay Ramp, Ruskin. End of Cockroach Bay Rd. Single ramp, roadside parking, marked channel to Tampa Bay.

Denny B's Bait & Tackle, (813) 885-9811, 9735 W. Hillsborough Ave, Tampa. Bait, tackle, and good up-to-the minute fishing reports for Old Tampa Bay.

Osprey Bay Outdoors, (813) 243-5737, 8808 Rocky Creek Dr, Tampa. Kayak sales, rentals, chartered fishing trips. www.ospreybay.com

Blue Water Fishing Supply, (813) 932-2707, 12403 N. Florida Ave, Tampa. Bait and tackle, repairs, marine and trailer supplies.

Tampa Fishing Outfitters, (813) 870-1234, 3916 W. Osborne Ave, Tampa. I agree with their claim of being "the largest and most complete tackle shop in West Central Florida." www.tampafishingoutfitters.com

Southeastern Fishing Tackle Liquidators, (813) 223-3775, 2907 N. Florida Ave, Tampa. Closeouts, over-runs, great prices. Tampa Fishing Outfitters may be bigger, but this place is more fun and always worth a visit.

Tampa Bay On The Fly, (813) 443-0660, 4203 El Prado Blvd, Tampa. Fly-fishing gear, tying materials, excursions.

T. A. Mahoney Company, (813) 241-6500, 4990 E. Adamo Dr, Tampa. Marine and trailer parts and service, bait and tackle.

Gandy Bait & Tackle, (813) 839-5551, 4923 W. Gandy Blvd, Tampa. This is the place to stop for bait, tackle, and supplies if you're launching at the Salty Sol Fleischman boat ramp.

Jack's Interbay Marine, (813) 831-3000, 4810 W. McElroy Ave, Tampa. Marine supplies and parts, repairs.

SouthShore Bait & Tackle, (813) 677-2575, 9851 US41, Ruskin. Live and frozen bait, tackle, repairs.

Local Fishing Guides

Capt. Marc Noe, (813) 363-1743. Inshore and near shore. www.floridafishingchartersonline.com

Capt. Ray Markham, (941) 228-3474. Inshore, light tackle, south Tampa Bay.

Capt. Sergio Atanes, (813) 541-2564. Inshore and near shore. www.reelfishy.com

Capt. Woody Gore, (813) 477-3814. Inshore and near shore. www.captainwoodygore.com

Capt. Mark Gore, (813) 434-5504. Inshore and near shore. www.captainmarkgore.com

Capt. Mike Gore, (813) 390-6600. Inshore and near shore. www.captainmikegore.com

Capt. David Rieumont, (727) 204-9723. Inshore. www.seascrapcharters.com

Capt. Wade Osborne, (813) 286-3474. Inshore. www.afishionado.com

Capt. Dan Malzone, (813) 833-0312. Inshore light tackle and fly-fishing, tarpon specialist.

Capt. Nick Angelo, (813) 230-8473. Inshore, light tackle and fly-fishing.

Capt. Matt McDuffee, (813) 841-4126. Inshore and offshore.

Capt. James Rouse, (813) 817-7868. Inshore light tackle fishing.

Capt. Jim Lemke, (813) 917-4989. Inshore light tackle fishing.

Capt. Tony Frankland, (813) 915-8541. Light tackle fishing.

Capt. Michael Anderson, (813) 244-9397. Light tackle inshore fishing. www.thunderbaycharters.com

Capt. Billy Nobles, (813) 299-5563. Light tackle inshore fishing. www.captbillynobles.com

*   *   *

Many fishing guides from the coastal communities on the Pinellas peninsula are familiar with all the waters of Tampa Bay. If necessary, please check the listings in chapter 4 for more recommendations. Also, the website of the Florida Guides Association (www.florida-guides.com) has a complete listing of USCG licensed and insured fishing guides.

Before You Leave Home

Be sure to check this guide's companion website, www.salt wateranglersguide.com, for updates to local information.

6

Manatee and Sarasota Counties— The Gateway to Tropical Florida

Mango, avocado, and key lime trees will grow north of Tampa Bay, and if you're lucky, they'll bear fruit. But it's only a waiting game until they're hit by a cold snap. On the other hand, to the south of the bay, the weather is warmer, allowing tropical flora and fauna to flourish.

The Sunshine Skyway, with its visually stunning main span, at the southern end of Interstate 275, crosses just inside the mouth of Tampa Bay and deposits southbound travelers onto Terra Ceia Island in Manatee County. Inland, this county is largely agricultural, but its shoreline includes the mouth of the Manatee River, Anna Maria Island, about half of Longboat Key, and miles and miles of "fishy" mangrove islands. All these potential fishing spots are conveniently located, for anglers at least, in the direct path of the tide's flushing action on Tampa Bay. Just look at a chart of Tampa Bay and you'll begin to understand why the fishing's so great here.

I'd be remiss here in not mentioning lonely Egmont Key, which sits squarely in the middle of Tampa Bay's entrance. This outpost of the Tampa Bay pilot boat fleet is actually in Hillsborough County and closer to Pinellas County's Mullet Key (at Fort DeSoto State Park), but its south side, toward Manatee County, offers the best fishing.

At first glance (or perhaps on your first visit), Sarasota County's Gulf shoreline seems pretty overdeveloped, with lots

The main ship channel runs close to the southern shore of Tampa Bay. (Map courtesy of Waterproof Charts, Inc.)

of snazzy beachfront hotels and resorts. That's mostly true about the northern part of the county, but as you head south toward the towns of Osprey, Venice, and Englewood, life gets simpler. The Intracoastal Waterway (ICW) runs behind the barrier islands of Manatee and Sarasota counties before heading inshore at Venice. It then resumes its path into Lemon Bay at South Venice, where Manasota Key protects the busy channel and the Lemon Bay Aquatic Preserve. Lemon Bay was designated as an aquatic preserve in 1986. It is long, narrow, and shallow. Two Gulf passes and 7 tributaries flow into the aquatic preserve, creating a diverse network of mangroves and marsh grass, and vast expanses of seagrass meadows that cover most of the underwater habitats.

There's also fishing on the outside of the beach islands, but almost all of Florida's beachfront and bayfront land has now been developed; however, a slow ride down one of the island roads might find you a good spot to surf fish from the beach while avoiding private property. Just pretend you're an early explorer!

Inshore and Near Shore Fishing

I often envy my friend Capt. Ray Markham. Not so much for his good looks and youthful energy level, but for the fact that he's able to make a living as a fishing guide, sometimes never leaving the 21,000-acre Terra Ceia Aquatic Preserve. This area, stretching from Port Manatee to the Manatee River, encompassing shallow and deep waters, represents what many consider the last bit of pristine shoreline in Tampa Bay.

Trout, redfish, and snook are probably the most popular species of sport fish found near the south end of the Sunshine Skyway Bridge. Here, with the weather a bit warmer than the in the northern parts of Tampa Bay, you'll find these fish willing to bite most of the year. Tarpon arrive and travel the shorelines in spring too, usually heading up into Tampa Bay by midsummer. Reef fish, like grouper and snapper, are attracted to the deep structure of the Skyway and its South Fishing Pier. Pelagics, mostly king mackerel, Spanish mackerel, and bonito, follow bait schools into the bay, sometimes surprisingly close to shore. Other species, some edible like sheepshead and flounder and others just plain fun, like ladyfish and jacks, also cruise the

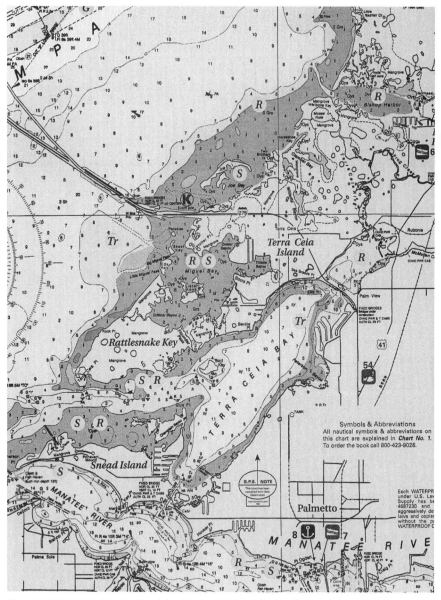

Terra Ceia Bay and the mouth of the Manatee River offer good protection from wind and cold weather. (Map courtesy of Waterproof Charts, Inc.)

Terra Ceia Bay is an excellent place to canoe and kayak.

shorelines of the bay and are often found inside local bays and in bayous and rivers.

There's a long line of shallow grass flats extending south from Port Manatee and into Bishop Harbor, Miguel Bay, and Terra Ceia Bay. Most of this grass is covered by 1–4 feet of water, but deeper potholes can be found between mangrove islands and alongside shell bars. When the weather's tolerable (meaning you can comfortably wade in short pants), expect to find seatrout on any of these flats. In the early hours of spring and summer, toss noisy topwater plugs over sand holes or alongside deeper cuts through the grass. These are the spots from which seatrout ambush their prey. As the day warms, expect the fish to move to slightly deeper and cooler water, especially along the outside of the grass banks, where they'll eat many types of baits. If you're not adept at using topwater or subsurface plugs, try a 3- or 4-inch soft plastic bait rigged to a 4/0 Daiichi ButtDragger hook or a light jig head. Simply throw it along the deep edge, make it hop along the bottom or just over the grass—and hold on. Another bait that works well here (and on any close-in waters on Florida's Gulf Coast) is the 3-inch D.O.A. shrimp. This artificial lookalike can be rigged under a cork with just enough clear fluorocarbon leader to glide it over the grass tops. An alternative method is to use D.O.A. Lures' pre-rigged "Deadly Combo." By "popping" its cork, you create a sound similar to the one made when a fish strikes a natural bait, attracting others to the "feed." Otherwise, you can simply retrieve a free-lined D.O.A. shrimp slowly over the grass tops, twitching it frequently—a technique that works well during summer months when trout are plentiful. Live baits also work well for trout. Live shrimp are excellent, but pinfish, another good bait for trout, like them, too. I just hate feeding bait to bait! In the morning hours, as the weather cools here (it rarely gets "cold" here), trout seek shelter in either backwater holes or in the 6- to 8-foot depths, just off the bayside edges of the shallow flats. Here, the sun shines a surprising number of days each winter, and by afternoon, trout will move into shallower water, seeking the warmth of dark flats and oyster bars.

As a general rule, each cast and each strike can bring a surprise to every saltwater angler. That's why so many freshwater anglers become fascinated with saltwater fishing. Here, at the bottom of Tampa Bay, it's spotted seatrout that attract lots of anglers to the water, but it's the reds and snook that really keep them focused. These species flourish here, the result of slow speed zones, unspoiled shorelines, temperate climate, and a general lack of angler pressure.

As winter ends and spring waters warm, snook and reds move from the backwaters and begin searching the flats for bait attracted to the shallows. Both are excellent targets for sight-fishers, but stealth is always an issue. Reds may be feeding, head down, on top of the flats or along shoreline shell bars. Snook, usually more aggressive ambush-feeders, will be cruising deeper cuts in search of swimming baits. If you intend

Don't miss any opportunity to fish shallow backwaters.

to catch these species, think about how your prey senses its predators before you start splashing around while wading or rocking your flats skiff or kayak while casting flies. What you think is a simple "push" of shallow clear water can mean much more to a 5-pound fish.

If you're looking for a place to start, you can't go wrong by launching your small boat or kayak at the Bishop Harbor ramp, exploring its backwaters, or heading out onto the flats near its mouth (N27 36.522 W82 34.261). Anglers in bigger boats might consider Terra Ceia Bay, entering from Tampa Bay using the marked channel. Depending on the tide, try fishing the north shoreline from Terra Ceia Point (N27 32.859 W82 37.837) to the docks at Sea Breeze Point (approx. N27 34.219 W82 34.462). There are also some good protected flats on the north side of Snead Island, south of Rattlesnake Key and the bay's mouth. Last, and certainly not least, don't overlook Miguel Bay, located just south of the Skyway Bridge Causeway. This is an exceptional backwater fishery that's popular with kayakers and other paddle-fishers, some even making trips from the north side of Tampa Bay to fish here. Its protected waters make for easy paddling and fly-fishing in almost any conditions as it's easy to find a shoreline in the lee of the wind.

Summer means "outside—but not offshore—fishing" in this part of the bay. The backwaters and near shore flats still hold trout, reds, and snook, as well as Florida's State Insect, the mosquito. If your hide's tough, fish "inside" and close to shore. If not, head to the deeper waters, including those near the Sunshine Skyway and the mouth of the Manatee River for more bug-free action. Bridge structures, like the Skyway, its long South Fishing Pier, and those inside the river, attract bait, and that bait brings with it some pretty good fishing. Tarpon roam the deeper edges of the shoreline or hang out behind bridge pilings and fenders. Grouper, mostly Goliaths, lurk anywhere there's something on the bottom that offers them an ambush point. And overslot snook, much bigger than those found up in the bays and backwaters, inhabit the depths under bridges and in deep channels. You don't even need a boat to fish these spots either, as certain bridges allow fishing from their catwalks or fishing piers. Even shorebound anglers have opportunities to catch lots of fish this time of year.

The Manatee River is wide and long, and because of the push and pull of the nearby Gulf of Mexico, its tides move well upstream of the Interstate 75 bridge. That being the case, anglers find snook and sheepshead around structures and under docks on the riverbanks almost year-round. In cooler weather, trout and snook will seek the comfort of the deeper channels near the mouth of the Braden River, the Manatee River's largest tributary. Try drifting the river channel between markers #24 and 28. Here, fish sinking plugs, like MirrOlure TTs, slowly along the bottom on overcast days or during early morning hours. As

The pilings and abutments of the bridges and structures over and along the Manatee River are excellent places to fish for snook, redfish, and tarpon.

the afternoon sun warms the day and the water, move toward and onto the shallows on either side of the river and try slow-moving, slow-sinking lures like Paul Brown Corkys. Redfish are more likely to adapt to the moderate ranges of temperatures here and tend not to move so much as the water cools or heats. Expect to find them closer to the river's mouth, hunting solo or in small groups until the late summer, when they school up for their annual spawning trip to offshore waters. Lower water temperatures won't give redfish pause to eat but will slow their actions. Expect them to be more interested in lures or bait that don't move very fast, a reason many anglers successfully catch them with live or artificial shrimp drifted under corks. When the waters get above about 75 degrees, however, it's time to get out the topwater plugs and enjoy the sight of reds chasing them down.

Anna Maria Island is at the northernmost tip of the long string of Gulf beach islands extending from Tampa Bay to

Sanibel Island, off Fort Myers. Some are connected by bridges and causeways. Others are separated by passes (Florida has "passes" on its west coast and "inlets" on its east coast), many with legendary fishing status. With Florida's growth and the need to fulfill the waterfront dreams of new residents, the beach islands have become crowded and, to some extent, over-built. I'd like to think that the developers and planners who built (by dredging and filling) the deep ICW and residential communities here would be surprised to see how generally clogged things have become, but I doubt it. Profit has always been a motive, and it's just in the first decade of the twenty-first century that muck-bottomed residential canals and channels are starting to become healthy again. Much of this improvement is due to renewed public interest in conservation and the hard work of groups like Sarasota Bay Watch (www.sarasotabaywatch.org).

With few exceptions, inshore fishing techniques and tactics don't change much from those mentioned earlier in this chapter as you proceed south from Tampa Bay. Bays, sounds, and structures differ, and for the most part, the fishing's the same, only the places change. The exceptions and additions to the mix of potential fishing spots are the beaches and the passes.

Beach fishing can be very democratic. Anyone can park a car, unload a rod and reel, and wade knee-deep into the surf in search of snook or pompano. That's the theory anyway, as the concept of "private property" often interferes with an angler's desire to walk a particular stretch of beach. Luckily, many of Florida's Gulf counties offer good access at parks and public beaches, offering anglers a chance to fish from shore. Of course, at many of these locations, anglers must share the beach with sunbathers and swimmers. Gulf-front fishing piers do offer some the opportunity to wet lines near busy beaches, but the best work-around seems to be boat-fishing close to shore. You will find some boat exclusion zones along beaches, but there are plenty of spots to fish that allow you access within just a few yards of shore. It's just as easy to see a snook just inside the surf "trench" from the water as it is from the land, and you've always got the chance to toss bait to larger prey, like tarpon or pelagics, roaming just out of beach-casting range. Beach fishing is, in my opinion, light tackle fishing. I often see folks fishing with spinning combos more geared to the Outer Banks of North Carolina than to the Gulf's clear, shallow shore. Unless there are snags or rock jetties nearby, you *can* land a 10-pound snook or a 3-pound pompano with light spinning tackle and 10-pound test line. You don't need to make long casts from either the shore or boats, as most of the "good" fish are cruising the surf in search of small baitfish or crustaceans (sand fleas and small crabs) churned up by the turbulent waves. D.O.A.'s 3-inch "glow" shrimp and light-colored Terror Eyz jigs are excellent choices for anglers wishing to quickly cover long stretches of beachfront. Beaches are also good places for fly-fishing, especially from shore. Capt. Rick Grassett's Snook Minnow fly, available locally at CB's Saltwater Outfitters, is an excellent fly for snook on the beaches. Seven to 9-weight fly tackle is sufficient for most beach fishing—just watch your back-cast if there are sunbathers behind you!

To become a successful pass angler, you must understand the action of the tides and the general "construction" of the pass you intend to fish.

Tidal strength can vary from pass to pass, depending mostly on the size of the bay or sound behind it, and on how far it is to the next pass. But for the most part, assume that any Gulf pass will offer you good water flow, even on weaker neap tides. The overall concept is simple: rising tides push bait and predators into the backwaters, and falling tides suck them out. Knowing that, along with the location of fish attractors like artificial reefs close to shore, rock jetties, broken seawalls, and inshore grass flats, can give you a game plan for a successful day of pass fishing. It's those places where most of the fish are caught in or near the passes, as structure is the all-important factor. As

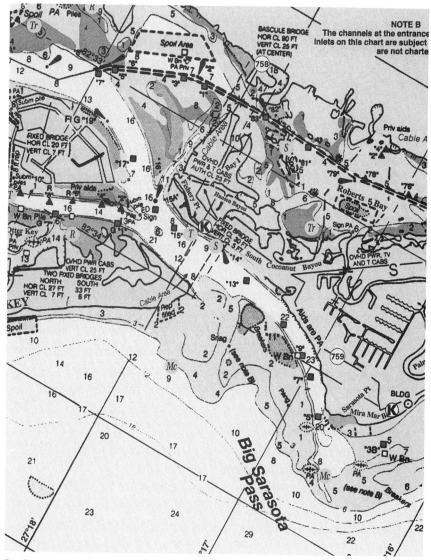

Big Sarasota Pass leads from the Gulf of Mexico into the heart of urban Sarasota. (Map courtesy of Waterproof Charts, Inc.)

The mix of water from Tampa Bay and the Gulf of Mexico provides forage for many species, like this redfish.

a general rule, and almost independent of the direction of the tides, expect to find trout, reds, flounder, and snook on the inside flats. Big summertime snook will also hang around bridge pilings and rock jetties, especially on stronger tides, and, on their springtime northern migration, tarpon will eat nonstop as they transit deep passes. Fishing the inshore flats behind passes can be a light-tackle exercise, but bigger rods and reels are needed if you plan to fish near pilings or rocky structure. Here, 5000- to 6000-class spinning gear is adequate, spooled with 30- to 50-pound PowerPro. For bait, consider live crabs for tarpon and live white bait for snook—or keep your hands from smelling bad and simply cast a deep-running MirrOlure TTR or a D.O.A. Bait Buster.

If you're fishing the 40-mile stretch of water from Anna Maria Island to the Charlotte County line, just south of Englewood, your techniques won't change much from the ones I've outlined; however, structure and waters will change, so I'll concentrate on geographic and hydrologic features for the remainder of this inshore fishing discussion.

The triangle of land making up Anna Maria Island has one side on the Gulf of Mexico, another on Tampa Bay, and a third on the Anna Maria Sound backwaters. This unique location allows the shore not only to feel the exchange of fresh Gulf and bay waters through the Passage Key Channel, but also to be influenced by the outflow of the Manatee River, just a few miles to the east. Inshore anglers should concentrate on the expansive grass flats bounded by Bean Point (N27 32.342 W82 44.643, at the tip of Anna Maria), Mead Point (N27 30.874 W82 40.914, at the mouth of shallow Perico Bayou), and the Bradenton Beach Bridge. On these flats, you'll find an active fishery for trout, reds, and snook, but don't be surprised if a Spanish mackerel, pompano, or permit takes your bait. It's sometimes hard for these species to resist the bait that's attracted to the area. In spring and early summer, you'll also see big schools of tarpon moving through the area, especially along deeper edges of the flats. A word or two about etiquette is in order about this, or any, tarpon fishery.

The area around Bean Point is fished regularly by professional guides hired by anglers wishing to catch tarpon on light or fly tackle. Be aware of this and give wide berth to anyone poling a skiff or casting to tarpon. If you're a visitor and intend to chase these big fish, watch the guides for a few days before you go and learn their routines. Even better, consider hiring one of the guides who fish there on a regular basis—as they know the "rules."

If you're looking for a side trip from the Anna Maria area, consider Palma Sola Bay. With its shallow flats and residential docks, this 2-mile-wide body of water offers some pretty good snook and redfish action, especially near the oyster bars and mangroves along the southern shores of the Cortez Channel or the main body of the bay. Entry to Palma Sola Bay is easy, with a channel leading east just south of ICW marker #50 at Cortez.

A day of fishing in Palma Sola Bay can be an adventure. (Map courtesy of Water-proof Charts, Inc.)

The narrows between Cortez and Bradenton Beach mark the northern end of Sarasota Bay, which extends south past downtown Sarasota to Big Sarasota Pass and Roberts Bay. Longboat Pass, dividing Anna Maria Key and Longboat Key, is the main source of clean Gulf water for the upper bay. Its edges are also good to wade, especially on the beach side, where snook and pompano feed during warmer months. Longboat Pass and the Longboat Key beachfront also offer excellent opportunities for tarpon anglers. There are some artificial reefs close to shore in fairly shallow (25 feet) of water to the north of the pass, at about N27 29.392 W82 43.758. Here, you may find small reef fish, but more likely Spanish mackerel, bonito, and bluefish chasing bait schools attracted to the structure below.

Jewfish Key and the Sister Keys, just inside and south of Longboat Pass, are examples of the amazing restoration of Sarasota Bay. Here, you'll find areas restricted to either slow speeds or nonmotorized craft only. Despite those restrictions, this is what Sarasota Bay used to look like, and it's a great fishery. The flats, cuts, and channel edges are excellent places to wade or kayak-fish. And you can take a break, head to shore, beach your kayak or tie up your boat, and have a great grouper sandwich at Ed Chiles's Mar Vista Restaurant on Longboat Key.

Fishing the shoreline flats within the main body of Sarasota Bay is always a good bet for trout, reds, and snook. One popular area is the Long Bar. It stretches from the shoreline at Long Bar Point (approx. N27 25.616 W82 37.191) to the edge of the ICW at marker #22. Popular means busy, but this is a big place. I'd recommend wading the south edge that faces the deeper water of the bay. Two other spots are the flats off Stephens Point (N27 22.583 W82 34.029, south of the Ringling Museum) and those between Bishops Point (N27 22.685 W82 36.904) and Whale Key (N27 23.628 W82 37.664). At these places, you'll likely catch trout, reds, snook, or a pompano.

The flats, potholes, and channels inside Sarasota's main Gulf passes, New Pass and Big Sarasota Pass, offer good angling as

There are thousands of residential docks lining the edges of the Intracoastal Waterway. Each is worthy of a cast or two.

a result of the constant flow of Gulf water. However, like the roads and beaches here, these are busy places often crowded with recreational boaters, personal watercraft, and other anglers. Depending on time of year and tide phase, you'll likely find trout over the grass and snook in deep cuts or around structure—and if you're fishing in the late summer or fall, keep your eyes peeled for the schools of Spanish mackerel that wash in and out of these passes with the tide.

Finally, regarding Sarasota Bay (and any other developed shoreline in Florida), give dock-fishing a try. Pitching small baits, like live or D.O.A. shrimp, under and around docks during early morning hours will produce good catches of snook, or keeper redfish, flounder, and trout. Or head out after dark, and fish each and every lighted dock you can access. Stealth is important here, and the use of a paddle or a trolling motor on your boat will greatly increase your chances of a good evening. At night, toss your bait just to the edges of the circle of light and await the bite of a predator using the dark for cover.

The 12-mile stretch of inshore backwater between Roberts Bay (behind Siesta Key) and Venice is anything but "more of the same old stuff" when it comes to fishing. Formed by Little Sarasota Bay and Blackburn Bay, it's narrow and busy with boat traffic, but its shorelines and docks offer some excellent snook fishing, and its flats attract trout, reds, flounder, and redfish. Beach anglers will find limited access on Siesta Key, but a trip down Midnight Pass Road to Turtle Beach Park will put you close to Midnight Pass and some good angling.

The boat ramp at the Turtle Bay Park also offers excellent access to anglers wishing to fish the Jim Neville Marine Preserve and the Bird Keys, inside Midnight Pass, which is now shoaled up. There are restrictions to motor use here, but paddlers find it an excellent area to fish for reds and snook almost year-round.

Blackburn Bay, south of Blackburn Point (at N27 10.790 W82 29.613) offers good fishing opportunities, especially inside the residential canals off South Creek. Its entrance is north of marker #28 on the ICW. Here, docks and mangrove overhangs provide shelter for snook, and oyster bars along deep edges provide forage for redfish.

At Venice, the ICW takes a turn eastward into Dona Bay and (yet another) Roberts Bay, where it resumes its course inland until it joins Lemon Bay, south, near Englewood. Here, Venice Inlet (for some reason it's an "inlet" rather than a "pass") provides fresh Gulf water to these backwater bays, as well as nearby Lyons Bay. All have docks, oyster bars, and flats providing some good angling for reds, trout, flounder, and snook. In warm months, look for bait schools passing through the inlet, and don't forget that it's a pretty good place to fish for snook or sheepshead. Shorebound anglers will also find the inlet's rock jetty or the Venice Fishing Pier (about 2 miles south) convenient places to fish.

Just north of Alligator Creek, where there's some pretty good snook fishing in the winter months, the ICW enters the Lemon Bay Aquatic Preserve. The preserve, with 8000 submerged acres, is the smallest of five aquatic preserves in the Charlotte Harbor area. With any boat travel outside the ICW limited to idle speed, this area has remained rich with mangroves, oyster bars, and lush grass flats. All these backwater structures, including bridges, residential docks, and canals, attract all species of inshore fish, including tarpon, as the bay widens toward Stump Pass, south of Englewood. Englewood's backwaters are, in the opinion of many anglers, some of the best places to catch big snook, especially at night during summer months. Beachfront sight-fishing for snook is good here too, with access for waders at Manasota Beach and Blind Pass Beach on Manasota Key.

Lemon Bay is shared by two counties, Sarasota and Charlotte, but that means nothing to the fish. Heading south just means more good fishing in Charlotte Harbor and near its Gulf islands.

Offshore Fishing

Despite this area's excellent inshore and near shore fishing, not all anglers want to stay close to land. Offshore and blue water fishing are excellent all along Florida's Gulf Coast, especially south of Tampa Bay, where deep water comes closer to the shore.

Anglers with bigger boats (or chartering offshore captains) leaving the Manatee River and Anna Maria Sound have the deep waters at the mouth of Tampa Bay within easy reach. It's a

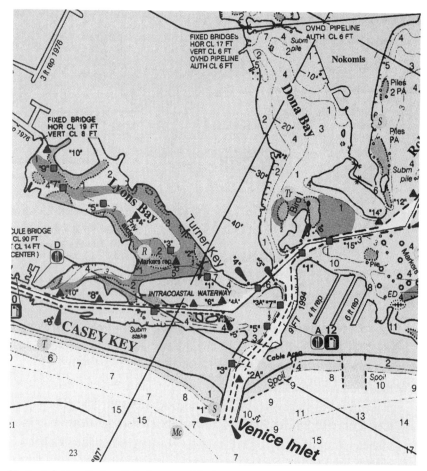

Venice Inlet is called an "inlet"—one of the few passes so named on Florida's west coast. (Map courtesy of Waterproof Charts, Inc.)

relatively short trip to the Egmont Reefs (approx. N27 35.080 W82 44.540) on the east side of Egmont Key, where you're just as likely to catch grouper, snapper, and king mackerel as you are 20 miles offshore in 80 feet of water. A couple of other good "offshore" spots within Tampa Bay are the areas of Sunshine Skyway bridge rubble near the north and south fishing piers, as well as the edges of the Mullet Key and Port Manatee channels. The edges of channel spoils can also produce surprising catches of grouper and kingfish, especially for anglers trolling big deep-diving plugs.

From Anna Maria to Venice, access to the Gulf is limited to just a few cuts through the barrier islands. Longboat Pass, New Pass, Big Sarasota Pass, and Venice Inlet are busy with boats heading westward in search of deepwater species like grouper, snapper, king mackerel, wahoo, billfish, and whatever other species are at home in deep water. There are literally hundreds of offshore places to fish here, and many are within 30 miles, and in less than 100 feet of water. Some feature natural structure or depressions; others, wrecks or reefs. Most offer some sort of fishing action year-round, as Gulf waters are warm here. This book includes lists of reefs, arranged by county, in chapter 11. Anglers fishing from Manatee and Sarasota ports should consult them, as well as the lists for Pinellas and Charlotte counties; however, if you're visually oriented and need a chart for reference, you can't do much better than having a copy of Waterproof Chart's chart #155F, Clearwater to Venice Fish/Dive (www.waterproofcharts.com) in front of you when you plan your offshore outing. Not only does this chart show several hundred reefs, wrecks, and depressions, but it also gives accurate waypoints and good visual clues as to where they are.

Getting Around

The two most important north-south routes in Manatee and Sarasota counties are Interstate 75 and US41, the Tamiami Trail (*Tampa* to *Miami* Trail). Interstate 275 and the Sunshine Skyway end at Terra Ceia and join up with I-75, which heads south, eventually crossing the state and dead-ending in Ft. Lauderdale. In Manatee County the important cross routes to be aware of are SR64 and SR684 from Bradenton to Anna Maria Island, Bradenton Beach, and the north end of Longboat Key. In Sarasota County, Fruitville Road (SR780) runs west to the John Ringling Causeway (SR789), Lido Key, and the south

Marinas, like this one at Bradenton, can be busy, especially during winter months.

end of Longboat Key. Bee Ridge Road (SR758) and Clark Road (SR72) feed traffic to Siesta Key and its beaches. US41 runs right through the middle of Venice and there's easy access to the shore via the established Business Route. US41 makes an eastward turn in South Venice, but there, following Englewood Road (SR776) will keep you oriented to the Gulf shoreline.

Roads and highways are good here, but as is the case with most of Florida, much of the development has taken place close to the Gulf shore. Expect traffic, lots of it, especially if you arrive during tourist season.

Where to Stay

Pirate's Point Resort, (813) 641-2052, 1800 Kofresi Court, Ruskin. "Resort" may be a stretch, but it's still a good place to stay near the mouth of the Little Manatee River. www.pirates pointeresort.com

Rod & Reel Resort, (941) 778-2780, 877 North Shore Dr, Anna Maria. One-room kitchenettes, on ICW inside of Bean Point, at Rod & Reel Pier and Restaurant.

Cannon's Cottages, (941) 383-1311, 6051 Gulf of Mexico Dr, Longboat Key. Private, simple beachfront cottages owned and operated by Cannon's Marina. Good beach fishing too!

Addy's Nokomis Villas, (941) 488-7990, 330 N. Tamiami Tr, Nokomis. 2- and 4-bedroom villas with full kitchens. Closer to Venice than to Sarasota.

Englewood Bay Motel and Apartments, (941) 475-1769, 69 W. Bay St, Englewood. Efficiencies and condos available. Reasonable daily, weekly, and monthly rates.

Buchan's Landing, (941) 474-5100, 599 W. Dearborn St, Englewood. Across the street from the Dearborn Corner Market. On Lemon Bay at marker 28a. Efficiencies and motel rooms come with free boat slip and trailer parking. Boat rentals available. Near the Indian Mounds boat ramp.

Where to Eat

I really enjoy eating seafood while I'm fishing in this part of Florida—and here, you'll find an almost endless number of seafood restaurants, ranging from shacks to 5-star eateries. I've listed a few local favorites for you to try.

*   *   *

Star Fish Company, 12306 46th Ave W, Cortez. Cortez hasn't changed much in the past 50 or 60 years. Eat some great fried shrimp and drink some cold beer on the working docks here. Don't miss this place!

Don't miss the fried shrimp at Star Fish Company at Cortez.

Cortez Seafood Market, (941) 794-1547, 4528 119th St W, Bradenton (off Cortez Road). If you can't catch dinner, pick up some really fresh seafood to take home!

Rod & Reel Pier, 875 N. Shore Dr, Anna Maria. A fun restaurant at the end of the fishing pier. Eat at the bar, if there's room.

Rotten Ralph's, locations at 902 S. Bay Blvd, Anna Maria, and Bradenton Beach Pier, Bridge St. Breakfast, lunch, and dinner.

Anna Maria City Pier, Pine Ave, Anna Maria. A good view of pier anglers while you're eating!

Mar Vista Dockside Restaurant & Pub, 760 Broadway, N. Longboat Key. Tie up your boat or beach your kayak, eat one of their famous grouper sandwiches, and leave a dollar bill on the wall. This place is well worth the visit.

Moore's Stone Crab Restaurant, (941) 383-1748, 800 Broadway, N. Longboat Key. Enjoy some crabs (in season) or seafood here.

Dry Dock Grill, (941) 383-0102, 412 Gulf of Mexico Dr, Longboat Key. Fresh seafood, patio dining.

Captain Eddie's Family Seafood Restaurant, 107 Colonia Lane, Nokomis. Take-out and fresh seafood available.

Sharky's on the Pier, Venice Fishing Pier, 1600 Harbor Dr S. Good seafood and a good view of the "green flash."

Wee Blew Inn Restaurant, 590 US41 By-Pass S, Venice. Breakfasts and diner food. Closed Sundays.

Left Coast Seafood Company, (941) 485-5064, 750 US41 By-Pass, Venice. A good choice for seafood. Family-style dining.

Snook Haven Restaurant, 5000 E. Venice Ave, Venice. An "old Florida joint" with decent, high-quality bar-type food. The scenery and decor are fun.

Marinas, Marine Supplies and Service, Bait and Tackle Shops, and Launching Ramps

Sunshine Skyway South Fishing Pier. At 8860 feet long, this is one of Florida's best fishing piers. Open 24 hours, 7 days a week. There's a bait shop, and the modest admission fee lets you drive onto the pier. "Sightseeing" passes are also available.

Skyway Bait & Tackle, 4808 US19 N, Palmetto. Tackle, live and frozen bait.

Discount Tackle Outlet, (941) 746-6020, 3113 First St E, Bradenton. Excellent selection of tackle, gear, and fishing kayaks, rod and reel repairs.

Annie's Bait & Tackle, 4334 127th St W, Cortez. At east end of Cortez bridge. Dock here for gas, bait, tackle, a beer, and a sandwich.

Rod & Reel Pier, 875 N. Shore Dr, Anna Maria. On Tampa Bay.

Anna Maria City Pier, Pine Ave, Anna Maria. Good fishing in Tampa Bay. Pier has restaurant and bait shop.

Bradenton Beach Pier, end of Bridge St, Bradenton Beach. 300-foot pier, restaurant (breakfast only), bait and tackle, restrooms, on the north end of Sarasota Bay.

Island Discount Tackle, 5503 Marina Dr, Holmes Beach (Anna Maria). Excellent selection of tackle and marine supplies.

Catcher's Marina, (941) 778-1977, 5501 Marina Dr, Holmes Beach (Anna Maria). Fuel and dockage.

Cannon's Marina, (941) 383-1311, 6040 Gulf of Mexico Dr, Longboat Key. At ICW marker #33. Full service marina, fuel, boat rentals. Beachfront cottages available.

Ingman Marine, (941) 360-0088, 8311 N. Tamiami Tr, Sarasota. Excellent service, parts and accessories. Locations in Placida and Port Charlotte too.

Sara Bay Marina, (941) 359-0390, 7040 N. Tamiami Tr, Sarasota. East of ICW marker #16 on Bowlees Creek. Full service marina.

Sarasota's deep-sea fishing fleet gives everyone access to good offshore fishing.

CB's Saltwater Outfitters, (941) 349-4400, 1249 Stickney Point Rd, Siesta Key. Orvis-endorsed fly shop, complete tackle shop. A good source for up-to-date information on "the bite." Some of the area's top guides call this place home. www.cbsoutfitters.com

Silent Sports Outfitters, (941) 966-5477, 2301 N. Tamiami Tr, Nokomis. Fishing kayak outfitters. www.silentsportsoutfitters.com

Mahi Mac's Discount Bait & Tackle, (941) 615-7485, 1011 Tamiami Tr, Nokomis. Live and frozen bait, tackle, repairs, custom rods.

Venice Fishing Pier, Brohard Park, Venice. 700-foot fishing pier with restaurant, restrooms, and bait shop.

Cook's Sportland, (941) 493-0025, 4419 Tamiami Tr S, Venice. Lots of tackle, good fishing know-how, rod and reel repair, canoes, and kayaks. A good place to while away a few hours on a stormy day!

Englewood Bait House, (941) 475-4511, 1450 Beach Rd, Englewood. Live and frozen bait, tackle.

Dearborn Corner Market, 598 W. Dearborn St, Englewood. Bait and tackle. A good source for live shrimp, especially after the other bait shops have closed for the evening.

Bishop Harbor boat ramp, Bishop Harbor Rd, off US41, Terra Ceia. Primitive ramp with excellent backwater access for canoes, kayaks, and shallow draft boats.

Riverside Park boat ramp, Palmetto. Paved ramps on Manatee River, at north end of US41 bridge.

Palma Sola boat ramp, 9000 Manatee Ave, Bradenton. Shallow paved ramp on north end of Palma Sola Bay.

Kingfish Ramp, west end of SR64 bridge, Anna Maria. On Anna Maria Sound.

Coquina Bayside ramp, S. Gulf Dr, Bradenton Beach (Anna Maria). Two ramps on upper Sarasota Bay.

Centennial Park, 11th St at US41, downtown Sarasota. Excellent, 3 ramps, lots of parking. Good access to New Pass and Big Sarasota Pass.

Ken Thompson Park, Lido Key, 3 paved ramps. Excellent parking, good access to New Pass.

Turtle Beach ramp, 8918 Midnight Pass Rd, Siesta Key. 2 ramps on Little Sarasota Bay north of Neville Marine Preserve.

Blackburn Point Park ramp, Blackburn Point Rd, Osprey. Shallow ramp, good canoe and kayak access to Blackburn Bay.

Higel Marine Park ramp, Venice Ave, Venice. On Roberts Bay.

Marina Park ramp, Venice. Single paved ramp on ICW.

Manasota Beach ramp, 8570 Manasota Key, Englewood. Single paved ramp on ICW.

Indian Mounds Park ramp, 210 Winson Ave, Englewood. 2 ramps, good parking, good canoe and kayak launch.

Local Fishing Guides

Capt. Ray Markham, (941) 228-3474. Inshore and light tackle fishing.

Capt. Rick Grassett, (941) 923-7799. Inshore, light tackle, and fly-fishing tarpon specialist. One of the area's top guides. www.snookfin-addict.com

Capt. Jonnie Walker, (941) 232-4970. Inshore, near shore, and offshore fishing. In the area since 1974. www.baywalkerchar ters.com.

Capt. Geoffrey Page, (941) 586-3756. Inshore and light tackle specialist.

Capt. Scott Moore, (941) 713-1921. Inshore, light tackle fishing.

Capt. Justin Moore, (941) 720-6408. Inshore, light tackle fishing.

Capt. Ed Johnson, (941) 321-1567. Offshore fishing. www.fish -factor.com

Capt. Michael Anderson, (813) 244-9397. Light tackle inshore fishing. www.thunderbaycharters.com

Capt. Billy Nobles, (813) 299-5563. Light tackle inshore fishing. www.captbillynobles.com

Capt. Jeffri Durrance, (941) 915-2933. Inshore and near shore fishing.

Capt. Pete Greenan, (941) 232-2960. Inshore, light tackle, and fly-fishing. Pete also operates the Boca Grande Fly Fishing School, www.floridaflyfishing.com.

Capt. Van Hubbard, (941) 697-6944. Inshore and near shore fishing. www.captvan.com

* * *

Many fishing guides from the Tampa Bay and Charlotte Harbor areas are familiar with the waters here. If necessary, please check the listings in chapters 4, 5, and 7 for more recommendations. Also, the website of the Florida Guides Association (www.florida-guides.com) has a complete listing of USCG licensed and insured fishing guides.

Before You Leave Home

Be sure to check this guide's companion website, www.salt wateranglersguide.com, for updates to local information.

7

Charlotte Harbor and Her Gulf Islands

Expressing my true feelings about this stretch of Florida's Gulf Coast is likely to get me tarred and feathered in my traditional fishing grounds. It's not that I don't like fishing the Big Bend, where I fish now, or Tampa Bay, where I grew up. I just love Charlotte Harbor.

The Charlotte Harbor area is, as explained to me by my good friend Capt. Ralph Allen, three separate and distinct fishing environments. There's the "upper harbor" that reaches from Cape Haze Point to Punta Gorda and Port Charlotte and includes some of the Myakka and Peace Rivers. Then, there's the "middle harbor" that includes the area inside Boca Grande Pass as well as some of the north end of Pine Island Sound. And finally, not to be excluded, are the beaches and backwaters of the barrier islands from Englewood to Redfish Pass, south of Cayo Costa Island.

Punta Gorda, or "fat point," is both a small city and a place where the Peace River flows into upper Charlotte Harbor. Quiet and quaint, the city's been steadily rebuilding since devastated by Hurricane Charley in October of 2004. The more commercial city of Port Charlotte is to Punta Gorda's north, just across the US41 Bridge. It offers excellent amenities for anglers as well. Many visitors to Florida assume that the state's history is based on oranges and animated big-eared rats; however, the

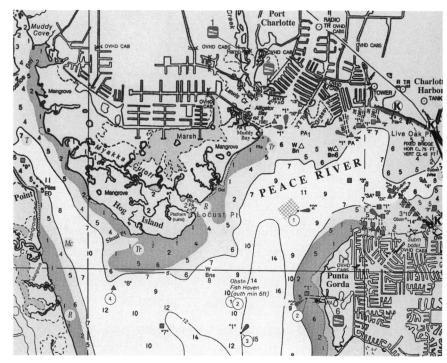

The confluence of the Peace and Myakka Rivers form upper Charlotte Harbor. (Map courtesy of Waterproof Charts, Inc.)

history of settlements in the upper harbor reminds us of the importance of cattle and fish to the early economy. What is now the city of Port Charlotte was once ranch land, and cattle were regularly shipped from docks on the Peace River. And at Punta Gorda, oysters, fish, and cattle all kept early settlers busy.

Boca Grande Pass, the cut between the south end of Gasparilla Island and the north end of Cayo Costa Island, is less than a mile wide and not much more than 50 feet deep at its deepest point. With the exception of some "leakage" to the Gulf through Gasparilla Sound to the north and Pine Island Sound to the south, much of the tidal flow into and out of Charlotte

Punta Gorda's riverfront has recovered nicely from several bad hurricanes in the 1990s.

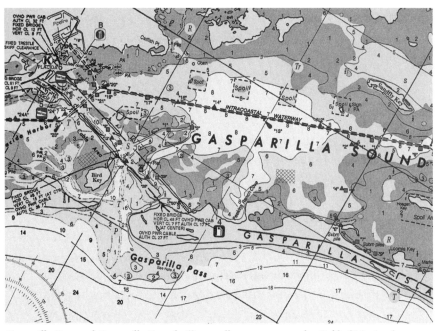

Gasparilla Pass and Gasparilla Sound offer excellent passage to the Gulf of Mexico from upper Charlotte Harbor. (Map courtesy of Waterproof Charts, Inc.)

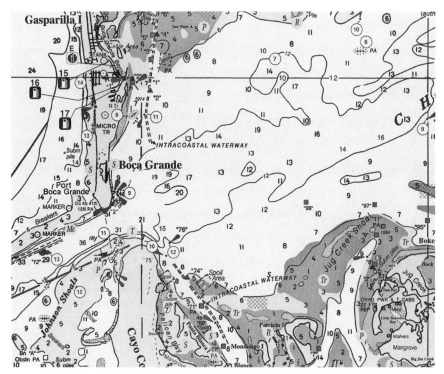

Huge amounts of water and bait pass through Boca Grande Pass on each tide cycle, making it one of the best fishing destinations in Florida. (Map courtesy of Waterproof Charts, Inc.)

Harbor runs through the pass. That's extreme, but likely the cause of some generally excellent fishing all the way back to Cape Haze, about 7 miles to the east.

Pine Island is about 15 miles long. Its size and adjacent shallow waters serve to block some of the tidal flow in and out of Charlotte Harbor; however, don't be fooled into believing that Pine Island Sound, which reaches south to Sanibel Island, is an insignificant body of water. The northern half of the sound is peppered with islands and islets, much like those to the north across the mouth of Charlotte Harbor in Gasparilla Sound.

These, divided by channels, surrounded by oyster and shell bars, and rimmed with mangroves, provide some of the best inshore fishing in Florida. This chapter will cover the northern end of Pine Island, Bokeelia, and Pineland. Chapter 8 will continue with coverage of the middle and southern parts of the island (including Matlacha and St. James City).

I can't think of many other areas in Florida that offer not only a tremendous diversity of angling opportunities but also a full range of amenities for the visiting angler. Here, expect to find excellent marine facilities, experienced and friendly fishing guides, helpful tackle shop personnel, a wide range of lodging possibilities, and some great places to eat and drink. The bottom line is that Charlotte Harbor is all about fishing and making anglers comfortable.

Inshore and Near Shore Fishing

Florida's most popular inshore fish species are probably spotted seatrout, snook, redfish, and tarpon—in that order. "Lesser" species, a category that includes sheepshead, flounder, Spanish mackerel, pompano, and tripletail, are not necessarily rare and often caught by anglers targeting the "big four."

The exclamation, "Let's go fishing!" translates to "Let's go trout fishing!" in most of Florida, and I suspect that's the same in the Charlotte Harbor area. Spotted seatrout (not "speckled trout" or "specks"!) can be caught here throughout the year.

Fish never stop eating. They do change their eating habits depending on structure, time of day, and water temperature. Those habits involve heading into deep water, sometimes up rivers and creeks, as the water cools in fall and winter, or into shallower waters, near grass flats and bars, when it warms. And the sudden onset of cool mornings or sweltering afternoons can change a fish's course, independent of the season. Here in southwest Florida, where the leaves don't change color in the fall and flowers bloom all year, understanding those subtle changes is the thing that makes some fishermen more successful than others.

Spotted seatrout are good barometers of any fishery, as they move in subtle ways, dependent on the water temperatures. Trout are plentiful here in Charlotte Harbor and relatively easy to catch. In spring, as waters begin to warm, bait like shrimp, pinfish, and minnows will lure them onto the grass flats, but just a few days of cool weather will drive them back into channels, creek mouths, and residential canals.

As water temperatures stabilize, expect to find trout on the "flats," setting up ambush points that maximize their feeding. They like sea grass, but they especially like small sandy potholes that give them a clear view of their prey. They are also attracted to the structure of docks that provide the advantages of shady hideouts during the day and brilliant edges of shadows at night. For the most part, trout don't "school up" but do tend to gang up with others of similar size. If you start catching small ones, move along, try another spot, and hope for bigger slot-sized versions. Big "gator" trout, those more than 20 inches, don't necessarily gather with others of their own size and are caught mostly while feeding solo along channel edges or bars, just as the sun comes up.

If it weren't for all the different ways anglers can catch spotted seatrout, folks in tackle stores would have nothing to do, or to sell. Many anglers own tackle boxes stuffed with all varieties of "trout killers," and each angler has his or her favorite method of catching these fish.

The great divide among trout fishers is drawn along a line that separates those who use live or natural baits and those who fish with artificial lures. Both methods have advantages, and I suggest anyone heading out on a trout-fishing trip be prepared to use either, or even a combination of the two.

Here, live bait is plentiful, especially in warmer weather. White bait schools, or pods, are easily found, and it's not difficult, using a small-mesh cast net and some chum, to fill a live well with hundreds of frisky minnows. Live pinfish can also be netted or trapped on grassy banks, and live shrimp are available at almost every bait shop. The advantage of using these baits is that they represent natural forage for trout, essentially "matching the hatch." The disadvantage is that you must deal with keeping them alive, not an easy task if the water temperature is high and its oxygen level low. Live wells are essential tools for keeping white bait and pinfish fresh. Live shrimp will stay frisky for hours if kept dry, bagged in a cooler, and separated from ice with the day's "society" section of the local newspaper. The simplest way to use live bait is to "free-line" it, hooked without a weight and allowed to swim or drift over flats, near bars or around structure. This natural presentation is excellent, but long casts can be difficult, even if there's no wind. Another popular method of trout fishing involves the use of what are generally called "popping corks." These, floating high enough above the bait to keep it just above the bottom, make a loud noise when they hit the water and when they are "popped" by the angler. The noise they make attracts trout (and other species) by simulating what they think is another fish striking bait. The best depth to use these corks is 3 to 4 feet. Anything deeper means a longer leader, and the whole rig gets unwieldy. Easy-to-cast, light spinning combos, in the 2000 to 2500 class, spooled with 8- or 10-pound-test Power Pro line, are preferred by many successful trout anglers. A 2/0 hook is sufficient for trout fishing with live bait, and near-invisible fluorocarbon leader (20-pound test) is essential. Snaps and swivels just mess up the action of your bait, so learn to tie your leader directly to your line with either a surgeon's knot or a Uniknot. And finally, learn to tie a loop knot to attach your leader to your hook—and to most terminal tackle.

Tossing artificial baits like plugs keeps you active making lots of casts and retrieves, but watching a trout strike a topwater lure is just about as exciting as trout fishing gets. Topwater plugs are popular trout lures and used mainly in shallower water. Despite the rumors, they will catch trout at any time of the day, but are especially useful at dawn and dusk, retrieved along shallow shorelines and over grass flats. MirrOlure's Top Dog and Top Pup lures seem to have just the right mix of rattle and action. If you find trout in deeper water, where they either cool off in the heat of summer or stay warm in the dead of winter, try a lure that sinks into the water column. Here, it's hard to beat a 3-inch D.O.A. shrimp (light colored if the water's clear, or dark if it's stained or muddy) retrieved slowly with a simple twitch every few feet. MirrOlure 52's or MirrOdine hard baits are also effective, as they really do mimic live baitfish. Jigs or hooks rigged with soft tails are also popular for trout. These baits come in a myriad of colors and styles, but I'd recommend you find one brand and a couple of colors you like, so as not to confuse your tackle box. Light colors work well in clear water, and I don't think the color of the jig head makes a bit of difference, so long as it's red or chartreuse. "Work" your jig and soft-tail combination along the edges of sandy potholes on grass flats, along channel edges, or under docks, day and night. Jigs can also be suspended under popping corks, a method especially useful if you have difficulty casting about a thousand times a day. Another option for jigging for trout is to use flavored and scented plastics like Berkley's GULP!, Bass Assassin's BLURP!, or FishBites. Another technique is to "sweeten" your jig with a small piece of cut-up shrimp. Adding some "stink" or flavor can often help attract fish, especially if they're unable to visually tune in to the bait in dark or cloudy water.

Any fishing trip here can start as a trout-fishing trip and end up a success with the bagging of a prize from a totally different species, like snook. Snook roam the same flats as trout,

Snook are certainly the most popular inshore fish found in Charlotte Harbor waters.

but they generally prefer slightly warmer water and are usually more interested in structure like snags and pilings, even if the currents are strong. They'll also get closer to shore than trout, often lying under overhanging mangrove branches in just a foot or so of water, waiting for their prey to get within range. And the biggest specimens can often be found at night, feeding around bridges and big lighted docks, sometimes on small bait-fish. For the most part, snook eat the same baits as seatrout,

Boca Grande Pass can be busy, especially during tarpon tournaments.

but here they seem to take particular interest in jumbo shrimp or in big white baits, free-lined and frisky.

Redfishing is popular here, especially for sight-fishing enthusiasts. On warm winter afternoons or early summer mornings, casting to reds with light spinning or fly tackle is lots of fun. Look for tails or backs out of the water, and be careful not to create any wake by rocking your boat. Your best bet, if it's shallow enough and you've got some wading shoes, is to get overboard and approach these fish on foot. If the reds are feeding on the bottom (tails up), along an oyster bar, or in a creek, try fishing with live or D.O.A. 3-inch shrimp, free-lined in front of them. Or, drag a weedless gold spoon, like the Eppinger Rex, in their path, moving it slowly and erratically along the bottom. These small baits help you avoid making a big fish-spooking splash near your prey. If reds are in deeper water (or if you don't see them and need to "prospect"), try a MirrOlure Catch 2000, which runs under the surface and looks like a small baitfish or mullet. Topwaters work well for redfish but you sometimes have to trick redfish into eating one. Reds' downturned mouths make it hard for them to strike a surface plug as they must often turn upside down to eat it. Teasing a charging red into eating sometimes involves slowing or speeding your retrieve, or stopping it altogether.

While Boca Grande Pass, at the southern end of Gasparilla Island, is considered by many anglers to be "tarpon central," it's not the only place in the Charlotte Harbor area to catch a silver king. Yes, in May and June, especially at the times of the "hill tides" (new and full moon), the tarpon fishing in the pass is excellent. Tarpon take particular interest in the small crabs that wash out of the harbor on those tides. Also, on those busy days, expect to compete with more than a hundred boats in the narrow pass. Over the last twenty years, rules for tarpon fishing in Boca Grande Pass have been established by the Boca Grande Fishing Guides Association. These rules make good sense and are officially endorsed (and enforced) by the FWC. The BGFGA rules are published online (www.bocagrandefish ing.com) and in their brochure, *Tarpon Fishing & Boat Operation at Boca Grande*, available at tackle shops locally. Pass fishing involves knowing the drift, the depth, and the bait that

Getting a big tarpon to your boat's side is a matter of angling skill and just plain luck.

tarpon are eating that day. Hiring a local professional tarpon guide makes perfect sense if you want to fish this pass.

Tarpon are found throughout the summer months in the deep holes in the middle of Charlotte Harbor and well up into the Myakka and Peace rivers, feeding along the edges of grass flats, channels, or bridge and pier structures. Some, including smaller fish, often range up into deep creeks and residential canals and spend the winter months there. Others leave the passes in late spring and travel close along the Gulf Beach shoreline, targets for sight fishers tossing small jigs, live baits, or flies.

A trip dedicated to chasing tarpon can be fun, but often frustrating. If you're not a seasoned tarpon angler, I recommend you be prepared for them and consider them an incidental and valued catch if you get one to your boat. Being prepared means fishing for trout, reds, or snook and having a big 6000 size spinning outfit rigged with 30-pound Power Pro line, an 80-pound fluorocarbon leader, and your favorite tarpon bait handy. Many "live baiters" keep a live white bait or pinfish at the ready in their live well just in case a school of tarpon is spotted. Others (myself included) have full confidence in the D.O.A. Bait Buster, a single-hook soft bait that tarpon readily strike. In either case, don't run up on the fish, but carefully put your boat in a position so the school will pass by within casting range. An electric motor or push pole will give you a better chance of successfully allowing tarpon to approach you.

The adjective "lesser" I use to describe sheepshead, flounder, Spanish mackerel, pompano, and tripletail really has nothing to do with the quality of these fish, but the frequency with which they're caught or targeted. All five, especially flounder and pompano, are excellent table fare.

Big sheepshead are mainly a cool-weather target and found on inshore reefs and around structure like bridges and docks. Smaller versions are caught year-round on flats and in inshore potholes. Favorite baits for this species are fiddler crabs and frozen or live shrimp. The smaller fish are sometimes difficult to hook, but the larger ones eagerly attack whole shrimp rigged on lead jig heads. Chumming seems to help concentrate the fish and encourage them to bite.

Flounder lie on the bottom, both eyes pointed upward, and wait for small baits to pass overhead. They particularly savor small live mullet and shrimp but will usually attack plastic jigs or shrimp imitations. Areas near creek mouths and oyster bars seem to be their favorite haunts, but some are even caught along the edges of shallow artificial reefs. Flounder can be found anywhere in the area and are always a welcomed bycatch of a close-to-shore trout or redfish trip.

Schools of Spanish mackerel are easy to spot. Usually, wheeling birds give away their location as the birds scavenge scraps of the white bait the mackerel are ravaging. Don't run into the middle of the bait pod, but fish the edges with any rig you're willing to lose to the mackerels' sharp teeth. If you have time, beef up your terminal tackle with wire leader, but otherwise, just take your chances and put a few tasty mackerel in the fish box.

Pompano and their larger and smarter cousins, permit, are members of the "jack" family, except they're edible. You'll sometimes find pompano when they attack your trout bait, but they're prone to feed in numbers along channel edges, in passes, or in beachfront surf. If you "skip" a pompano in the wake of your boat, stop and bounce a jig along the bottom. Special "pompano jigs" like Doc's Goofy Jig work best, but whatever's handy will do in this case. Live or artificial shrimp will work in a "pompano emergency," as will short-tailed soft baits. If you know you're in an area that's likely to hold pompano, like a beach or pass, fish with live sand fleas or the special "pompano" jigs. Permit are likely to be found over wrecks in the Gulf, but it's not unusual to find them within the vast reaches of Charlotte Harbor, especially around the shallow artificial reefs.

Do you remember when Junior Samples (of *Hee Haw* TV fame) took a gag grouper home to Georgia from Florida and convinced everyone there that it was a world-record largemouth bass? He might have done the same had he caught a tripletail, which looks much like a freshwater aquarium fish known as an oscar. Not sleek or pretty, this fish can be found near pilings, channel markers, and crab trap floats. Looking much like pieces of flotsam or jetsam, many are often missed by anglers in search of other species. Seasoned anglers will stop at every potential tripletail lair and toss a live or artificial shrimp near it, just to see if anyone's home. Tripletail rival sheepshead and triggerfish when it comes to difficulty in cleaning, a task usually aided by use of an electric knife. But they're worth the effort when it's dinner time.

Above Cape Haze Point (N26 47.156 W82 09.061), on the eastern shore, the main body of Charlotte Harbor is 4–6 miles wide. Hog Island, at the top of the harbor, is at the confluence of the Myakka and Peace rivers. The Peace River is the larger of the two, with the cities of Port Charlotte and Punta Gorda near its mouth.

The shoreline between Cape Haze and the mouth of the Myakka River is straight, lined with shallow flats and interrupted by only a few small bays and one mangrove-lined creek. At any of the bays' entrances, or at the mouth of Trout Creek (N26 55.182 W82 10.839), you can expect to find trout or redfish during warmer months. As the weather chills, expect these fish to move up into whatever protected water they can find. As you move up into the Myakka River toward El Jobean Bridge, you've probably got a better chance of catching a snook at Cattle Dock Point (N26 56.288 W82 10.994) or along the shoreline of Hog Island, across the river. El Jobean Bridge and the fishing pier also offer structure that's attractive for summertime (nighttime) snook and cool-weather sheepshead, as well as trout, redfish, and flounder. Above the bridge, the Myakka River heads to North Port, where fishing for saltwater

There are miles and miles of residential canals along the edges of Charlotte Harbor. Expect to find snook in almost every one!

species depends largely on their ability to survive in fresher water. Luckily, snook, trout, reds, and tarpon are all euryhaline and not affected by any lack of salt in the brackish river water. Upriver, all are good targets, especially when the water's cool.

Shoal Point (N26 55.481 W82 09.188) is at the southern tip of Hog Island, marking the middle of the rivers' confluence. The deeper edges of the flats there, especially on the Myakka River side (west), attract bait schools midsummer and make for some good trout fishing all the way out to marker #4 (N26 54.650 W82 09.531). There's also a shallow channel behind Hog Island (the Myakka Cutoff) that offers some protected fishing water, especially at either end, on falling tides.

At the top of Charlotte Harbor, even the more "urban" areas offer some good fishing. There's good access for trailer-boaters at Port Charlotte Beach (in Alligator Bay) or Laishley Park (in downtown Punta Gorda). On the north side, at Port Charlotte, you can expect to find trout and reds on the flats and near the shoreline from the east end of the Myakka Cutoff to the mouth of Alligator Bay. In the bay, and near docks and residential canals that stretch almost all the way to the US41 Bridge, add snook to your list. And there are literally miles of canals here, each worth a fishing trip, particularly during cool weather. If you don't have a boat, consider fishing from the piers at Bayshore Live Oak Park or Port Charlotte Beach.

The pilings of the US41 Bridge offer some good night fishing for tarpon and snook. Not only are these species found here, but upriver well past the I-75 bridge near Bird Key and Long Island. Depending on the river's flow, which is dependent on rainfall to the east as well as on the tide, you'll find good fishing on the upstream side of islands and bars in slower water. Ruined docks are always worth a peek, and dredged-out residential canals attract fish in cooler times of the year.

The shoreline and canals at "fat point" from just west of the Fishermen's Village complex, around the point past Ponce de Leon Park (and boat ramp) to the mouth of Alligator Creek (N26 52.630 W82 03.890) are easy to reach. The shallows often hold snook or reds, and the outer canals of Punta Gorda Isles offer some good wintertime fishing. There are entrances to this maze of canals at N26 55.626 W82 04.927 (on the north shore), at Mangrove Point (N26 53.614 W82 05.564), or from Alligator Creek.

Unlike the west shore, the east shore of Charlotte Harbor is not so straight and smooth. Here, the coast is peppered with small keys, creeks, and a series of shallow bars. In late spring or summer, the edges of the close-in flats (which sometimes stretch as much as a half-mile into the harbor) attract predators chasing schools of baitfish. A good tactic to fish this 8-mile shoreline is to use your push pole or electric motor to make a north-south drift while casting to potholes or cuts along island or bar edges. This stretch of shoreline can be busy with anglers, but there's plenty of room and plenty of fishing potential here. The shoreline gets a bit less "confused" as you head south from

Look for snags—and snook—along Charlotte Harbor's eastern shoreline.

Key Point (N26 47.476 W82 03.774) and the Burnt Store Marina Channel (N26 45.700 W82 04.041) to the "Two Pines" area at the top of Matlacha Pass. Anglers might consider morning trips to this area, especially in summer, as afternoon sea breezes can create choppy seas here and on the way back to the boat ramp or dock.

For no reason other than they are generally included by marine chart makers on products depicting Charlotte Harbor, a discussion of the northern end of Pine Island, Cayo Costa Island, and the smaller islands between them is appropriate here. Bokeelia, at the island's north tip, is an excellent place from which to shove off for a day of inshore fishing either in southern Charlotte Harbor or in Matlacha Pass. You'll have good access to some nice shallow flats that extend off the shore, as well as both shorelines of upper Matlacha Pass. Expect to find snook and reds closer to the mangroves here, and trout to the outside of the bars and near shoals. One such shoal is just off Jug Creek on the northwest corner of the island (approx.

N26 42.599 W82 11.479). Also, any of the small bays (Little Bokeelia, Smokehouse, and Indian Field) along Pine Island's north and east sides are good fisheries for snook and reds. Just remember that the close-to-shore waters here can be very shallow on extremely low wintertime tides, and that mosquitoes as big as mockingbirds are commonplace here in spring and summer months.

Cayo Costa Island and the numerous small islands to its east are best reached from either Boca Grande or from Pineland, on the western shore of Pine Island. I can't overemphasize the quality of the year-round fishing here. Gulf waters entering Pine Island Sound through both Boca Grande and Captiva Passes bring both bait and clean salty water to the shores of these weather-protected islands. The general lack of human encroachment doesn't hurt either. I suspect that greater numbers of early Native Americans, the Calusa, lived here and plied these waters at the time of Florida's discovery than do fishermen and boaters now. The trip from the Tarpon Lodge at Pineland, past the north end of Part Island and on to Useppa Island and Cabbage Key, is an easy one. If the weather's bad, the mile-long section in the middle of the sound can be sloppy, but once you're west of Useppa Island and into the ICW, you're protected. This triangle of shallow waters formed by Cayo Costa to the west and Useppa and Patricio Islands to the east is generally shallow and less windblown. Cabbage Key has my recommendation as the starting point for a fishing adventure here. The lodging is good; the food is superior, and the fishing's close by. In fact, on one October trip here, we tossed topwater plugs from our skiff, within trolling motor distance of the dock, and caught limits of snook, trout, and reds, all before breakfast. Of course, there are other options here too. The entire eastern shoreline of Cayo Costa will produce snook and reds almost year-round, as will the bars to the southeast of Mondongo Island at N26 40.603 W82 12.642. There's also a stretch of deeper water in Primo Bay, to the northwest of Cabbage

Key. Consider approaching this area from Punta Blanco and the small swash channel there (it enters the ICW at about N26 40.581 W82 13.476) rather than running the more direct, but shallow, route from Cabbage Key.

Boca Grande Pass, which separates Cayo Costa and Gasparilla islands, is widely known for its tarpon fishery—but that's only for a few months in late spring or early summer. As that action slows, anglers turn their attention to the snook that cruise the pass's shores and the beaches of both islands. They also back off into Charlotte Harbor and begin concentrating on the backwaters and islands that stretch from Cape Haze across the mouths of Turtle Bay, Bull Bay, and Gasparilla Sound and into the lower reaches of Lemon Bay. Snook, reds, and trout all move—with the tide, the bait, and the water temperature—from the deeper southern edge of the Boca Grande Channel north up into more protected and comfortable waters. Places of note here include the deeper backwaters in Turtle Bay, and those to the east of Cayo Pelau at about N26 46.642 W82 13.131, at Bull Bay. Your fishing success here depends on just how shallow your boat can float, and how much stealth you can maintain while maneuvering these mangrove islands and shorelines. Oyster bars, small channels, cuts, and mangrove shorelines all hold fish, and catching them is a matter of getting close enough to cast to them without spooking them. Kayak fishermen often launch at Placida and head here to take advantage of their crafts' stealth. And here, even in cooler weather, you've a good opportunity to use topwater lures, especially in the extreme backwaters of mangrove-lined and shallow Whidden, Catfish, and Coral creeks.

The settlements of Placida and Cape Haze are both good places to set up a fishing expedition's base camp. This area, inside Gasparilla Pass, and the entire Charlotte County shore north toward Englewood, offers visiting anglers some respite from the busy residential development to the east. If you go here, enjoy the peace and quiet while you're on the water, but

The backwaters near Placida are excellent for paddling and paddlecraft fishing.

be sure to take a trip over to the planned development of Rotonda, just for the experience. I like the fact that fishing, like much of life, is unpredictable, and I have no desire to live in a community that's shaped like a 2-mile-wide wagon wheel.

At Placida, you can take advantage of some bridge or pier fishing, or you can kayak and fish the backwaters. Snook still hang out around the old railroad trestle, the fishing pier, and the flats behind Little Gasparilla Island support good trout and redfish populations. While narrower than Boca Grande, both Gasparilla and Stump passes attract snook and tarpon. Snook are usually found along the channel edges, while tarpon lurk offshore of the passes, especially as falling tides wash baits out from Placida Harbor and Lemon Bay. At Cape Haze (the town), and north toward Englewood, Lemon Bay begins. This narrow backwater, with the busy ICW running down its center, holds great potential for anglers targeting seatrout, and as stated earlier, anything that bites. If you're fishing here, from either Englewood or from the south end of the bay, don't miss an opportunity to fish the mouth of Buck Creek (south of Stump

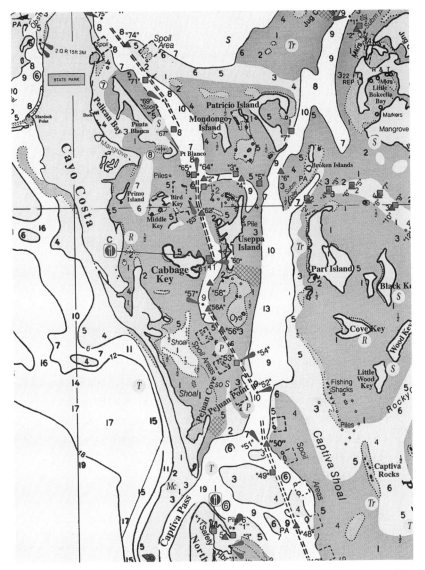

Stay a few days at Cabbage Key and fish the protected waters along the western edge of Charlotte Harbor. (Map courtesy of Waterproof Charts, Inc.)

Pass, at N26 53.517 W82 19.182) or Peterson Cut (between Whidden Key and Peterson Island, north of Stump Pass).

Charlotte Harbor's barrier islands, starting to the north at Manasota Key and ending at Captiva Pass, south of Cayo Costa Island, offer more than 20 miles of beach fishing. Anglers with boats have good access through the four passes (Stump, Gasparilla, Boca Grande, and Redfish) and can easily target snook, cobia, and tarpon along the shoreline or near Gulfside shoals; however, shorebound anglers still have opportunities to catch fish. Beach access is limited at places, but many parks, including the State Park at Cayo Costa Island (reached by ferry from Pine Island or Boca Grande), welcome beach fishermen. Light spinning or medium-weight fly tackle is all you need to catch fish here. You'll find pompano and snook in the surf, and you can always be surprised by a tarpon when wade-fishing along these shores.

Offshore Fishing

Southwest Florida has such a rich inshore and near shore fishery that it often overshadows what goes on in deeper waters. Historically, fishing here, unlike that in the northern Gulf of Mexico, where deep, thousand-foot-plus canyons are close to shore, has been centered on shallow coastal waters where even "big" fish can be caught by any angler.

Charlotte Harbor, much like Tampa Bay, supports an "offshore" fishery within its confines. The middle of this bay may be shallow, but it can be a treacherous place for a small boat on the wrong day. For the most part, the bottom here is flat and has but a few naturally occurring rocky spots. A few "inshore-offshore" spots are worth a mention as having potential for small reef fish like mangrove snapper or grunts. You might even be surprised by a keeper gag grouper. The shallow Charlotte Harbor Reef is a mile long and is marked at either end by buoys. Located about 3 miles south of the Ponce de Leon boat

Placida's fleet of offshore boats is ready and waiting.

ramp (centered at N26 51.054 W82 05.349), it's constructed of concrete rubble and regularly attracts pods of white bait and predators. A similar reef, the Cape Haze Reef, is located closer to Boca Grande at about N26 45.700 W82 09.613.

Years ago, Goliath grouper (then called Jewfish) were caught around many of the Harbor's commercial docks, especially at Boca Grande. These fish, often reaching hundreds of pounds, were brutes. You'll occasionally catch juveniles along the mangrove shores now, but special care must be taken to release them. The fish are now protected, and it's illegal to even bring one into your boat. And if you hook a big one, you'll first think you've snagged Mother Earth, but when it moves . . .

There's good access to the Gulf and deeper water through the passes, and some anglers head westward to look for reef species and blue-water pelagics. But anglers in search of offshore species, some in smaller boats, don't really have to travel too far. Here, as in other parts of southwest Florida, artificial reefs and wrecks play an important role as fish attractors inside the 6-fathom (36-foot) "curve" on charts. Anglers wishing to stay closer to shore often try Helens Reef, northwest of

Captiva Pass at N26 38.114 W82 17.261 or Marys Reef, off the middle of Gasparilla Island, at N26 46.081 W82 18.286. While neither reef is particularly deep, both attract bait pods, followed by spring and fall king mackerel and summertime cobia.

Gag and red grouper as well as feisty amberjacks are attracted to artificial reefs, live bottom, limestone ledges, and rock piles. Gags will head far offshore to spawn in midwinter, but as the weather warms into spring, they seem to move back toward the reefs and wrecks in the 40-foot range. Catches of tasty gags have been restricted in recent years, but a quick look online at www.myfwc.com will get you current information on closures for that species, as well as those for snapper.

Another reef species of note is the gray, or mangrove, snapper. Smaller versions of this fish can be found along inshore shorelines and are known to attack almost any lure. Larger specimens, in the 5-pound range, move around the passes, and some downright whoppers can be found offshore over limestone ledges in depths much greater than 100 feet. "Mangos" are excellent to eat, but sometimes difficult to catch. Small hooks, nearly invisible fluorocarbon leaders, frisky live bait (I prefer shrimp for smaller fish and pinfish for larger ones), and the ability to feel the bite before it happens will help you catch these fish.

Expect to reach 100 feet of water depth at about 50 miles offshore. Here, you'll begin to find some big natural depressions and structures on the Gulf floor. It's here that you (and your charter boat's captain) need to start thinking about billfish, wahoo, tuna, mahi-mahi, and other denizens of the deep.

Getting Around

The Charlotte Harbor area is easy to navigate by car, as it is by boat. Interstate 75 passes to the east of Port Charlotte and Punta Gorda on its way south from Sarasota to Fort Myers, Naples, and Ft. Lauderdale. US41 (the Tamiami Trail), runs closer to the coast from Sarasota, heads westward at Venice, and crosses the Peace River at Punta Gorda. SR776 leaves US41 at Murdock, heads south to El Jobean at the Myakka River, where it changes numbers to SR771. It leads to SR775 at Placida and is the main route north to Englewood and south to Boca Grande on Gasparilla Island. Just south of downtown Punta Gorda, SR765 (Burnt Store Road) runs due south to Cape Coral. From there, you can take SR78 west to Pine Island.

Where to Stay

Lodging options in the Charlotte Harbor area vary from "luxurious" to "Mom and Pop." Be sure to call ahead regarding boat and trailer parking, as well as availability, especially during the busy winter months.

*   *   *

Banana Bay Waterfront Motel in Charlotte Harbor has something for everyone.

Best Western Waterfront, (941) 639-1165, 300 Retta Esplanade, Punta Gorda. On the harbor, convenient to the Laishley Park Marina, with excellent parking for boats on trailers.

Vacation Villas at Fishermen's Village, (800) 639-0020, 1200 W. Retta Esplanade, Punta Gorda. Daily and weekly condo rentals, overlooking Charlotte Harbor. An excellent choice if you're planning to fish with the King Fisher Fleet, which is headquartered there.

Banana Bay Waterfront Motel, (941) 743-4441, 23285 Bayshore Rd, Charlotte Harbor (just off US41),

Comfortable waterfront efficiencies and motel rooms. A 500-foot fishing pier on the harbor. Boat trailer parking and boat rentals available. www.bananabaymotel.com

Wyvern Hotel, (941) 639-7700, 101 E. Retta Esplanade, Punta Gorda

Sheraton Four Points Harborside, (941) 637-6770, 33 Tamiami Tr, Punta Gorda.

The Wyvern and the Sheraton are luxurious and perhaps better suited to anglers not needing to park boats on trailers.

Grove City Motel, (941) 474-3436, 2555 Placida Rd, Englewood. Comfortable efficiencies near Stump Pass Marina and Capt. Van Hubbard. Next door to The Egg & I restaurant. www.grovecitymotel.com

Gasparilla Inn & Club, (941) 964-4500, 500 Palm Ave, Boca Grande. One of the great hotels in the area. Pricey, but close to Boca Grande Pass. Adjacent marina. www.the-gasparilla-inn.com

Tarpon Lodge, (239) 283-3999, 13771 Waterfront Dr, Pineland. One of the great fishing lodges in southwest Florida. On the west side of Pine Island, it offers easy access to lower Charlotte Harbor and Pine Island Sound. Dockage and 4-star dining available. www.tarponlodge.com

Bokeelia Tarpon Inn at Bocilla Island Seaport, (239) 283-8961, 8241 Main St, Bokeelia. Bed & breakfast, with fishing pier and boat ramp.

Cabbage Key Resort, (239) 283-2278, on Cabbage Key, at ICW marker #60. Cottages, rooms, restaurant, bar, dockage for guests. An excellent place to begin your backwater fishing adventure. Accessible by boat only.

Where to Eat

You won't go hungry here. There's a wide variety of restaurants serving everything from hands-on boiled crabs and shrimp to European-inspired haute cuisine. Here are a few of my favorites.

*   *   *

Peace River Seafood & Crab Shack, (941) 505-8440, US17, Punta Gorda. Excellent fresh local seafood in an authentic Florida setting. Try the steamed blue crabs if they're available.

The Captain's Table, (941) 637-1177, at Fishermen's Village, 1200 W. Retta Esplanade, Punta Gorda. Local seafood with a great view of the harbor.

You can't go wrong with a meal from Peace River Seafood & Crab Shack.

Village Fish Market Restaurant & Lounge, (941) 639-7959, at Fishermen's Village, Punta Gorda. Casual seafood, salads, and sandwiches. They'll cook your catch!

Benedetto's, (941) 639-1165, adjacent to the Best Western Waterfront, Punta Gorda. Good food and a great bar!

Trattoria Limoncello, (941) 639-6500, 10361 Tamiami Tr, Punta Gorda. Authentic home-style Italian food and pizzas.

Burnt Store Grille Family Restaurant, 3941 Tamiami Tr, Punta Gorda. Breakfast, lunch, and dinner.

Myakka River Oyster Bar, (941) 423-9616, Tamiami Tr at the Myakka River, South Venice. Fresh local seafood, daily specials.

The Egg & I Restaurant, (941) 475-6252, 2555 Placida Rd, Englewood. Breakfast and lunch, next door to Grove City Motel.

Bay Pointe Grill, (941) 460-0500, 264 N. Indiana Ave, Englewood. Family-style restaurant serving breakfast, lunch, and dinner.

Stump Pass Grille, (941) 697-0589, on Lemon Bay at Stump Pass Marina. Great bar food and drinks, inside and outside.

The Fishery Restaurant, (941) 697-2451, Fishery Rd, Placida. Very good local seafood. Grilled is good; fried is always best!

PJ's Seagrille, (941) 964-0806, 321 Park Ave, Boca Grande. Upscale lunch and dinner. "Steak Dinner Served Anytime."

Eagle Grille, (941) 964-8000, at Boca Grande Marina, Boca Grande. Upscale, lunch and dinner.

Miller's Dockside, (941) 964-8000, at Boca Grande Marina, Boca Grande. Casual, lunch and dinner.

Tarpon Lodge Restaurant and Bar, (239) 283-3999, 13771 Waterfront Dr, Pineland. Excellent food at a 4-star restaurant. www.tarponlodge.com

Raymary Street Grill, Stringfellow Rd, Bokeelia. Affordable breakfasts and lunches.

Lazy Flamingo Restaurant, (239) 283-5959, at Four Winds Marina, Bokeelia. Lunch and dinner, casual, seafood.

Red's Fresh Seafood House & Tavern, (239) 283-4412, 10880 Stringfellow Rd, Bokeelia. Family owned, serving fresh local seafood.

Cabbage Key Restaurant, (239) 283-2278, at Cabbage Key Resort, ICW marker #60. Famous for "cheeseburgers in paradise." Lunch and dinner, access by boat only.

Marinas, Marine Supplies and Service, Bait and Tackle Shops, and Launching Ramps

Waterproof Charts, (941) 639-7626, 320 Cross St, Punta Gorda. If you have some free time, stop by Waterproof Charts' main office in downtown Punta Gorda and see their newest offerings.

Fishin' Franks Bait & Tackle, (941) 625-3888, 4425-D Tamiami Tr, Port Charlotte. One of the best in the area, stocking lots of tackle, live and frozen bait, and fishing accessories.

Bayshore Live Oak Park Fishing Pier, 23157 Bayshore Rd, Port Charlotte. Fishing pier at the mouth of the Peace River.

Port Charlotte Beach Fishing Pier, 4500 Harbor Blvd, Port Charlotte. Fishing pier on Alligator Bay.

Laishley Park Municipal Marina, (941) 575-0930, downtown Punta Gorda. Ship's store, live and frozen bait, dockage, boat ramp.

Laishley Marine, (941) 639-3868, 3415 Tamiami Tr, Punta Gorda. An excellent source for tackle, marine supplies, clothing, and gifts. www.laishleymarine.net

Black Tip Bait & Tackle, 4352 El Jobean Rd, Port Charlotte. Live crabs, pinfish, shrimp, frozen bait, tackle.

West Marine, (941) 625-2700, 4265 Tamiami Tr, Port Charlotte. West Marine, (941) 637-0019, 700 Tamiami Tr, Punta Gorda. West Marine stores are excellent sources of marine supplies, including repair parts and materials.

Ingman Marine, (941) 255-1555, 1189 Tamiami Tr, Port Charlotte. (941) 697-1000, 15001 Gasparilla Rd, Placida. Marine service and parts.

Mariner's Trading Company, (941) 639-1340, 1035 Elizabeth St, Punta Gorda. A source for all kinds of consigned marine items. Worth a visit on a rainy day.

Rio Villa Bait & Tackle, (941) 639-7176, 113 Rio Villa Dr, Punta Gorda. Live shrimp and pinfish.

Grande Tours Kayak Rentals, (941) 697-8825, 12575 Placida Rd, Placida. Kayak sales, rentals, guided fishing trips, tours. www.grandetours.com.

Stump Pass Marina, (941) 697-4300, 260 Maryland Ave, Englewood. Dockage, fuel, live and frozen bait, marine repairs.

Boca Grande Fishing Pier, 5810 Gasparilla Rd, Placida. A popular inshore fishing pier. Great snook action here.

Eldred's Marina, (941) 697-1431, 6301 Boca Grande Causeway, Placida. Bait, tackle, $5 unpaved boat ramp, good trailer parking.

Gasparilla Marina, (941) 697-2280, 15001 Gasparilla Rd, Placida. Full service marina, fuel, dockage, bait and tackle, boat rentals and sales.

Affinity Tackle, (941) 697-4343, 2290 Gasparilla Rd, Port Charlotte. Tackle and fishing kayaks.

Fisherman's Edge, (941) 697-7595, 4225 Placida Rd, Grove City. Bait and tackle, fly-fishing gear, repairs, excellent up-to-the-minute fishing reports.

Palm Island Marina, (941) 697-5456, 7080 Placida Rd, Cape Haze. A "big boat" marina, fuel, supplies, storage.

El Jobean Fishing Pier, alongside the SR776 El Jobean Bridge, on the east side of the Myakka River. Good parking, bait and tackle available at Gump's Bait and Tackle.

Gump's Bait and Tackle, (941) 276-7445. Next door to El Jobean Fishing Pier, 4370 Garden Rd, El Jobean. Live shrimp, pinfish, crabs.

The Inn Marina (Gasparilla Inn & Club), (941) 964-4620, Boca Grande. Dockage, fuel, bait, and marine supplies

Boca Grande Outfitters, (941) 964-2445, 375 Park Ave, Boca Grande. Light tackle and fly-fishing gear.

Gasparilla Outfitters, (941) 964-0907, 431 Park Ave, Boca Grande. Gear for fly-fishing, pass fishing, beach and back country fishing.

Whidden's Marina, (941) 964-2878, between ICW markers #2 and 3, Boca Grande. Fuel, ice, bait and tackle, dockage.

Capt. Russ' Boat Rentals, (941) 964-0708, at Whidden's Marina. Deck and bay boat rentals.

Boca Grande Marina, (941) 964-2100, between ICW markers #2 and 3, Boca Grande. Bait and tackle, fuel, transient slips, restaurants (Eagle Grille and Miller's Dockside).

Burnt Store Marina, (941) 637-0083, 3197 Matecumbe Key Rd, Punta Gorda. Full service marina with boat ramp, dockage, fuel, bait and tackle. On the eastern shore of Charlotte Harbor.

Pineland Marina, (239) 283-3593, 13921 Waterfront Dr, Bokeelia (on Pine Island). The boat ramp fee and daily parking for trailers is expensive, but this is one of the closest places to launch to reach Boca Grande from Pine Island.

Four Winds Marina, (239) 283-0250, Stringfellow Rd, Bokeelia. Full service marina.

Bocilla Island Seaport & Fishing Pier, (239) 283-8961, 8241 Main St, Bokeelia. Marina, boat ramp and fishing pier at Bokeelia Tarpon Inn Bed & Breakfast.

Laishley Park boat ramp, 100 E. Retta Esplanade, Punta Gorda. Paved ramps on the harbor near downtown. Excellent parking.

Ponce de Leon Park boat ramp, 4000 W. Marion Ave, Punta Gorda. Paved ramp on the eastern shore of the harbor. Good parking.

Darst Park boat ramp, 537 Darst Ave, Punta Gorda. Paved boat ramp, small fishing dock. Good access for canoes and kayaks.

El Jobean boat ramp, 4224 El Jobean Rd, Port Charlote. Excellent ramp, 75 cents per hour to park.

Port Charlotte Beach boat ramp, 4500 Harbor Blvd, Port Charlotte. Paved ramps. Good access to upper harbor.

Sunrise Park kayak and canoe launch, 20499 Edgewater Dr, Port Charlotte. Good access to backwaters and mangrove shoreline.

Placida Park boat ramp, 6499 Gasparilla Rd, Placida. Paved boat ramps. Parking lot can get crowded at height of tarpon season in May and June.

Ainger Creek Park boat ramp, 2011 Placida Rd, Englewood. Single paved ramp. Good access for canoes and kayaks.

Bokeelia boat ramp, 7290 Barrancas Ave NW, Bokeelia. Paved ramp, $5 launch fee, $10 per day parking with 3-day maximum.

Matlacha boat ramp, 4577 Pine Island Dr, Matlacha. 2 paved ramps on Matlacha Pass.

Local Fishing Guides

King Fisher Fleet, Punta Gorda, (941) 639-0808. Headquartered at Fishermen's Village, this charter boat operation, owned by Capt. Ralph Allen, offers inshore, bay, and offshore fishing. www.kingfisherfleet.com

Capt. Van Hubbard, (941) 697-6944. Inshore and near shore fishing. www.captvan.com

Capt. Travis Ormond, (941) 374-1669. Offshore fishing. www.pelagiccharter.com

Capt. Rick Grassett, (941) 923-7799. Inshore, light tackle, and fly-fishing. Tarpon specialist. www.snookfin-addict.com

Capt. Pete Greenan, (941) 232-2960. Inshore, light tackle, and fly-fishing. Pete also operates the Boca Grande Fly Fishing School. www.floridaflyfishing.com

Capt. Rick DePaiva, (239) 246-8726. Inshore light tackle and fly-fishing. www.saltwaterflyfishing.org

Capt. Mike Manis, (941) 628-7895. Inshore and backwater fishing. www.flatscaptain.com

Capt. Gregg McKee, (239) 565-2960. Light tackle and fly-fishing, Pine Island Sound. www.wildflycharters.com

Capt. Robin Leach, (941) 916-3207. Light tackle inshore and back bay fishing. www.puntagordacharters.com.

Placida Queen Deep Sea Fishing, (941) 698-6999. Offshore party boat. www.placidadeepseafishing.com.

Capt. Josh Harvel, (239) 233-0655. Kayak fishing charters. www.swflkayakcharters.com.

*   *   *

Many fishing guides from the Fort Myers area are familiar with the waters here. If necessary, check the listings in chapter 8 for more recommendations. The website of the Florida Guides Association (www.florida-guides.com) has a complete listing of USCG licensed and insured fishing guides. Also, if you plan to fish for tarpon at or near Boca Grande, consider hiring a guide who's a member of the Boca Grande Fishing Guides Association, www.bocagrandefishing.com.

Before You Leave Home

Be sure to check this guide's companion website, www.salt wateranglersguide.com, for updates to local information.

8

Fort Myers, Estero, Sanibel, and Captiva

Lee County and the Fort Myers area always intrigues me. It's a study in opposites. You can be driving down Stringfellow Road, the main north-south artery on Pine Island, and find yourself in the middle of farmland, and then suddenly realize that you're only about 5 miles away from a huge traffic jam on Sanibel Island. Seasons change here, too. Not that you'll see autumn leaves, but condos and homes in Fort Myers and Cape Coral with storm-shuttered windows are signs that tourist season is over and the "snowbirds" have migrated north. However, lots of visitors to the area, Thomas Edison and Henry Ford included, have seen just too many warm and sunny winter days and have set up permanent residence here.

From an inshore fisherman's point of view, Lee County's coastline is a dream come true. Pine Island Sound is the estuary of the Caloosahatchee River, bounded on the south and west by the barrier islands of Sanibel and Captiva. Fifteen-mile-long Pine Island sits right in the middle of the shallow sound. Offshore anglers don't have to run a great distance in search of deeper water after exiting the sound through Captiva Pass, Redfish Pass, or San Carlos Bay to the south. San Carlos Bay itself is also worthy of mention as it, Estero Island, and the backwaters all along the coast south of Fort Myers serve as the natural drain of the Estero River, the Imperial River, and numerous creeks. From Punta Rassa, at the eastern end

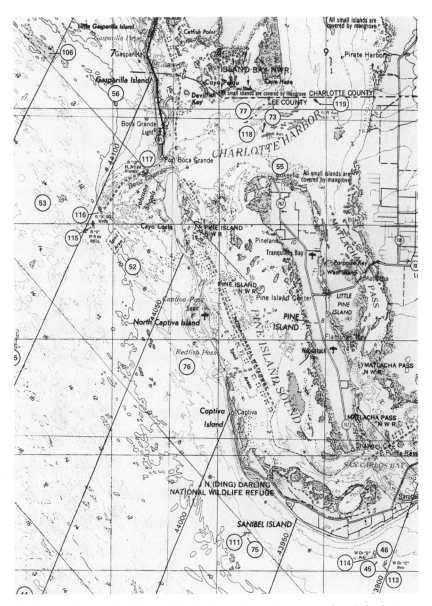

The barrier islands of Sanibel and Captiva form the southwestern edge of Charlotte Harbor. (Map courtesy of Waterproof Charts, Inc.)

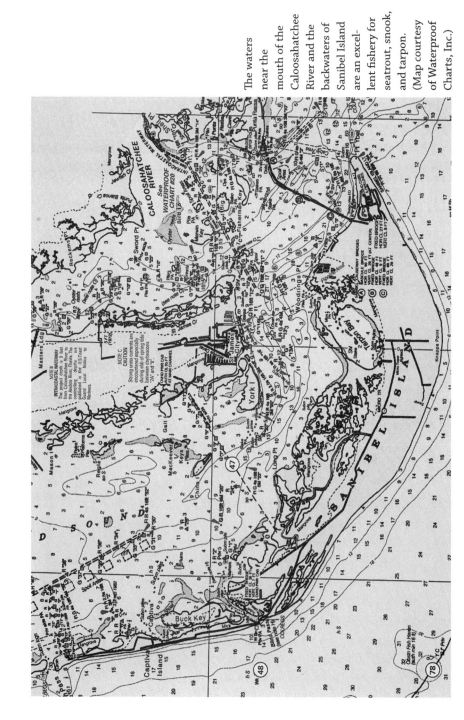

The waters near the mouth of the Caloosahatchee River and the backwaters of Sanibel Island are an excellent fishery for seatrout, snook, and tarpon. (Map courtesy of Waterproof Charts, Inc.)

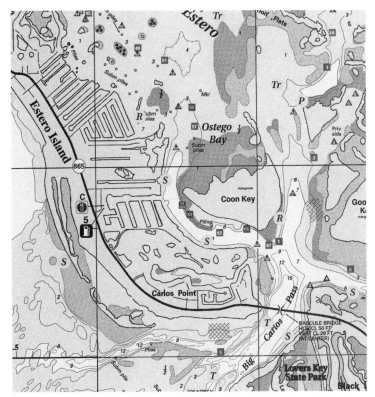

Big Carlos Pass feeds the backwaters of Estero Bay, south of Fort Myers.
(Map courtesy of Waterproof Charts, Inc.)

of the Sanibel Bridge, south to Bonita Beach, you'll find some
incredible fishing. Fed with Gulf water by four passes (Matanzas, Big Carlos, Big Hickory, and New), the waters of Estero
Bay are legendary. An inshore angler could fish a lifetime here,
in all seasons, and never leave the backwaters unless he or she
wanted to look for striking fish or tarpon along the beach.

"Grown up" may not be the best term to use when talking
about any town or city on Florida's Gulf Coast. Many of us na-
tives were perfectly happy when, 50 years ago, these places
were in their infancy. Less crowded, with fewer amenities, was
not bad, but all of Florida has matured to the busy place we see
now. Some cities have outgrown their potential and become

"too big for their britches," but the Fort Myers area is a pretty nice place to live or visit—especially if you love to fish.

Inshore and Near Shore Fishing

There's no doubt in my mind that Florida's most popular inshore fish is the spotted seatrout (not "speckled trout"!). I'm sure I would get arguments from many anglers in southwest Florida that snook are more fun to catch, and if in season, better to eat. I'm no fan of eating trout but find that just about all the popular inshore species, except tarpon and certain members of the jack family, are excellent to eat. Redfish, sheepshead, flounder, Spanish mackerel, pompano, and tripletail have all made appearances on our dinner table. The arguments for trout's popularity may be based on the fact that they're easy to catch and probably more plentiful and far ranging than any of the other species.

Spotted seatrout come in all sizes and bite all year. And they bite a wide variety of baits, including mullet, shrimp, pinfish, and any number of "guaranteed" artificial lures. Techniques vary too, but catching trout is an everyman's game in that lighter, less-expensive tackle is usually adequate for catching one's daily bag limit.

Expect the best trout fishing during the spring and fall months when the water temperatures are moderate. Both hot summer water and cool winter water will send fish to deeper, more protected waters. In the summer, expect trout to seek the depths of offshore grass flats, and in the winter, expect to find them in deep river and dredged channels.

I'd wager that the most popular trout fishing method statewide involves the use of a rattling or popping cork. The purpose of this device is twofold. One, it holds the bait above the bottom, eliminating snags, and two, it allows the angler to make some noise that mimics the striking action of game fish. The first reason is obvious, and the second plays off the fact that trout are voracious—and stingy. Upon hearing the rattling or popping noise created by the cork's action, trout within "earshot" are immediately attracted. Their assumption seems to be that there's a mullet jumping with his gill plates rattling—or that one of their brethren has attacked a school of tasty baits. In either case, corks attract bites as predators find your bait at hand and attack it. Live shrimp, live pinfish, shrimp imitations, and even lead-head jigs all work at the terminal end of cork rigs. In fact, D.O.A. Lures even makes several versions of their "Deadly Combos"—popping corks factory-rigged with their highly effective artificial shrimp.

The use of noisy corks in the search for seatrout is looked down upon by many alleged "sport fishermen," claiming that the technique gives anglers an unfair advantage. Whether there's any truth to that matter, there are certainly hundreds of other choices of baits made specifically to catch trout. At any tackle store, you'll find hard- and soft-bodied baitfish imitations, usually called "plugs," that sink, suspend, or float. And there's a time and a place for each. Topwater plugs are particularly effective on seatrout in the early or late hours of the day, especially in water less than 3 feet deep. You'll find bigger topwater lures more effective than smaller ones if the water's surface is choppy. If the prevalent live bait is small minnows or "white bait," consider using smaller plugs. If it's mullet, use larger. Many manufacturers make their topwater lures in various sizes. MirrOlure, for example, makes both big "Dogs" and small "Pups" as part of their topwater lure series. Suspending lures are popular in situations where floating grasses might snag topwater lures, or when it's just too deep for a topwater lure to be effective. Suspending lures also offer the advantage of being worked very slowly, a good technique in winter months. MirrOlure's Catch 2000 and Paul Brown Corky lures are both highly effective suspending lures. Sinking plugs also have a place in any angler's lure inventory. When the trout are deep, in either summer or winter, try working deep-running plugs like MirrOlure's TT or D.O.A.'s Bait Buster just above the bottom.

And just in case you have any room left in your tackle box or boat, don't forget that, thanks to freshwater bass anglers, there are literally hundreds of lead-head and soft-body "jig" combinations that are absolutely essential when it comes to catching seatrout. These can be worked over grass tops, in and out of deep holes, and even hung under popping corks—all with great success. If you read the ads of the manufacturers of these products, any day and time and situation might just determine that you need one combination rather than another. Simply put, the company line is that you need to own enough different lead-head jigs and soft bait bodies to make up just over a million combinations. Of course, I'm exaggerating here, but you can easily fill a tackle box (or three) with tens of pounds of these lures. Me, I keep it simple and keep a bunch of ¼-ounce jigs painted red and chartreuse with some chartreuse and root beer–colored tails with me at all times. I suspect that with the combinations I can make from that selection, I can handle 90 percent of the trout-fishing scenarios I encounter statewide. I may miss a few fish, but my back and my bank account thank me.

In spite of my preference for artificial lures, I won't argue with any angler about the effectiveness of live or fresh bait for seatrout. Personally, I don't enjoy spending money on shrimp or frozen bait or time netting live pinfish before I get on the water. Nor do I relish the smell of cut bait on my hands and clothing. And then there's the by-catch issue. Sometimes you'll catch a trout, but junk fish likely to eat your fresh offering include catfish, ladyfish, jacks, and stingrays. Of course, if you're a gambler, consider that good trout by-catch can be redfish, flounder, mackerel, pompano, and cobia.

Snook can roam the same flats as trout, but generally prefer slightly warmer water temperatures and are usually more interested in structure like snags and pilings, even if the currents are strong. They'll also get closer to shore than trout, lying under overhanging mangrove branches in just a foot or so of water, waiting for their prey to swim within range. And the biggest specimens can often be found at night, feeding around bridges and brightly lighted docks, sometimes on small trout. For the most part, snook eat the same baits as trout, but here they seem to take particular interest in jumbo shrimp or big white baits, free-lined and frisky. Obviously, snook tackle for bridge, dock, and pier fishing needs to be heavier than what you'd use for flats or beach fishing. Big snook that live around structure have an uncanny ability to make their first run, after being hooked, around a piling or into a barnacle-encrusted snag.

Fishing for redfish has become more popular here in recent years, due mainly to anglers' interest in sight fishing. Of course, like snook, many are caught by anglers "just fishing" over flats, around shell bars, and along mangrove shorelines. But to me, the real "sport" of redfishing involves sight fishing in the shallow backwaters. On warm winter afternoons or early summer mornings, casting to reds with light spinning or fly tackle is lots of fun. Look for tails or backs out of the water, and be careful not to create any wake by rocking your boat. Your best bet, if it's shallow enough and you've got some wading shoes, is to get overboard and approach these fish on foot. If the reds are feeding on the bottom (tails up) of grass flats, along an oyster bar, or in a creek, try fishing with live or D.O.A. 3-inch shrimp, free-lined in front of them. Or drag a weedless Eppinger gold spoon in their path, moving it slowly and erratically along the bottom. Using these small baits helps you avoid making a big, fish-spooking splash near your prey.

If reds are in deeper water (or if you don't see them and need to "prospect"), try a MirrOlure Catch 2000 or a Heddon Swim 'n' Image. These lures run under the surface and resemble small baitfish or mullet. Topwaters work well for redfish, but you sometimes have to trick redfish into eating them. I'm partial to the Heddon Super Spook Jr., in bone or nickel color. The downturned mouth of redfish makes it difficult for them to strike a surface plug as they often need to turn upside down to eat it. Teasing a charging red into eating any artificial lure sometimes involves slowing or speeding your retrieve, or stopping it altogether.

Other species abound here, and tarpon, the "silver king," is one that many anglers put atop their list of favorites. In summer months, expect to find these fish roaming the inshore waters or along beachfronts, eating almost any bait in their path. Tarpon are surprisingly omnivorous but can at times be picky eaters. Usually it's not necessarily what they eat, but when! White bait, pinfish, crabs, squirrelfish, shrimp, and mullet are their favorites, but at any time (just when you've made the perfect presentation of a live bait to them) they're likely to turn away from the same tasty morsel they ate a day earlier. Tarpon can also be taken by artificial lures, including small MirrOlures, D.O.A. Bait Busters, simple bucktail jigs, or flies. While tarpon can be fought and landed on relatively light tackle, I recommend you pick a rod and reel combo that allows you to land these fish quickly; 5000 to 6000-class spinning reels filled with 30-pound line will do the job. Tired tarpon are often the prey of big sharks, especially during the spring and summer months.

In cooler months, expect to find sheepshead, notorious for bait stealing, schooling near structure. You'll find smaller ones on the flats and the larger ones near deep bridge pilings or offshore reefs or wrecks. Without a doubt, crustaceans such as shrimp, sand fleas, and fiddler crabs are their favorite fare. You'll find that rigging your light rod and reel with braided line will help you better feel the soft bite of these striped "convict fish."

You'll find flounder mostly near creek mouths and along the edges of shell and oyster bars, but don't be surprised to find them inhabiting offshore artificial reefs. Flounder feed, both

Lee County offers many opportunities for anglers to put a bend in their fishing rod.

eyes upward, from these strategic hiding places, so targeting them usually involves dragging small live or artificial baits slowly over the bottom.

Unless you see birds diving over large schools of baitfish, the first sign of Spanish mackerel is usually marked by the disappearance of your favorite trout lure. These toothy critters can appear almost by magic and cut a piece of 25-pound fluorocarbon before you feel the bite. Should this happen and you wish to take a few "macks" home for dinner (they're excellent table fare, if fresh), strengthen your leader—or better yet, replace it with a short trace of light wire. Soft baits, spoons, brightly colored jigs, and all varieties of live bait will catch mackerel.

Members of the jack family of fish, pompano are certainly the most edible of that group. Look for pompano along channel edges and just outside beachfront surf, places they're able to forage for sand fleas and small crustaceans. Live baits, rigged freely at the end of light tackle, work well. You might consider keeping a few specialized pompano jigs, available at most tackle shops, near the top of your tackle box—just in case. Pompano are cousins to the hard-fighting, and much larger, permit.

Tripletail are not pretty fish. In fact, they resemble freshwater oscars, the same fish you see in freshwater aquariums. Cobia *are* pretty in that they're sleek and shiny, not lumpy and scaly like a tripletail. Of course, these species are not related at all, but they do have some of the same habits. Most anglers are on a mission to get to their favorite fishing hole and often pass lots of good cobia and tripletail habitat on the way. Both species have a penchant for holding close to channel markers (big tripods in particular), bridge fenders, pilings, and mats of floating grass. Tripletail even like the company of crab trap floats. Neither is necessarily hiding, as you can often see tripletail or cobia near the surface as you pass by structures.

If you spot a tripletail, set your boat to drift within casting range and throw a free-lined live or D.O.A. shrimp to him. More than likely, he'll attack, then jump, and then try to wrap you up in the structure. Many anglers who target tripletail stop and fish every structure they find, as the fish sometimes are deep and out of sight. I'd estimate that most tripletail are caught by sight-fishers.

Cobia, swimming on the surface or hanging around on the bottom, are not very spooky. In fact, some of these curious fish will be attracted to your boat by motor noise or talking. I've even had them come up and peck at chum bags while I was snapper fishing over shallow inshore reefs. But, while not afraid of you or your boat, cobia are often reluctant to eat any offering you make them. If you're fishing a particular marker or structure that's known to hold these fish, try a pinfish floated under a cork and another pinned to the bottom with a slip-sinker and circle hook. If you can see them, try tossing free-lined live pinfish, shrimp, or white bait. Chumming with live white bait or processed chum (in a bag or box) can get cobia feeding and increase your chances. No matter where you fish, you're likely to be surprised by a cobia. As they can appear over

Keep a big spinning rod handy, just in case a tarpon or cobia swims into range.

shallow grass flats, near channel edges, and even over deep reefs, every angler should be always "on the ready" to tangle with a cobia, especially in warmer months. Many anglers keep a big spinning outfit rigged with an eel imitation just in case a curious cobia swims near the boat. Eels are known far and wide to be "cobia candy."

When planning a fishing trip to any new area, it's best to first take a look at some nautical and fishing charts, like Waterproof Charts' #15F, 20F, and 25F. These charts cover a lot of water and shoreline, from Pine Island to Estero, and can often intimidate even the best and most experienced angler. However, taking a look at the big picture can be helpful, and understanding that you can't fish the whole area on one day (or even in a year of fishing!) is a good start. I advise that you take your time, learn an area or chase a particular species, have fun, and then move on as needed.

Catching even a small redfish is fun, especially if it eats a topwater plug.

For no reason other than it's approachable from Charlotte Harbor and the north, I've included the top half of Pine Island, Pine Island Sound and Matlacha Pass in chapter 7, "Charlotte Harbor and Her Gulf Islands." An imaginary line drawn from the settlement at Matlacha along Pine Island Road toward Captiva Pass pretty much marks the middle of the island. I'll use that boundary for this chapter and include a discussion of the bottom half of the island here.

Local anglers often argue about which side of Pine Island has the better fishing. The fact is that Pine Island Sound and Matlacha Pass are both good, but different, based on depth and ease of access. Pine Island Sound is wide, usually deeper, and directly affected by water moving through the passes to the Gulf of Mexico. On the other hand, Matlacha Pass, between Pine Island and the mainland, is much narrower and shallower and usually considered a backwater.

Exact names in this neck of the woods are often vague. I've always assumed that Buzzard Bay is north of Matlacha and Pine Island Road and that Matlacha Pass extends "officially" from there to Saint James City at the southern tip of Pine Island. There's a marked channel down the middle of Matlacha Pass, but the areas of most importance to anglers are the shorelines. Snook, seatrout, and redfish are the species you're likely to catch here, almost year-round. Both the eastern and western shorelines are lined with mangroves, and small creeks and a few deeper holes offer some protection to fish from extreme cold weather, which rarely happens. Of course, snook are much more intolerant of cold water than reds and trout, especially when it gets below about 55 degrees, but if they "feel" a cold front approaching, they can usually find a place to ride out the storm. This is also a place where having a shallow draft boat gives you an advantage. A push pole and electric motor are helpful if you plan to sight-fish, fish around residential docks, or fish in canals and creeks.

The mangrove-lined shoreline south of Matlacha to Underhill Point (N26 34.135 W82 03.705) is a good place to begin. In warm weather, expect snook to be hiding under the overhanging branches and reds to be moving from point to point. Finding just the slightest depression in the bottom can clue you to a route that fish take either on a falling or rising tide. For example, there's a long slough of deeper water behind McCardle Island (at approx. N26 35.428 W82 03.210) that holds fish most of the year. A 5-mile run south of Matlacha will take you to the end of Little Pine Island and some interesting deeper water and oyster bars. Look for snook up into Pine Island Creek and around the islands there. You can expect to find some seatrout on the deeper (3-foot) flats or along the edges of the channel that runs south from Pine Island Creek to the mouth of the Caloosahatchee River, at Sword Point (N26 31.517 W82 02.445). Just remember that many fish seek warmth in winter and cool comfort on hot summer days, and that determines their seasonal hideouts and eating habits. Learning to think like a fish is a good goal for any angler.

The southern stretch of Matlacha Pass, reaching to Saint James City, is sometimes influenced by the flow of the Caloosahatchee River, which can vary because of release of water from Lake Okeechobee. The eastern shore and the flats to the south of Sword Point attract snook, trout, and redfish. As Matlacha Pass joins with the river and the channels that run westward into Pine Island Sound, you're likely to have your fishing influenced by the flow of water from San Carlos Bay. Pompano and Spanish mackerel are common catches here, and depending on their springtime migration, tarpon can be an exciting target.

Lower Pine Island Sound, the part adjacent to the sound sides of North Captiva, Captiva, and Sanibel islands is a big chunk of water, with many opportunities for both bay and backwater fishing. Captiva Pass, Redfish Pass, and sometimes-open Blind Pass serve to round out the fishing opportunities here.

The deepest water in this part of the sound is only 10 to 15 feet deep (and some of that includes the dredged ICW channel), and it's the relationship between this deep water and the shallows that attracts bait and anglers' prey. Deeper sloughs and holes, like those inside Captiva Pass, give gamefish protection on both cool or sweltering days, while the adjacent shallows, sometimes only a foot or so deep, provide them a steady flow of food in the form of white bait, pinfish, and shrimp. Fishing here has much to do with understanding the edges of the flats, the structure of the bottom, and the tides. Even shallow flats have structure, and the slightest indention, channel or close-by mangrove island or shoreline can make a difference. A good example is the "deep-ish" tongue of water to the west of Panther Key (N26 36.646 W82 08.690). It is surrounded by very shallow flats and even has some rocky structure, the

Captiva Rocks and Shoals (N26 37.347 W82 11.009), along its northwest edge. It's a tricky spot to reach if the tide's low, but usually a good fishing hole for trout, tarpon, and even a cobia. Another good spot is the edge of the natural deep water to the east of North Captiva Island's Foster Point (N26 35.097 W82 12.352). Here, the grass flats fall off into the deeper water that's freshened daily by the flow from Redfish and Captiva passes. Snook, flounder, pompano, and redfish all hunt this edge, especially in summer months.

As their spring migration gets under way, tarpon can also be found in Pine Island Sound, usually along the edges of deeper water or in holes, like the one to the west of Regla Island centered at about N26 32.063 W82 07.872. Depending on the number of fish that swim into the sound (and not along Sanibel's beaches) on their northbound trip, this place can be popular with tarpon anglers using cut or live bait. This type of fishing is usually a "bait-and-wait" process, and by-catches of big rays and sharks are not uncommon.

The 5000-plus-acre J. N. "Ding" Darling National Wildlife Refuge takes up much of the northern shoreline of Sanibel Island and about half of smaller Captiva Island. The refuge stretches from Woodrings Point (N26 28.087 W82 03.753) on Sanibel to the north end of Buck Key (N26 30.858 W82 11.035) on Captiva and includes backwaters such as Tarpon Bay, McIntyre Creek, Hardworking Bayou, and Blind Pass (if it's not silted-in). Each of these places offers spectacular backwater fishing for snook, redfish, and trout. Mangrove shorelines, bars, old pilings, and docks all attract these fish, and none should be passed by without a cast, night or day. The refuge is usually protected from evening sea breezes, but not from the mosquitoes for which the area is famous. Never forget your bug spray. Visiting anglers should also be aware of certain slow speed zones, and of areas where motorized craft are prohibited in the refuge. The U.S. Fish & Wildlife Service publishes an excellent guide to fishing in the refuge, available at Refuge Headquarters or online at http://www.fws.gov/southeast/pubs/Ding-Darling-fish-broch.pdf.

It's a toss-up as to whether "beach snook" or "pass snook" are responsible for attracting anglers to Sanibel and Captiva—and for getting them to come back year after year. Of course both these fisheries are related, as it's the fast clear water of the narrow passes here that gives the big springtime and early summer snook access to the beaches. Pass fishing in Redfish Pass involves drifting a falling tide from the shallow inshore flats and casting jigs or live baits into the deep channel or along the jetties on the south shore. Captiva Pass moves more water than Redfish Pass, and snook often hug the northern side of the channel and then move to the reefs to the south of the pass. Blind Pass is open infrequently, and there have been several recent efforts to dredge it; however, unless its shores can be effectively contained, it will continue to shoal up and close. That's unfortunate, as the Blind Pass Bridge has been an excellent spot to snook fish for many years. Pass fishing also involves other species than snook. Anglers drifting the passes in cooler weather often catch some nice mangrove snapper and sheepshead. To catch these fish, try "knocker rigs" and live shrimp, worked as slowly along the bottom as possible. Slower than new moon or full moon tides always make passes easier to fish. Tarpon are also in the passes. You'll have a good chance in Captiva Pass, fishing it much like Boca Grande and drifting squirrelfish or live crabs near the bottom. Outgoing "hill tides" (on the new and full moon) in May or June are probably the best ones for tarpon in this pass. That's when the most bait washes out of Pine Island Sound.

In spring, anglers wading the beaches or casting toward them from boats catch snook of all sizes under snags or in the trough just outside the surf. The clear water here demands that you exercise some stealth and choose your bait or lure carefully. Just as when you're fishing for snook and reds in shallow

Pass fishing doesn't always mean fishing from a boat.

clear water like that inside Redfish and Captiva Passes, be especially careful not to slam hatches or cooler lids. And avoid fishing in areas where there are multitudes of swimmers. Live bait enthusiasts seem to do well with white bait, free-lined with light spinning gear. I'd recommend either D.O.A.'s 3-inch "nite glow" shrimp or their TerrorEyz in the same color to anyone interested in tossing artificial baits. Both of these D.O.A. offerings are also excellent, day or night, for snook around mangroves, docks, or bridges. Fly anglers should make their first stop at Sanibel Island a visit with Norm Zeigler at his shop (see listing at the end of the chapter). Norm will give good advice about beach fishing, and you'll have the opportunity to purchase a handful of his Crystal Schminnow flies, a local favorite for snook and small tarpon.

Starting in May, the Lee County beaches attract vast numbers of tarpon. As schools of these fish continue their annual migration from Caribbean waters north toward Florida's Big

Bend, local anglers set up along the beachfronts, all hoping to intercept them and bring a "silver king" boatside. Of course, because of the mild climate here, some tarpon can be found in the back bays or up the Caloosahatchee River all year long, but it's May and June when everyone really gets excited.

One of the nice things about fishing the beaches for tarpon is the number of techniques that anglers can use to get them to bite. In summer, many of these fish are lazily "daisy chaining" and can be spotted easily in the gin-clear water. That makes them easy targets for light tackle enthusiasts casting flies or artificial baits. In fact, if you can get positioned in front of an advancing school of tarpon, you're likely to have a shot at whichever fish in the group you hope to catch. Stealth is important, and accurate casts count in this situation. The 10- to 15-foot depths here make push poles useless, but an electric trolling motor will help keep thing quiet.

Fly fishers typically use 12-weight gear and a variety of flies, including "destroyers," "toads," and "screamers" for tarpon. If you prefer spinning tackle, remember that, while there's plenty of room to fight big fish off the beaches, hungry sharks abound. Keep your spinning gear in the 40-pound class. Doing so will give you a good fight and not tire the tarpon too much, making him lunch for a hammerhead. Tarpon fishing is usually about the "hunt," and many anglers, including myself, are satisfied with just a spectacular jump or two from a big fish. Artificial lures like D.O.A.'s Bait Busters or TerrorEyz will almost always attract a bite but are small enough to give the fish a "fighting chance." If you're inclined to anchoring and soaking cut mullet, live pinfish, or shrimp, use a circle hook. You may get fewer hookups, but you're less likely to "gut hook" and kill a tarpon.

Captiva, Redfish, Matanzas, and Big Carlos passes all attract tarpon with the bait that washes out on falling tides. The shoals to the south of Captiva Pass can be especially productive, but sometimes crowded. In general, all the beachfront from Blind Pass (N26 28.769 W82 11.180) to Knapps Point on the south end of Sanibel (N26 25.447 W82 03.852) is worth exploring in late spring and early summer. Remember that while the bite may be better at dawn, sight-fishing gets better as the sun gets overhead, so plan your beach tarpon trip based on your fishing style.

The Caloosahatchee River empties some of its water into San Carlos Bay under the Sanibel Causeway and the bridges. The structures and lights of the causeway bridges attract spring and summer tarpon and offer good nighttime fishing. Be sure to look for tarpon schools heading into Pine Island Sound at Point Ybel (N26 27.062 W82 00.744) at Sanibel Island's eastern tip, too.

To the south, the barrier islands outside Estero Bay and Big Hickory Bay attract migrating tarpon, especially near the passes. New Pass and Big Carlos Pass have bridges, and there's some good nighttime tarpon and snook fishing near them. The same holds true for the fishing pier under the Matanzas Bridge and in Matanzas Pass at Fort Myers Beach.

The estuary of the Caloosahatchee River is a complicated place. I've already discussed fishing in Pine Island Sound, Matlacha Pass, and the shoreline of Sanibel Island. The fishing at these places, as well as the soon-to-be discussed areas of San Carlos Bay and Estero Bay, is a direct result of the river's flow into the Gulf of Mexico, about 12 miles downstream of downtown Fort Myers. According to my friend and outdoor writer Byron Stout, this estuarine system extends some 30 miles upstream to the first set of locks in the Okeechobee Waterway, of which the river is part, to the Franklin Locks at Olga. The net result to anglers is that the river offers some pretty darn good saltwater fishing, near its mouth and well upstream.

You can expect to find fish near bars, structure, and off points up and down the river. Near the river's mouth, concentrate on the docks near Punta Rassa for late spring and summertime snook. "Work" each structure carefully and silently, pitching 3-inch D.O.A. "nite glow" shrimp under the docks and near pilings. The flats and bars that flank the ICW between Shell Point (N26 31.543 W82 00.051) and Sword Point probably represent the very best of the fishery here. Snook, trout, and reds all feed over the flats and in adjacent cuts and swashes in warmer weather. Sheepshead are also popular targets here in winter, usually sharing deeper water with seatrout and redfish seeking solace from the cold. Tidal flow and range are very important factors in fishing the lower river here. I think it's safe to assume that the best bite will be on the "up tide" side of any structure, whether the tide is falling or rising. An example is the narrows between Shell Point and Cattle Dock Point (N26 31.886 W81 59.813), considered by Byron Stout "the best natural snook spot in Florida." Here, fish near Cattle Dock Point on an incoming summer tide for snook.

From Shell Point upriver, anglers should consider fishing the eastern, or Fort Myers, side of the Caloosahatchee shoreline. Understand that the less-ragged Cape Coral shoreline is the product of the creation of Cape Coral by dredging. That's not a bad thing, as residential canals run like spider webs several miles inland from the river, each offering inshore species cover and comfort in the form of docks and deeper water. Some canals here are busy waterways and others are all but deserted (except on warm weekends), but all have angling potential year-round, especially for those who are able to find a deep hole along a seawall or dock. But the east shore of the river, with its bars and scattered flats, is probably a better choice for anglers inclined to fish while drifting rather than anchoring and still-fishing. More structure simply means more places to fish, and drifting allows you to cover more ground. Of course, if you find a "honey hole" anywhere, drop your anchor and let the fun begin.

Several bridges cross the Caloosahatchee River, joining Fort Myers to Cape Coral. The Cape Coral Bridge and the Midpoint Bridge both cross some relatively wide natural river channels and offer some good summertime tarpon fishing. My suggestion is that you anchor with the tide at your boat's bow, and drift or cast live or artificial lures behind you toward the bridge structure. D.O.A.'s Bait Busters and bigger TerrorEyz lures work well for this technique, especially at night. As with most bridge fishing, you'll need heavier tackle, like spinning rods and reels lined with 40-pound-test Power Pro line and 60-pound-test fluorocarbon leaders. Cut mullet will work well, fished deep, but if white bait or big live shrimp are available, use them free-lined into the current like the artificial lures. As is the case in many of Florida's big rivers, expect other species than tarpon. Snook of all sizes lurk around the bridges in warmer weather, and sheepshead and small mangrove snapper will hide there when it's cool.

No matter how far upstream from the Caloosahatchee's mouth you travel toward the first lock at Olga, you're going to find saltwater fish to catch. Just look for structure and consider the time of year. In cooler weather, species like trout, reds, and snook will move upriver seeking protection even from what are usually mild winter temperatures here. As an example, the power plant warm water discharge near the confluence of the Orange River and the Caloosahatchee, above the Interstate 75 bridge, is an excellent cold weather spot for "resident" tarpon. Here, hundreds of tarpon are landed and released each year, mostly by anglers fishing cut bait.

Geologically speaking, Estero Bay's formation must have had something to do with the formation of Pine Island Sound and its barrier islands by the Caloosahatchee River. That was likely well before our time, and since then the brackish Estero backwaters, fed by Hendry Creek, the Estero River, Spring Creek, and the Imperial River have matured on their own into a rich fishery. Snook, redfish, seatrout, flounder, and tarpon can all be found behind the barrier islands that stretch from Matanzas Pass to Big Hickory Pass, just north of Bonita Beach.

It's hard to rank any particular feature of Estero Bay as more important than another. As with Pine Island Sound, there are mangrove islands and shorelines, oyster bars, points of land, natural and manmade channels, grass flats, and residential canals. And there are also the mouths of creeks and rivers, much smaller than the Caloosahatchee, each with its own estuary system.

Unofficially, Estero Bay seems to enclose about 15 square miles of fishable water. The fact that it's fed from the Gulf by four passes (Matanzas, Big Carlos, New, and Big Hickory) means that the rate of tidal exchange is good. It's better when the weather's dry, as in winter, but the freshwater creeks and rivers rarely overwhelm the salt, even if it rains inshore of the bay. In any case, expect the areas directly behind the passes to have a bit more water flow than those in the extreme backwaters, but expect the fishing for seatrout, redfish, and snook to be excellent throughout this eco-system.

Estero Bay hugs Florida's coast, oriented northwest, at Matanzas Pass, to southeast. Beginning at that pass, and in warmer months, anglers should expect to find trout and reds along the flats off Bunches Beach and toward the Matanzas Bridge that connects the mainland to Estero Islands and the beaches. The bridge and fishing pier underneath it keep wintertime anglers busy catching sheepshead and summertime anglers busy catching snook. Of course, just about any inshore species can be caught around the bridge, from the pier, or around nearby docks. The stretch of water behind Estero Island is shallow, but bigger boats can navigate the channels there; however, anglers in shallow-draft skiffs, canoes, or kayaks might have more success fishing for snook and reds in backwaters like Hurricane Bay or Hell Peckney Bay. There's access to Hurricane Bay by a privately marked channel from marker #6 on the Matanzas Channel at about N26 27.325 W81 56.543.

Similarly, there's a channel from marker #25, west of Julies Island (N26 26.484 W81 55.126) that leads up into Hell Peckney Bay.

The Matanzas Fishing Pier is conveniently located under the bridge at Fort Myers Beach.

The largest expanse of Estero Bay lies behind the south end of Estero Island and the mouth of Hendry Creek, to the north. There's a bit more deep water here, but it's still a shallow backwater. Big Carlos Pass does feed channels that surround Goombs Key, but they eventually end on shallow flats. Anglers should spend time investigating (and fishing) the shoreline of Rocky Bay, at the mouth of Hendry Creek. The edges of the "deeper" water between Goombs Key and Coon Key and that between Coon Key and Estero Key are good places to look for cruising snook, especially on falling summertime tides. Seatrout anglers should try the grassy area to the southeast of Monkey Joe Key (N26 24.421 W81 51.610) where the deeper water from Big Carlos Pass pushes onto the flats. Likewise the big trout flats inside Long Key, which are easily accessed from the Lovers Key boat ramp.

New Pass and Big Hickory Pass feed the lower range of Estero Bay as well as Big Hickory Bay. Either backwater offers good trout fishing, spring through fall, on the grass flats to the south of Bird Island, beginning at about N26 22.835 W81 50.909. Summertime snook and even a few pompano can be found in the inner channel of New Pass and in the Broadway and Hogue channels behind Big Hickory Pass.

The unofficial end of Estero Bay is at Bonita Beach, near the mouth of the Imperial River. Here, in smaller Fish Trap Bay, you can catch trout and reds near the bars and over the flats. And, though some species prefer staying closer to the Gulf, you can expect to find snook well up the river and into the residential canals south toward Wiggins Pass.

Offshore Fishing

I'm sometimes amazed by the number of offshore-style fishing boats I see leaving Matanzas Pass, Big Carlos Pass, or heading south through San Carlos Bay into the broad expanse of the Gulf of Mexico.

Despite the number and variety of inshore species here, some anglers head westward to look for reef and blue-water species. Getting to bottom that has enough natural structure, like ledges and rocky outcrops, involves long trips far offshore, and long trips involve bigger boats than you'd normally use in the Caloosahatchee River, Pine Island Sound, or Estero Bay, sometimes overnight and sometimes in heavy seas. Party boats or big offshore charter boats are an option, but with gas prices rising and reef-fish bag limits restricted more and more in recent years, I'll take a tarpon trip along the beach any day. Then, after the fun's over, I'll have a grouper dinner ashore at a nice restaurant.

But if you're determined to look for reef fish, there are

several shallow-water artificial reefs within easy reach of the beaches here. Lee County has had an artificial-reef program since the early 1990s, and more reefs are under construction or planned. You many not catch whopper gag grouper or your limit of red snapper on these close-to-shore structures, but you might catch some excellent table fish like gray (mangrove) snapper, sheepshead, or even a cobia. You will see some small grouper close to shore, particularly in warmer months, but expect most of your catch to be smaller reef fish. Migrating pelagics like Spanish or king mackerel will inhabit the reefs in spring and fall, as will permit and amberjacks. The Redfish Pass Reef (N26 33.167 W82 13.927) is in about 25 feet of water and was created by the sinking of two small barges. It's only a couple of miles from the pass and on a calm day easily accessed by smaller boats. Paces Place Reef is a bit deeper, at N26 31.120 W82 17.000, and made up from construction debris and machinery. Expect some species, particularly snapper and grouper, to move away from shore in the late fall, and this is a likely spot to intercept them. Another big (and popular) artificial reef is the Belton-Johnson Reef. This is actually several small adjacent reefs, made up of concrete rubble and debris. It's located at N26 25.507 W82 11.673, about 8 miles due west of Knapps Point at the south end of Sanibel Island. If you're fishing from the Estero area, try the "MAY" Reef, at N26 22.680 W81 55.400. It's in about 20 feet of water, slightly more than 2 miles southwest of Big Carlos Pass and a favorite haunt of both reef and pelagic species. Finally, the Edison Reef (N26 18.700 W82 13.400) is a longer run to the southwest of Fort Myers Beach and a good spot for king mackerel, amberjack, and even permit.

Getting Around

If you're approaching the Fort Myers area from the north, use US41 or Interstate 75. If you're heading to Cape Coral or Pine

Island, don't cross the Caloosahatchee River, but take Pine Island Road (called Bayshore Road in North Fort Myers) to the west. If you're coming from Punta Gorda or Charlotte Harbor, an alternative to US41 is Burnt Store Road. On Pine Island, Stringfellow Road is the main north-south route. In Cape Coral, you can cross the river using either of the two bridges over the river to Fort Myers.

If you're driving to Fort Myers, Fort Myers Beach, Estero, Sanibel, or Captiva, cross the river. US41 runs through the city and turns into McGregor Boulevard, which will get you to Sanibel and Captiva Islands. If you're heading to Fort Myers Beach or Estero, watch for signs and take San Carlos Boulevard south. From Interstate 75, Colonial Boulevard or Daniels Road will take you west to Fort Myers or toward the beaches.

Where to Stay

When Henry Ford and Thomas Edison vacationed here, they didn't have trouble finding a place to stay (or to park their boat trailer!). Now, this part of Florida's Gulf Coast can be crowded, so be sure to call ahead for reservations.

*   *   *

Matlacha Island Cottages, (239) 283-RENT, 4756 Pine Island Rd, Matlacha. Historic cottages, some with kitchens, near Matlacha Pass. www.islandcottages.com

Southernmost Inn, (239) 283-4519, southern end of Stringfellow Road, Pine Island. Boat access from ICW marker #16.

Knoll's Court Motel, (239) 283-0616, 4755 Pine Island Rd, Matlacha. Efficiencies on Matlacha Pass. Dockage available. www.knollscourtmotel.com.

Holiday Inn Express Cape Coral, (239) 542-2121, 1538 Cape

Coral Pkwy E, Cape Coral. Predictable lodging close to the Yacht Club boat ramp and the bridge to Fort Myers.

Country Inn and Suites/Sanibel Gateway, (239) 454-9292, 13901 Shell Point Plaza, Fort Myers. This hotel is 2 miles from the Punta Rassa boat ramp and the Sanibel Causeway. Good parking. Be sure to ask if they're offering an "angler's special."

Castaways Beach & Bay Cottages, (239) 472-1252, 6460 Sanibel-Captiva Rd, Sanibel Island. Cottages, efficiencies, and motel units on the water near Blind Pass. www.castawayssanibel.com

Matanzas Inn, (239) 463-9258, 414 Crescent St, Fort Myers Beach, on Matanzas Pass. A resort, but convenient to Matanzas Pass. Dockage available.

Lovers Key Resort, (239) 765-1040, 8771 Estero Blvd, Fort Myers Beach. Pretty snazzy, but near the Lovers Key ramp and State Park beaches. www.loverskey.com

Where to Eat

If you're not bringing along your personal kitchen and serving staff, as did Edison and Ford, give some of these places a try when you visit.

*　　*　　*

Tarpon Lodge Restaurant and Bar, (239) 283-3999, 13771 Waterfront Dr, Pineland. Excellent food at a 4-star restaurant. www.tarponlodge.com

Red's Fresh Seafood House & Tavern, (239) 283-4412, 10880 Stringfellow Rd, Bokeelia. Family owned, serving fresh local seafood.

Raymary Street Grill, Stringfellow Rd, Bokeelia. Affordable breakfasts and lunches.

Lazy Flamingo Restaurant, (239) 283-5959, at Four Winds Marina, Bokeelia. Lunch and dinner, casual, seafood.

Woody's Island Bar and Grill, (239) 283-5555, 3051 Stringfellow Rd, Saint James City. Fresh seafood, burgers, and dockside dining on the Monroe Canal, off ICW marker #13. Overnight dockage available. www.woodyswaterside.com

Hogfish Waterfront Grill, (239) 283-5300, 3135 Stringfellow Rd, Saint James City. Sandwiches, seafood, BBQ. On the Monroe Canal with dockage for boaters. www.thehogfishgrill.com

The Waterfront Restaurant and Marina, (239) 283-0592, Saint James City, at the southern tip of Pine Island, off ICW marker #12 on the Henley Canal. Excellent seafood, with easy access and dockage for boaters.

Sandy Hook Fish and Rib House, (239) 283-0113, 4875 Pine Island Rd, Matlacha. Like it says: "fish and ribs."

Cabbage Key Restaurant, (239) 283-2278, at Cabbage Key Resort, ICW marker #60. Famous for "cheeseburgers in paradise." Lunch and dinner, access by boat only.

Doc Ford's Rum Bar & Grille, (239) 472-8311, 975 Rabbit Rd, Sanibel Island. As only author Randy Wayne White could have imagined—good food and drink! There's a second location at 708 Angler's Wharf on Fort Myers Beach. Famous for mojitos.

Lighthouse Café, (239) 472-0303, 362 Periwinkle Way, Sanibel Island. Self-proclaimed "World's Best Breakfast." Capt. Rob Modys agrees.

Pincher's Crab Shack, locations at Fort Myers Beach (18100 San Carlos Blvd) and S. Fort Myers (15271 McGregor Blvd). Good local seafood. "You Can't Fake Fresh" is their motto. www.pincherscrabshack.com

KC's River Stop Snack Bar, (239) 549-5699, at Cape Coral Yacht Club Beach. Dock here for burgers and fries. Get gas (for your boat) too!

Marinas, Marine Supplies and Service, Bait and Tackle Shops, and Launching Ramps

Fishin' Tackle Outlet, (239) 731-8385, 18441 N. Tamiami Tr, N. Fort Myers. Excellent tackle at discounted prices, no bait.

Marine Trading Post, (239) 997-5777, 1156 N. Tamiami Tr, N. Fort Myers. Marine supplies and engine parts, open 7 days.

Lehr's Economy Tackle Shop, (239) 995-2280, 1366 N. Tamiami Tr, N. Fort Myers. An excellent source for quality tackle.

Rite Angler Tackle, (239) 466-7326, 16450 S. Tamiami Tr, Fort Myers, www.riteangler.com. Tackle and rigging supplies.

Marine Surplus Inc., (239) 332-0909, 2901 Palm Beach Rd, Fort Myers. Marine supplies and parts. www.marinesurplusinc.com

Fish-Tale Marina, (239) 463-3600, 7225 Estero Blvd, Fort Myers Beach. Full service marina with dockage, fuel, tackle, and boat and kayak rentals. www.thefishtalemarina.com

Getaway Marina, (239) 466-3600, 18400 San Carlos Blvd, Fort Myers Beach. Full service marina, just north of the Matanzas Pass bridge. www.getawaymarina.com

West Marine, (239) 267-3116, 17220 San Carlos Blvd, Fort Myers Beach. A good source of marine and boating supplies.

Fort Myers Beach Fishing Pier, 950 Estero Blvd, Fort Myers Beach. 560-foot pier.

The Bait Box, (239) 472-1616, 1041 Periwinkle Way, Sanibel Island. Live and frozen bait, tackle, fly rods and reels, rod and reel rentals, repairs. www.thebaitbox.com

Norm Ziegler's Fly Shop, (239) 472-6868, 2242 Periwinkle Way, Sanibel Island. Fly and spinning tackle, bait and excellent advice about snook fishing. "Norm's Crystal Schminnow" fly is one of the best flies for beachfront snook. www.normzeiglers flyshop.com

Sanibel Island Fishing Pier, near the lighthouse, Sanibel Island. Small inshore pier on San Carlos Bay. $2 to park.

Sanibel Marina, (239) 472-2723, 634 Yachtsman Dr, Sanibel. www.sanibelmarina.com. Located between the Sanibel Causeway and the lighthouse, on the southern tip of Sanibel Island at Point Ybel. Dockage, ship's store, boat rentals, fuel.

Tarpon Bay Explorers, (239) 472-8900, 900 Tarpon Bay Rd, Sanibel Island. Kayak rentals, guided kayak fishing trips, boat ramp, supplies. Licensed concessionaire of the J. N. "Ding" Darling NWR. At the south end of Tarpon Bay. www.tarpon bayexplorers.com

Castaways Marina, (239) 472-1252, 6460 Sanibel-Captive Rd, Sanibel Island. Dockage, fuel, bait, tackle, boat ramp. Near Blind Pass.

Estero River Outfitters, (239) 992-4050, 20991 S. Tamiami Tr, Estero. Full-service kayak and paddling store on the Estero River. Rentals available. www.esteroriveroutfitters.com

Master Bait & Tackle, (239) 992-2553, 4465 Bonita Beach Rd, Bonita Beach. Full selection of inshore and offshore tackle, frozen bait.

Bass Pro Shops, (239) 461-7800, 10040 Gulf Center Dr, Fort Myers. As expected, Bass Pro offers an excellent selection of tackle, marine supplies, and clothing.

D&D Matlacha Bait and Tackle, (239) 282-9122, 3922 Pine Island Rd, Matlacha. Live shrimp, pinfish, crabs, ice, tackle. Direct access to Matlacha Pass.

D. G.'s Hardware and Tackle, (239) 283-7533, 10523 Stringfellow Rd, Pine Island Center, Bokeelia. Marine and fishing supplies at the 4-way stop on Pine Island.

Old Pine Island Marine and Tackle, (239) 283-2548, 3187 Stringfellow Rd, Saint James City (up Monroe Canal from ICW marker #12). Marine supplies, live bait and tackle, ice, boat ramp.

Monroe Canal Marina, (239) 282-8600, 3105 Stringfellow Rd, Saint James City. Marine supplies, tackle, bait, boat ramp.

Bokeelia boat ramp, 7290 Barrancas Ave NW, Bokeelia. Paved ramp, $5 launch fee, $10 per day parking with 3-day maximum.

Matlacha boat ramp, 4577 Pine Island Dr, Matlacha. Two paved ramps on Matlacha Pass.

Cape Coral Yacht Club boat ramp, 3 paved ramps on Driftwood Pkwy at the Caloosahatchee River, $10 fee, good parking.

Horton Park boat ramp, 2600 SE 26th Pl, Cape Coral. A steep ramp 10 miles up the Caloosahatchee River. $10 per day parking fee. A rebuild was planned for 2011.

Franklin Lock boat ramp, at Franklin Campground, near Franklin Lock, upriver on the Caloosahatchee River. $3 fee, paved ramp. Camping available.

Punta Rassa boat ramp, 18700 Punta Rassa Rd, Fort Myers. Double paved ramps, $10 fee, at the east end of the Sanibel Causeway.

Sanibel Island boat ramp, at the island end of the Sanibel Causeway at Point Ybel. $2 per hour parking. Single paved ramp. Low tides may cause problems if launching bigger boats here.

Imperial River boat ramp, 27551 S. Tamiami Tr, Bonita Springs. $5 fee, paved ramps. Inland on Imperial River.

Lovers Key boat ramp, at Lovers Key State Park. Near Big Carlos Pass. Good ramp for bigger boats. Excellent parking.

Bay North boat ramp, Little Hickory Island, Bonita Springs. Free, but limited parking. Good canoe and kayak access to Big Hickory Bay backwaters.

Local Fishing Guides

Capt. Rob Modys, (239) 851-1242. Inshore, near shore, and backwater fishing in Pine Island Sound and Estero Bay. www.soulmatecharters.com

Capt. Paul Hobby, (239) 433-1007. Light tackle and fly-fishing. www.fishinghobby.com

Capt. Rick DePaiva, (239) 246-8726. Inshore light tackle and fly-fishing. www.saltwaterflyfishing.org

Capt. Josh Harvel, (239) 233-0655. Kayak fishing charters. www.swflkayakcharters.com

*   *   *

Many fishing guides from the Charlotte Harbor area are familiar with the waters here. If necessary, check the listings in chapter 7 for more recommendations. The website of the Florida Guides Association (www.florida-guides.com) has a complete listing of USCG licensed and insured fishing guides. Also, if you plan to fish for tarpon at or near Boca Grande, consider hiring a guide who's a member of the Boca Grande Fishing Guides Association, www.bocagrandefishing.com.

Before You Leave Home

Be sure to check this guide's companion website, www.salt wateranglersguide.com, for updates to local information.

9

~~~~~~~~~~~

Naples, Marco, and
the Ten Thousand Islands

Naples is a "little big city," with glamorous shops and big fancy hotels; however, it also has some excellent places to fish, and if you look hard enough, some places to stay and eat that won't break the bank. Fifty years ago, Marco Island, just south of Naples, was mostly uninhabited. Now, even with its big fancy hotels, condos, and high-end homes, it still attracts anglers. And Everglades City and Chokoloskee, both on the edge of the Ten Thousand Islands, are in the middle of nowhere, south of Marco Island and north of the Everglades. Of course, "nowhere" can be a good thing—if you're an angler.

Gulf access to the bay and harbor at Naples is through Gordon Pass. The three passes (Wiggins, Clam, and Doctors) to the north, between Naples and Bonita Beach, are smaller and offer limited access to backwaters. Boaters making a north-south transit along this stretch of coast must travel away from shore, as the protected Intracoastal Waterway (ICW) makes an easterly turn up the Caloosahatchee River at Fort Myers, 40 miles to the north; however, there is a channel that begins in Naples Bay and heads south behind Keewaydin Island toward Marco Island and Big Marco Pass.

Marco Island lies just south of Naples and north of Cape Romano, where the Ten Thousand Islands begin and the shoreline takes a southeasterly turn toward the Florida Keys. Despite the high-rise condos, the area around the island remains

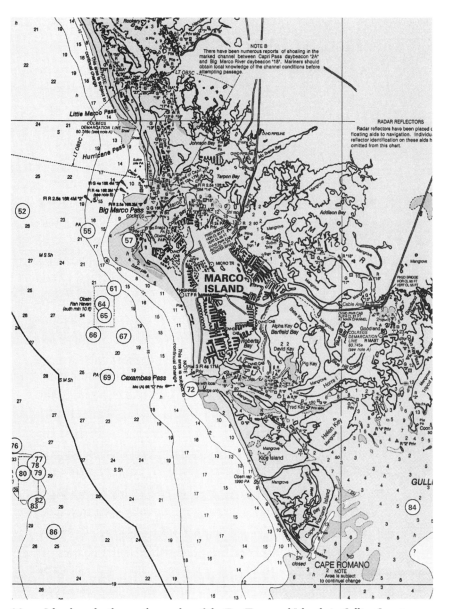

Marco Island marks the northern edge of the Ten Thousand Islands in Collier County. (Map courtesy of Waterproof Charts, Inc.)

largely unspoiled and an excellent fishery. The backwaters near Marco are flooded and drained by several Gulf passes, including Big Marco Pass and Caxambas Pass. To the south, the backwaters open up into Gullivan Bay, at the northern edge of the Ten Thousand Island area.

If you really want to prove to yourself that there are ten thousand islands in the Ten Thousand Islands, take a boat ride along the 45-mile stretch of Florida's coastline between Cape Romano and the western tip of Cape Sable. You'll probably lose count of the islands you pass, but will certainly be tempted to fish each and every cut, channel, and mangrove shoreline you see. With the exception of a few outposts like Port of the Islands, Everglades City, and Chokoloskee, this is barren country that should not be taken lightly or navigated without caution.

These are places that every angler should visit. If you plan to come to this stretch of Florida's Gulf Coast for just a few days, you may want to consider hiring a professional fishing guide to show you the variety of angling opportunities, inshore, near shore, and offshore. If you've the luxury of a season, or all four, get your own boat wet and expect to stay busy each and every day you're here. In Collier County, it's easy to forget about anything but fishing.

Inshore and Near Shore Fishing

The "big four" on my list of southwest Florida's most-sought-after inshore species are snook, redfish, tarpon, and spotted seatrout. There are, of course, lots of other "fish in the sea." Sheepshead, silver trout, tripletail, cobia, pompano, and permit are commonly caught in inshore waters. Pelagics like Spanish mackerel, king mackerel, and bluefish make appearances along the shorelines and beaches, often chasing bait well into bays and inshore channels. There are also reef species that come close to shore. Mangrove (gray) snapper can be found in passes as well as around inshore snags and structures, and the

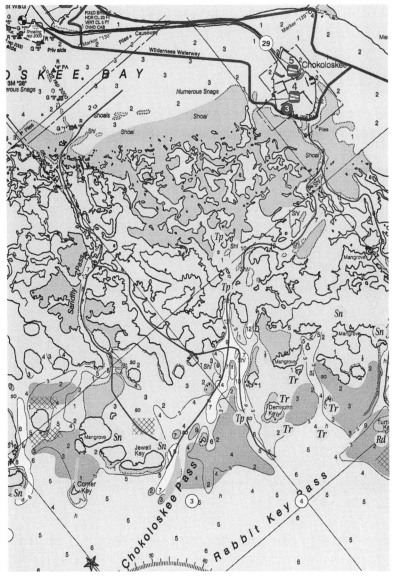

Chokoloskee means literally and figuratively "at the end of the road."
(Map courtesy of Waterproof Charts, Inc.)

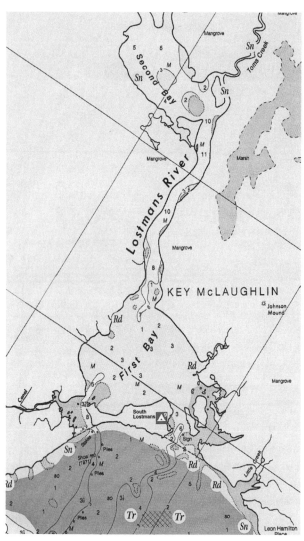

They don't call it Lostmans River because it's easy to get around in this wild back country. (Map courtesy of Waterproof Charts, Inc.)

A happy angler with a nice Ten Thousand Islands sea-trout.

dense mangroves serve as the nursery for almost all the Gulf's Goliath grouper.

Unlike the other areas covered in this book, where spotted seatrout seem to head the list of most-desired species, anglers here seem to spend more time in search of snook, reds, and tarpon. It's not that there are fewer trout here. Limits of seatrout are caught, but it's the other species that bring anglers to the area, over and over. I'd put snook at the top of my list, probably followed by tarpon, redfish, and trout, in that order. Why? Because the backwaters, passes, and beachfronts here lend themselves so well to sight-fishing techniques that have become so popular among sports anglers in recent years. Snook, reds, and tarpon are, in these shallow and clean waters, relatively easy to spot swimming, tailing, and rolling. Seatrout

The mangrove-lined shorelines of the Ten Thousand Islands offer some excellent fishing for snook and tarpon.

are here, and in great numbers, but are masters of deception and hide themselves in deeper sloughs and channels and on grassy flats. Sight fishing for seatrout just doesn't happen too often, and simply put, snook, reds, and tarpon are one helluva lot more fun to catch than trout.

Here, from Naples south to the top of Everglades National Park, you'll find yourself in a place where extended cold fronts are rare, even in the deep of winter, and the waters stay warm and inhabited by bait and game fish all year. Natural disasters like late-summer hurricanes and outbreaks of red tide, not freezes, are often the most serious factors when it comes to the health of this fishery. And for the most part, seasons really don't mean much here, unless you compare the number of mosquitoes or no-see-ums in July to those in February.

Early in the calendar year, the waters in this part of Florida are still warmer than Lake Michigan's are in summer. Here, 55 or 60 degrees is cold for water—cold enough to send sport fish high-tailing far into the backwaters or deep channels. But that cold usually doesn't last long. There are sometimes as few as four or five "cool spells" here each winter, and after a few sunny days the water warms and the fish return to their usual haunts. There are no shortages of sunny winter days either, and even if it's cold, the fish are attracted to areas that absorb more solar radiation, like oyster bars, muddy flats, and the western shorelines of mangrove islands. Afternoons make better wintertime fishing, so sleep in and have a nice breakfast before you head out on the water.

Spring arrives here early, often as early as February. Then, fish move from the backwaters toward the Gulf, spreading out onto shallow flats or into passes in search of bait that appears, almost by magic, as the water warms. Snook, reds, and trout are all on the move during the short transition from winter to summer, but the absolute proof that spring has arrived are the Spanish mackerel. They arrive, usually following schools of white bait, and are quickly followed by their bigger cousins, the king mackerel.

Summer in southwest Florida doesn't wait for the June solstice. Water at 70 degrees soon warms to 80-plus degrees, and every species is active, from the backwaters to the beaches. Redfish can often be sight-fished along the edges of bars, and trout move onto whatever grass flats they can find. Snook of all sizes cruise the beaches, sidle up alongside seawalls or rock jetties, or hide under docks, just waiting for a lively bait to cross their field of view. Migrating tarpon usually move north in early summer, but a few hang around in the passes and along the beaches. As opposed to wintertime fishing, your summertime pursuits can begin early, as the first two hours of daylight are often the times when the fish feed best. But in more developed areas, where there are lighted docks and structure, fishing is sometimes best in the very early and cool pre-dawn hours.

During fall (which many local anglers laughingly say begins here at Thanksgiving and ends at Christmas), expect game fish to feel the waters cooling and instinctively start eating heartily. Snook will move away from the beaches and head into passes, and redfish will gather along coastal mangrove points in advance of their trip offshore to spawn. Trout will move to shallower flats early in the season, following bait into warmer water, and eventually move to deeper, more protected waters. Tarpon "season" is over, but a few resident fish, stragglers from the big migration, are still found well up into backwaters and residential canals.

Snook are voracious eaters. They readily attack all sorts of baits, including live minnows, shrimp, pinfish, hard and soft-bodied plugs, and flies. And they can usually be found somewhere in the area, year-round. Snook are considered sport fish, and while they're good to eat, regulations regarding closed seasons and size limits confuse many anglers, encouraging them to practice catch-and-release when fishing for the species.

When you find snook along the beaches here, expect them to be eating small fish and crustaceans that wash in and out with the action of the waves. There will usually be a mix of large female fish and smaller males. Scattered snags, consisting of driftwood or large tree roots, offer cover to these fish, but sometimes give them an advantage if you're using light spinning tackle or fly gear. If you're fishing from a boat and casting toward shore, fill your live well with lots of white bait or shrimp and free-line them toward the beach and the cruising fish. If you're wading, lugging a bucket of live bait is impractical, so a D.O.A. 3-inch shrimp or ¼-ounce TerrorEyz jig ("nite glow" is a good color) is a better choice. Fly fishers should stick with a fly that's "light or white," like Norm Zeigler's Crystal

Schminnow or a chartreuse-and-white Clouser minnow. To many, beach fishing for snook is sight fishing at its best.

Backwater and "pass" snook are generally in water that's somewhat murky or stained. If the fish are in canals or channels, try bouncing jigs off the bottom or using live baits on "knocker" rigs. If you're fishing near structure like docks, free-lined live or artificial shrimp work well. At night, under lighted docks, let your bait drift across the edge of the light cones. During the day, look for the edge of shadows, as that's where the snook will set up their ambush. As you head south from Naples, the most common backwater snook habitat will likely be the structure of mangroves. Depending on your casting skills, this is when learning to flip noisy topwater plugs under overhanging branches and into the small gaps between mangrove islands pays off. If lots of treble hooks get you in trouble with the branches, you might consider a lightweight jig head and a brightly colored plastic tail, like the D.O.A. C.A.L. "Silver Glitter" Shad. If you prefer using live bait, free-lined white baits work well along mangroves. The downside of using live white bait is that you have to deal with catching them, keeping them alive, and rebaiting your hook after every snook you catch!

Redfish sometimes feed with their mouths oriented toward the bottom, rooting around for crustaceans. Other times, they'll chase small mullet along shorelines and attack from below. A good visual clue to anglers should be whether they see a red's tail or his back in shallow water. Tail wagging means the red is feeding along the bottom, and its back showing means it's feeding above the bottom. Big wakes mean one of two things: (1) you've spooked a red, or (2) he's attacking your lure. Reds are partial to shrimp and mullet and readily eat live or fake ones, like MirrOlure Catch 2000 plugs and D.O.A. shrimp. Live shrimp can be free-lined or used under popping corks, depending on your casting prowess. Reds also eat cut bait, with ladyfish, pinfish, and mullet topping the list of their favorites.

But remember that cut bait will attract other species, including small sharks and rays, considered pests by many anglers.

Spotted seatrout will eat just about anything, including their own young, and they'll also turn up in a surprising number of places. For "slot" trout, a favorite habitat is shallow grass flats where they can hunt around the edges of deeper sandy potholes. Here, the fish will be plentiful and you'll often catch a limit quickly, using any number of a thousand-or-so baits guaranteed to catch the species. Live shrimp, pinfish, and white bait all work, as do jigs, artificial shrimp, and hard-bodied plugs. Rigging live bait or jigs under corks is popular, and free-lining works so long as accurate casts can be made. Slot trout don't seem reluctant to feed 24 hours, 7 days a week. Big, or "gator," trout travel in smaller numbers, with the exception of the cooler months when they school up to spawn. These are the fish you'll find along the edges of oyster and shell bars, along seawalls, or under lighted docks at night. An important thing to remember if you plan to target big trout is that little trout don't grow up to be big trout because they're stupid. These fish can hear a boat's live-well hatch slam a thousand feet away, and even if hooked, can use their fingers and toes to unhook themselves!

A day of tarpon fishing can be a lonely one, especially if you're of a "catching," not "fishing" temperament. However, here in the Naples and the Ten Thousand Islands, you've probably a better chance of catching a silver king than in any other place in the state, including Boca Grande Pass or on the flats at Homosassa. Migratory schools of tarpon, traveling the beaches in spring and early summer, are easily targeted by sight casters in the clear Gulf water off the beaches. Some single fish move into passes and channels and are caught using cut or live bait. Others, sometimes smaller, move into moderate depths to hunt along the edges of inshore mangrove islands, targets for plug and fly anglers. Many local anglers avoid the potential disappointment of a slow day of tarpon fishing by always being prepared for tarpon while fishing for snook or other species. Unless you're crowded into a kayak or canoe, there's always room in your boat for a big spinning rod rigged with a D.O.A. Bait Buster or a MirrOlure 52M18—just in case a hungry tarpon swims by.

Tripletail and cobia hide in the relative shade of crab pot floats and channel markers, hoping to snag a passing meal. For a tripletail, that meal can be your lure, but only if you show interest and stop at every marker or float to toss a live shrimp or an imitation. These fish often resemble a piece of floating trash and are often passed by as anglers head to more "productive" waters. Cobia can be spotted near the surface, too, but are just as likely to swim around the bases of big tripod-shaped markers. If you stop at a marker in search of these "crab eaters," fish one live bait (a crab or a pinfish) down deep and another under a cork near the surface. Medium-weight spinning tackle works well for tripletail, but use your big spinners for cobia, as their first run will be to cover. Both of these species are excellent at table, and unlike many fish, bigger specimens taste as good as smaller ones.

Three other popular inshore fish you're likely to catch here are sheepshead, pompano, and Spanish mackerel. You'll find sheepshead over structure, sometimes on close-in artificial reefs, in cooler weather. They're also found in the deeper passes and along rock jetties in warm weather. Pompano like to feed on crustaceans, particularly sand fleas, along the edges of fast-moving currents in channels and in the rolling surf at beaches. Many of these fish are caught by anglers tossing small jigs for snook, but they're worth the diversion as they may be the tastiest fish in the Gulf. Expect the first "run" of Spanish mackerel to arrive off the Gulf beaches here in early March. Look for birds and troll or cast small jigs or spoons around the edges of the bait pods the mackerel are attacking. Mackerel do not freeze well but are excellent to eat the day they're caught. They're also lots of fun, and usually hang around until late fall.

This is a fishy bit of inshore water, so you can expect to catch any number of species other than those described above in detail. Flounder and whiting are good to eat and often the by-catch of a trout fishing expedition. King mackerel usually follow the Spanish mackerel to the area in spring, sometimes coming conveniently close to shore. Permit are the big cousins of pompano and often feed inside passes and over close-to-shore reefs, as do mangrove snapper and Goliath grouper. And baby Goliaths will often be found well back into the backwaters, along the mangroves where they grow up before heading out to the deeper 100-foot depths in the Gulf.

And then there are the jack crevalle, the ladyfish, and the small sharks that just make any fishing trip fun.

Knowing that you're going fishing is a good thing and knowing what species you'll be fishing for increases your excitement. But knowing *where* you'll find fish makes the difference between a day of "catching" and a day of just "fishing."

Collier County, which stretches from just north of Naples south to Chokoloskee, has a varied fishery, to say the least. The species remain the same, but the geography is significantly different, north to south.

The 12-mile coastline from Wiggins Pass at Vanderbilt Beach to Gordon Pass (at the Gulf entrance to Naples Bay) is best described as "the beach." The only breaks in the shoreline between those two passes are Clam Pass and Doctors Pass.

Wiggins Pass leads from the Gulf into Wiggins Bay and the mouth of the Cocohatchee River. The narrow pass, like others in southwest Florida, offers some good fishing for snook, sheepshead, mangrove snapper, pompano, and an occasional Spanish mackerel. When fishing outside the pass and along the beach to the south, look for daisy-chaining schools of tarpon during their annual spring migration. Inside the pass, expect to find snook (smaller in summer months and bigger as fall approaches) around the islands in Wiggins Bay, behind Wiggins Island. Or head up into Little Hickory Bay and fish that

Gordon Pass offers excellent deepwater access to the Naples area.

northern shore. Delnor-Wiggins Park, in Water Turkey Bay, is a good place to launch canoes or kayaks and fish south into the residential canals behind Gulfshore Drive and Vanderbilt Beach. There, concentrate your casts under docks and the 111th Avenue Bridge. Expect to find snook and reds in this backwater. Up the Cocohatchee River, between the Vanderbilt Drive Bridge and US41, fish the mangroves and edges of the channel in warmer weather for snook and reds. In cooler weather, there's some deeper water just upriver from the bridge that attracts some seatrout.

Clam Pass is sometimes non-navigable to boats other than kayaks or canoes. There is a small kayak launch at the park, and snook and reds are sometimes caught in Outer Clam Bay and the residential canals nearby.

Doctors Pass is active and feeds Venetian Bay and some residential backwaters. More important to anglers are the rocks that line the channel and the shoals just outside. You'll find the "usual" pass species, like snook, snapper, and sheepshead in the channel, and you may see tarpon along the deep edges of the shoals. There's also a pile of rocks about a mile to the west of the pass (at N26 10.382 W81 49.035) that is worth the trip during the spring and fall mackerel runs.

Gordon Pass is the main entrance to Naples "proper" from the Gulf of Mexico. The pass is lined by a rock jetty that attracts snook, mangrove snapper, and sheepshead. Shoals can develop at random, depending on storms, and should always be investigated for tarpon, especially during that species's migration. The channel dead-ends into an inland waterway that runs north to downtown Naples and south, behind Keewaydin Island, to Capri Pass at Marco. Look for snook in the small bay just to the south of the main channel (entrance at about N26 05.833 W81 47.754) or at The Cloisters, near the mouth of Haldeman Creek toward Naples, east of markers #23 and 24 on the inland channel. Of course, this is a densely populated area, with lots of lighted residential docks and channels, each with year-round, night-and-day fishing potential.

The beachfront between Wiggins Pass and Gordon Pass is also a good fishery for both shore-bound anglers and those with boats. Tarpon, during the spring migration, move between the 2- and 3-fathom (12- and 18-foot) curve, just offshore, often slowing to feed or "sleep," laid up, near the passes. Depending on beach activities and frolicking bathers, snook will cruise the shoreline, just outside the surf, feeding in the troughs for small fish and crustaceans. These fish are well within casting distance of wading anglers fishing with light spinning or fly tackle. And, in the fall and spring, particularly outside the passes, look for mackerel of the Spanish and king variety. Another beachfront option for anglers on foot is the Naples Fishing Pier, located about 2 miles north of Gordon Pass and within walking distance of downtown Naples. This structure attracts snook, whiting, seatrout, and even Spanish mackerel.

If you're leaving Gordon Pass and heading south by boat to fish near Marco Island, you have a choice of two possible

There's good angling year-round at Naples Fishing Pier.

routes. If the winds are calm and the water's warm, run on the outside of Keewaydin Island and keep an eye peeled for snook along the shoreline and near snags. If it's windy or cold, run the "inland waterway" behind the island; however, the inland route does offer some distractions that might get you fishing long before you get to Marco. In Dollar Bay, just south of Gordon Pass, look for snook along the mangrove shorelines to the east and trout nearer the channel. Fish the oyster bars across the channel from marker #53, in the mouth of Shell Bay, for redfish. This entire backwater system is generally an excellent fishery for trout, reds, and snook, but access can be tricky. Smaller boats should have no trouble getting into the channel to Rookery Bay from marker #47, but boaters should realize that the eastern end is shallow. Rookery Bay, all of Henderson Creek, and Sand Hill Creek are all worth a day or two of exploration and fishing. As I noted, this place can be distracting.

At marker #34, and depending on your boat, you can either take the main channel and jog east into Johnson Bay or go straight ahead into the channel west of Little Marco Island. There, on your way toward Little Marco Pass and Hurricane Pass, try some snook fishing along the edges of the deeper

Fly-fishing for snook along the Gulf beach at Keewaydin Island, south of Naples, can be rewarding.

water, especially if the tide's falling and washing bait out of the backwaters. If you take the main channel, you'll come to the southern entrance to Rookery Bay, where there's some good fishing too.

The inland waterway joins the Marco Channel at the confluence of Little Marco, Hurricane, Capri, and Big Marco passes off the northwest corner of Marco Island. If you're approaching from offshore, take note that Capri Pass is the main entrance to the back channels, but on some charts the whole complex is termed "Big Marco Pass." In this area, the shoaling is continuous and changing, but also be on the lookout for snook, tarpon, and even a cobia along the deeper edges.

It's hard to tell, when looking at a modern chart or map, which parts of Marco Island are original and which parts were dredged up as part of its development during the 1960s. Fifty

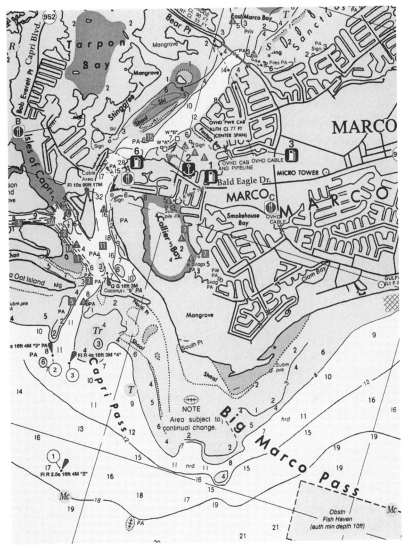

The inland waterway south of Naples leads to Marco Island and Big Marco Pass.
(Map courtesy of Waterproof Charts, Inc.)

years is a long time, and Marco has changed, not only in size, but also in the quality of the fishing there. While its beach-fronts are generally busy with swimmers, its deep residential canals and docks attract snook and trout. To the island's north, and behind Stingaree Island, the protected north and east shorelines of Tarpon Bay and the residential canals at Isles of Capri offer good backwater fishing for both reds and snook. The Collier Boulevard Bridge has now been in place long enough to attract nighttime snook and tarpon. The flats to the east of Charity Island in East Marco Bay (at approx. N25 57.728 W81 42.200) attract snook in cooler weather, as does the deep hole between markers #6 and 8. That 22-foot hole can also attract some summertime tarpon, if you're willing to anchor up and soak cut bait or live pinfish at night.

The Big Marco River and its channel run southwest below Turtle Island, under the CR92 Bridge and into Goodland Bay. From the community at Goodland, you have plenty of choices when it comes to backwater fishing. To the east, depending on your craft's draft, try the shore of Goodland Bay. Or run around Coon Key and Tripod Key and head up into the mouth of the Blackwater River. On your way, take some time to cast for snook along the edge of Tripod Key. Depending on the tide, you may have to come all the way out of Coon Key Pass into Gullivan Bay before you can head up into the Blackwater River by way of the Whitney Channel. The best entry is to the west of Brush Island at about N25 53.730 W81 37.754. While easing your way toward shore, start snook fishing from the private marker at Shell Key (N25 55.041 W81 36.768) to the end of the line of markers just inside the Blackwater River. This area is known to hold fish almost year-round.

Cape Romano Island and Cape Romano Shoals are separated from Marco Island by Caxambas Pass. This pass undergoes periods of shoaling, caused mostly by storms, and may not be navigable by larger boats; however, its easterly path leads into some deep water and some good fishing for redfish and snook

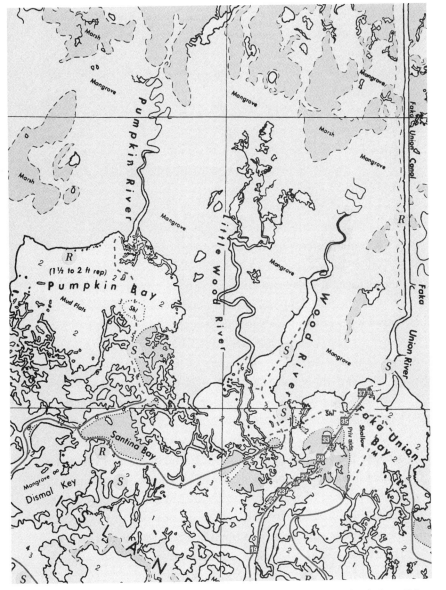

Take the Faka-Union Canal south from Port of the Islands and fish the islands from Faka-Union Bay to Pumpkin Bay. (Map courtesy of Waterproof Charts, Inc.)

The slow run out the Faka-Union Canal gives anglers time to plan their day.

along the mangrove shorelines of Fred Key and Helen Key, and the flat between them. Cape Romano Shoals has some of the few big grass flats in the area, to its east. Try drifting the "vee" of grass just to the east of Morgan Point (N25 50.722 W81 40.748) for reds, trout, and snook on a falling tide.

The Ten Thousand Islands area unofficially begins at Cape Romano. Here, the "shoreline" takes an easterly turn toward Everglades City and Chokoloskee. Until you actually see this place, it's hard to imagine its complexity. Vast areas of mangroves and tall grass extend well into the interior of the state, cut by small rivers and fringed by a series of bays, passes, and islands. Some of the bays are almost too shallow to navigate, and some of the passes seemingly go nowhere. But this is a place unlike any other. Known in the not-too-distant past as a hideout for outlaws and scalawags, it's now an angler's paradise.

Of the four named passes (Dismal Key, Fakahatchee, West, and Indian Key) below Cape Romano, only one is marked from the Gulf. That's Indian Key Pass, and it leads to Everglades City. One pass that's significant, but not named, runs from Gomez

Point on Panther Key (N25 50.751 W81 32.957) north to Faka Union Bay and into the Faka Union Canal.

The Faka Union Canal is about 4 miles long, beginning at US41 and Port of the Islands. Port of the Islands is an excellent jumping-off spot for a trip into the Ten Thousand Islands. It has lodging, food, a boat ramp, ship's store, dockage, and fuel, but the 4-mile idle-speed run to Faka Union Bay (or back) can be tedious, hot, and buggy. And don't get confused into thinking that Fakahatchee Pass will get you to the canal, as it simply dead-ends south of Fakahatchee Island to the east, where boat travel gets dicey, at best. If you're not sure about any of these passes, move between them outside the islands until you learn your way around. Waterproof Charts' #41F, Marco Island/Ten Thousand Islands Inshore, does show some good inshore and backwater routes, but seeing a plotted track on a map is very different from being in an actual location at sea level.

You can expect to find snook, redfish, and seatrout throughout the islands here. From the Faka Union Canal, you can easily reach Faka Union Bay, Pumpkin Bay, and Fakahatchee Bay. Concentrate your fishing efforts along the mangrove shorelines and near any snags or deep cuts between islands. As the area is essentially the drainage system for the Everglades, expect the water to be murky closer to shore, but to clear up as you approach the Gulf. Shallow waters don't allow reds, snook, and tarpon to go unseen, however, and there's some good sight fishing over shallow bars well into the bays. Seatrout will be found in calmer, deeper backwaters. On the Gulf front, island points near deeper water passes will hold redfish. Try the grass flats along the south shore of White Horse Key (approx. N25 51.424 W81 34.062) and those to the east of Panther Key (approx. N25 51.141 W81 32.555) for reds on falling tides. In early spring, look for tarpon to be holding inside Dismal Key Pass, in West Pass, and in the deeper cut between Gullivan and Turtle Keys (at about N25 52.711 W81 35.093.

Everglades City is located at the mouth of the Barron River, on Chokoloskee Bay. Its "suburb," Chokoloskee, is about 3 miles southwest, across a causeway and at the mouth of the mouth of the Turner River. From this point south, expect to be fishing within the confines of the Everglades National Park. Fishing from either of these places really doesn't involve much travel, but it does involve some directional skills. Of course, you can easily fish the islands alongside the Indian Key channel that leads to the Gulf, or the oyster bars on the southwest side of Chokoloskee Bay without getting too lost. But don't venture too far without a good mapping GPS unit and a chart or two. Waterproof Charts' #39F, Everglades City to Lostmans River, shows good detail as well as a few usable routes. The best advice I can give anyone fishing here for the first time is to hire a professional guide for a day or two before you take your own boat out. I was particularly impressed one day by local Captain Charles Wright as he guided his skiff home to Chokoloskee from the mouth of the Chatham River in a blinding thunderstorm. Just a little bit of local knowledge will go a long way when it comes to fishing unknown waters like these.

As in other places in the "islands," reds and snook can be found on points of Gulf-facing islands, especially those between Indian Key Pass and Chokoloskee Pass. Snook will also cruise shoals and any white sand beach they encounter. There's also some good tarpon fishing in the deep sloughs of Chokoloskee Pass. Trout are likely to hang around any place you can find a grass flat. There's a good flat to the east of Kingston Key (approx. N25 48.113 W81 26.835). Two others you should note are found to the northwest and southeast of Pavilion Key, east of the Huston and Chatham rivers.

Storter Bay is located at the confluence of the Huston and Chatham rivers. Both rivers are short, beginning in House Hammock and Huston bays. Some of the best snook fishing in the area is found up these rivers and in Storter Bay, but extreme caution must be taken to avoid shell bars that litter all these bodies of water.

A brief literary aside is in order here, as I discuss the Chatham River. If you've not read Peter Matthiessen's novel *Killing Mr. Watson*, now's the time—or take a copy on your next fishing trip to the Ten Thousand Islands. It's a great true account of early life in this area.

It's hard to imagine that the islands "thin out" along the shoreline from the mouth of the Chatham River to Lostmans River, but they do. In spite of that, the shoreline is still complex enough to attract snook, trout, and reds. Look for snook along the shore of the islands and along any part of the shallow mainland you can reach. As you get to the mouth of Lostmans River, pay special attention to the narrow entries on either side of the barrier island into First Bay and the deep river channel leading to Second Bay.

Finally, consider taking one of America's greatest fishing adventures, kayaking the Everglades. The Wilderness Waterway is 99 miles long and runs from Everglades City to Flamingo, on Florida Bay. The average time to finish the trip by kayak is 8 days, but it can be run (carefully) in a small boat in one day. There are campsites along the Wilderness Waterway as it meanders up the Lopez River, across a series of inland bays and down the Broad River. There are restrictions and rules for this trip, and complete information can be found online at www.nps.gov/ever/index.htm. Here, great fishing might delay your trip, so plan accordingly.

Offshore Fishing

Offshore fishing usually means you have the ability to get your boat into offshore waters. From Wiggins Pass, Doctors Pass, Gordon Pass, and Big Marco Pass, access isn't a problem. Caxambas Pass can be touchy, but to its south, consider inshore fishing to be your best bet.

There's lots of good blue-water fishing off the southwest Florida coast, but it's a long trip to reach the 100-foot-plus depths where you'll find billfish. It's also in those depths that you'll find the natural rock formations that attract reef fish, including all varieties of grouper and snapper, as well as pelagics like king mackerel, tuna, and wahoo.

A simpler option is to head out and fish the many artificial reefs and wrecks that lie closer to shore. Of course, closer means that they can be busy, but some of these reef areas are large and able to handle crowds. The species of fish you're likely to catch on these shallow reefs (usually in 50 feet of water or less) are grouper, mangrove snapper, cobia, and king mackerel. You'll also find that some of these areas attract species usually considered "inshore," like permit, Spanish mackerel, and sheepshead. You might even find what guides in the Marco area call "sea snook" at the shallower reefs.

From Wiggins Pass, try the reef at N26 18.612 W81 52.501 or the wreck site at N26 15.347 W81 56.172. If you feel like burning some fuel, head out 30 miles to the Edison Reefs, near N26 18.529 W82 13.332. This array of reefs is in 50 feet of water.

There are a number of old wrecks to the west of Gordon Pass. None seem to be stationary, but look for birds and baitfish schools. However, there is a good group of artificial reefs about 5 miles out, in 30 feet of water. Start trolling around the Evan Thompson Reef System (N26 20.280 W82 05.120), the bigger group, and then try the Jaycees Reef, just to the north at N26 20.080 W82 05.350.

To the south of Naples, there's a good close-in reef system at about N26 02.250 W81 49.855. These are the Keewaydin Boulders, a pile of rocks surrounded by some concrete construction rubble. Off Marco, try the Caxambas 1.5 Mile Reef. It's close in, at N25 54.166 W81 44.250, and is built up with old dredge pipe and construction rubble.

Getting Around

At Naples, Interstate 75 makes a hard easterly turn toward Miami. That leaves US41, the Tamiami Trail, as the main thoroughfare through Collier County. It also leads to Miami, but takes a more leisurely route. To reach the Wiggins Pass area you can take Immokalee Road west from US41 and then go north on Vanderbilt Drive. Doctors Pass is accessed by taking Mooringline Drive. Golden Gate Parkway is the best way to get into downtown Naples from the north if you're traveling on the Interstate.

Marco Island can be accessed from one of two highways that lead south from US41. Collier Boulevard (SR951) leads to the northern side of the island, and San Marco Road leads to the Goodland area.

Following US41 south will eventually take you past Port of the Islands and to Carnesville, where CR29 turns off toward Everglades City and Chokoloskee. From there, you're on your own!

Where to Stay

There's a broad range of lodging options in Collier County, but visitors should remember that lodging rates are often based on whether it's tourist season or not. At the southern end of the county, as you near remote Everglades City and Chokoloskee, the possibilities thin out, along with the population.

*   *   *

Lemon Tree Inn, (239) 262-1414, 250 9th St S, Naples. A small motel in downtown Naples. An excellent value. www.lemontreeinn.com

The Lemon Tree Inn in Naples is convenient to shopping, restaurants, and marinas.

Bayfront Inn, (239) 649-5800, 1221 5th Ave S, Naples. Downtown hotel with dockage.

Cove Inn, (239) 262-7161, 9th St, Naples. On Naples Bay, adjacent to the Naples City Dock. Efficiencies available.

The Boat House Motel, (239) 642-2400, 1180 Edington Pl, Marco Island. A 20-unit motel with dockage in "Olde Marco." www.theboathousemotel.com

GreenLinks Resort, (239) 732-9920, 7995 Mahogany Run Lane, Naples. Daily, weekly, and monthly villa rentals for those of you who have not yet made the choice between fishing and golfing. Conveniently located within easy reach of Marco Island, Port of the Islands, Isles of Capri, and downtown Naples. www.greenlinksnaples.com

Port of the Islands Everglades Adventure Resort, (239) 394-3101, between Naples and Everglades City, on the Faka Union Canal. Motel units with adjacent restaurant and marina. www.poiresort.com

Rod & Gun Lodge, (239) 695-2101, 200 Riverside Dr, Everglades City. A historic lodge and restaurant on the Barron River. Cottages available. www.evergladesrodandgun.com

Ivey House B&B, (239) 695-3299, 107 Camellia St, Everglades City. Several styles of rooms available. www.iveyhouse.com

Everglades City Motel, (239) 695-4224, 310 Collier Ave, Everglades City. Motel rooms and efficiencies with good boat trailer parking. Free cooler ice too! www.evergladescitymotel.com

Chokoloskee Island Park Marina, (239) 695-2414, 1150 Hamilton Lane, Chokoloskee. One-bedroom efficiencies and campsites. www.chokoloskee.com

Where to Eat

Don't worry about finding "good eats" in this neck of the woods. I've listed a range of eateries, from simple to fancy, and from sit-down to take-away. Some even have menus of more healthy-to-eat offerings. And if you need a fast food fix, I'm going to let you search for that on your own. Those places abound—at least until you get down into the Ten Thousand Islands.

*　*　*

Texas Tony's BBQ Shack, (239) 732-TEXAS, 4519 Tamiami Tr E, Naples. In my (humble) opinion, Florida has no BBQ tradition; however, Tony Phelan makes a great effort in that he smokes his delicious BBQ with citrus wood.

Randy's Fishmarket Restaurant, (239) 593-5555, 10395 Tamiami Tr (US41) N, Naples. Not on the water, but the seafood simply doesn't get better than at Randy's.

The Boat House Restaurant, (239) 643-2235, 990 Broad Ave S, Naples. Waterfront seafood on Naples Bay, adjacent to the Cove Inn.

Ric's Café Grill & Bakery, (239) 434-5999, 694 Tamiami Tr N, Naples. Breakfast, lunch, and great bagels.

Wynn's Market, 141 9th St N, Naples (next to Ace Hardware). An upscale grocery and fresh seafood market. Pick up some tasty take-away food today for your fishing trip tomorrow.

Capri Fish House Restaurant, (239) 389-5555, 203 Capri Blvd, Isles of Capri. Local seafood. Ask about their "all you can eat" fish specials.

Marco Island's Snook Inn is easily reached by water.

The Snook Inn Restaurant and Chickee Bar, (239) 394-3313, 1215 Bald Eagle Dr, Marco Island. "Come by boat; come by car; meet the dolphins at the Tiki Bar." The place to "see and be seen" in Marco. Dockage available.

Little Bar Restaurant, (239) 394-5663, 205 Harbor Place, Goodland. Great seafood and stone crabs (in season). See the website for their "Ends of the Earth Good Times Theory." www.littlebarrestaurant.com

Stan's Idle Hour Bar, (239) 394-4041, 221 W Goodland Dr, Goodland. Off the Marco River in Buzzards Bay. Home of the annual Goodland Mullet Festival.

Old Marco Lodge Crab House, (239) 642-7227, 401 Papaya St, Goodland. Crabs and other local seafoods. Dockage available. www.oldmarcolodge.com

The Camellia Street Grill, 202 Camellia St, Everglades City. Excellent seafood, but "if you're in a hurry, you're in the wrong place." Good stone crab bisque, too.

Rod & Gun Lodge, (239) 695-2101, 200 Riverside Dr, Everglades City. A historic lodge and restaurant on the Barron River. Dockage available. www.evergladesrodandgun.com

Joanie's Blue Crab Café, (239) 695-2682, 39395 Tamiami Tr E, Ochopee. Seafood and "swamp food," just south of the turnoff to Everglades City.

Marinas, Marine Supplies and Service, Bait and Tackle Shops, and Launching Ramps

Tall Tales Bait & Tackle, (239) 325-8284, 841 Vanderbilt Beach Rd, Naples. Tackle, repairs, frozen bait.

Sunshine Ace Hardware, (239) 262-2940, 141 Tamiami Tr N, Naples. One of the best selections of fishing gear in Naples.

Mangrove Outfitters Fly Shop, (239) 793-3370, 4111 Tamiami Tr E, Naples. Full service fly shop carrying top name-brand gear.

Naples Kayak Company, (239) 262-6149. Kayak rentals and tours. Locations at Isles of Capri (next to the Capri Fish House), Everglades City, and Naples Bayfront Inn. www.napleskayak-company.com

Naples City Dock on Crayton Cove, (239) 213-3070, 880 12th Ave S, Naples. Dockage and marina services near downtown Naples.

Naples Fishing Pier, on the Gulf at the end of 12th Ave S, Naples. This pier is within walking distance of downtown Naples.

Isles of Capri Marina, (230) 389-4626, 292 Capri Blvd, Isles of Capri. Full-service marina with good access to the waters near Marco Island and Rookery Bay. Dockage and kayak rentals available. www.islesofcaprimarina.com

Walker's Coon Key Marina, (230) 394-2797, 604 Palm Ave, Goodland. Wet and dry boat storage, dockage, repairs, fuel, bait, boat rentals.

Calusa Island Marina, (239) 394-3668, 385 Angler Dr, Goodland. Full-service marina with dockage, repairs, fuel. www.calusaislandmarina.com

Barefoot Willie's Pelican Pier Marina, (239) 389-2628, 1085 Bald Eagle Dr, Marco Island. On the Marco River, ¼ mile from Gulf of Mexico. Fuel, bait and tackle, ice, food.

Port of the Islands Marina, (239) 289-3143, between Naples and Everglades City, at the head of the Faka Union Canal. Full-service marina with dockage, food and lodging, fuel, boat ramp.

Glades Haven Marina, (239) 695-2579, 800 S Copeland Ave, Everglades City. Full-service marina, boat ramp, canoe and kayak rentals.

Win-Car Hardware, (239) 695-3201, 209 Collier Ave, Everglades City. A good source for fishing and marine supplies.

Chokoloskee Island Park Marina, (239) 695-2414, 1150 Hamilton Lane, Chokoloskee. Full-service marina with dockage, fuel,

ice, bait and tackle, boat ramp, lodging and camping. www.cho
koloskee.com

Cocohatchee River Park boat ramp, 13531 Vanderbilt Dr, Naples. 4-lane paved ramp. Concessionaire offers fuel, bait, and
tackle.

Delnor-Wiggins Pass State Park boat ramp, 11135 N Gulfshore
Dr N, Naples.

Naples Landing boat ramp, 9th St. S, Naples. 2-lane paved
ramp, limited parking.

Bayview Park boat ramp, 1500 Danford St, Naples. 2-lane
paved ramp, restrooms.

Collier Boulevard Boating Park, north of Marco Bridge. 2 paved
ramps, good parking.

Calusa Island Marina ramp, end of S Collier Blvd, Goodland.
2-lane paved ramp. Concessionaire offers fuel, bait, and tackle.

Caxambas Park, 900 S Collier Ct, Marco Island. 2-lane paved
ramp.

Faka Union Canal boat ramp, Port of the Islands Marina, between Naples and Everglades City.

Outdoor Resorts of America ramp, SR29, Chokoloskee.

Local Fishing Guides

Capt. Charles Wright, Chokoloskee, (239) 695-9107. Backwater and inshore fishing (kayak and boat). www.evergladesarea
tours.com

Capt. Mark Ward on the lookout for big Marco Island tarpon.

Capt. Mark Ward, (239) 450-9230. Orvis endorsed, Mark is one of the best fly-fishing guides in the Naples area. www. evergladesangler.com

Capt. Bill Baldus, (239) 272-8027. Bill specializes in fly-fishing from Naples to the Everglades. Based in Port of the Islands. www.flyfish10k.com

Capt. Bill Blanton, Chokoloskee, (239) 253-8899. Fly-fishing in Chokoloskee and the Everglades National Park. www.flyfish theglades.com.

Capt. Tom Shadley, (239) 793-3370. Naples-based fly-fishing guide and owner of Mangrove Outfitters.

Capt. Harry Julian, Naples, (239) 298-1116. Bay and offshore fishing. www.cruisenaplesflorida.com

Capt. Gene Luciano, Naples, (239) 450-4870. Offshore fishing.

Capt. Jack Lloyd, (407) 376-6803. Backwaters fishing in the Ten Thousand Islands.

Capt. Jesse Karen, (239) 298-2626. Inshore and offshore fishing, Naples to the Everglades. www.madsnookin.com

Capt. T. J. Reuther, (239) 450-4427. Backcountry fishing, Ten Thousand Islands and Everglades.

Capt. Stacey Mullendore, (239) 793-4442. Light tackle and fly-fishing. www.fishingfloridaeverglades.com

*   *   *

The website of the Florida Guides Association (www.florida-guides.com) has a complete listing of USCG licensed and insured fishing guides, some of whom are not listed here.

Before You Leave Home

Be sure to check this guide's companion website, www.saltwateranglersguide.com, for updates to local information.

Expect good kayak fishing in the backwaters of the Ten Thousand Islands.

PART 2

Practical Matters

10

It's All About the Fish . . .

Popular Inshore and Near Shore Fish Species

Inshore and near shore fishing along Florida's Gulf Coast has as much to do with economics as it does with species. Of course, many inshore anglers long to be aboard a big sport fishing boat trolling the depths of the Gulf for fish of mammoth proportions. The reality, however, of a round trip that has a fuel cost approaching that of the purchase price of a small outboard motor is staggering to many anglers. Inshore fishing, which includes small boat, bridge, bank, beach, and pier fishing, is much more accessible to the general public. So many game fish species come close enough to Florida's Gulf shoreline that most anglers need only expend a minimum effort in catching dinner on a low-impact, low-cost outing.

Flounder

An inshore angler friend once commented, "It's easier to catch a flounder than to clean one." That's a good assessment, as flounder are easily targeted and attack both live and artificial baits enthusiastically. Found all along the Gulf coastline of Florida, these flatfish lie along the edges of rock piles, shell bars, and channels and in sandy holes on grass flats waiting for passing prey. Small baitfish, shrimp, soft plastic jigs, and suspending plugs all catch flounder. If a tasty treat passes overhead, flounder will eat it. Not great fighters, flounder are renowned for

Flounder are best caught by anglers dragging soft baits slowly over potholes or under docks.

holding onto the end of a soft plastic lure only until the angler approaches with a landing net. They do, however, have the unfortunate habit of dropping immediately to the bottom after letting go of the bait and will usually strike a second time.

Flounder are plentiful and excellent table fare. Stuffed with shrimp or crabmeat or fried as filets or whole, their firm white flesh is hard to beat. And they're not really that hard to clean—just imagine a trout that's been run over by a pickup truck and you'll figure it out!

Pompano and Permit

If you can find white sand and clean moving water, you'll likely find pompano. And if you're fishing over an offshore reef or wreck, you'll likely find his larger cousin, the permit.

Pompano seem to enjoy feeding where there's water churning up the edges of white sand, uncovering small crabs and sand fleas. They also feed in passes and inlets, but it's rolling surf that brings more bait into the open. The attraction of pompano to the surf also makes them an attractive target for shore-bound anglers.

The trick to catching pompano is to get the bait to the bottom and to bounce it along very slowly. Small jigs like the ¼-ounce D.O.A. TerrorEyz in bright colors or stubby "pompano jigs" do well, but the best all-around bait seems to be live sand fleas rigged on simple jig heads. While sand fleas are available at some bait shops, most anglers prefer to catch their own, using a variety of rakes and strainer baskets. Live shrimp work well, but sand fleas are better.

Given their choice of fish to eat, many anglers put pompano at the top of their list. Fresh filets, broiled with olive oil and salt and pepper, are hard to beat.

Permit are game fish; they are rumored to taste like pompano, but anglers should take special care to release them after a trophy photo is taken. A few permit are found closer to shore, but they mostly roam around wrecks and reefs looking for wayward crabs and other crustaceans. If you hope to find permit, be sure to pack a heavy rod, fly or spin, and some live crabs or

Pompano are found along edges of bars and Gulf passes.

crab imitation flies. And remember, permit are not always as hungry as you think they should be.

Redfish

Red drum, puppy drum, channel bass, and redfish—they're all the same—it just depends on where you fish. In Florida, we call them redfish. They are prized by all inshore anglers, not only for their table appeal, but also for their great fighting ability. The redfish population was almost decimated by the culinary craze for blackened redfish in the 1990s, but it has rebounded since then. Many professional guides and conservation-minded anglers practice catch-and-release when fishing for reds in hopes of increasing fish stocks for future generations of anglers.

More finicky eaters than spotted seatrout, legal-size redfish cruise the shallow waters all along Florida's Gulf Coast, devouring everything from crustaceans to small baitfish. Their downward-facing mouths give the impression that they feed only on the bottom—on oyster bars, rock piles, and grassy flats. Crabs and shrimp are certainly part of their everyday diet, but make no mistake: small baitfish and commercial imitations attract quick and upward-oriented strikes. There's nothing like the sight and sound of a big red turning upside down in 2 feet of water to inhale a noisy topwater plug.

With the exception of wintertime fish found in deep channels or residential canals and big spawning fish found well offshore, reds, sometimes in schools, generally cruise the edges of flats, grassy shorelines, and shell bars in search of food. On lower tides, they can be found on sun-drenched shallow flats with their tails or backs out of the water, nudging dinner from grass patches or rocks. These fish are prime targets for sight-fishing anglers using light tackle or fishing with fly rods.

While many anglers insist that live bait is essential to catching large redfish, others believe that the smell of cut mullet or pinfish attracts them better. Smell seems to be important, but slashing lures do well too. Shrimp, stinky in its natural, live condition, is a statewide favorite. Before hooking a whole shrimp, tear off the tail and push the hook up through the body toward the head. This will enhance the scent and attract more fish. Plastic jigs, sometimes "sweetened" with a small piece of fresh or frozen shrimp or synthetic bait, bounced slowly across the bottom near shell or oyster bars, are also a sure way to catch reds. The use of a super-strong invisible leader, such as those made of fluorocarbon, is important, particularly in clear waters. Redfish have a second sense when it comes to recognizing solid fishing line and for rubbing leaders ragged on oysters, sharp rocks, or barnacle-encrusted pilings.

Redfish can be wary prey if found on the flats in very clear water. Any loud noises aboard a boat or from wading anglers can signal reds that predators are nearby. Many professional guides argue that undue rocking of a boat by casters, particularly fly anglers, pushes a wave of water out toward redfish, making them move away. Movement by boats, splashing wade anglers, or hungry dolphins—the reds don't know the difference.

No discussion of redfish is complete without mention of their close cousin, the black drum. Many an angler swears they've seen redfish tailing on top of a flat or oyster bar, only to have encountered big black drum. They are also seen in the backwaters and creek estuaries throughout the state. Black drum feed on crustaceans and are wary of biting artificial baits. Smaller, juvenile fish fight well, but not with the enthusiasm of the redfish. Big ones simply lumber off with the hook in their mouths and need to be tugged rather than played by the angler. Black drum have limited table appeal. Smaller ones are edible—if you're really hungry. Big ones, sometimes reaching 50 pounds, are wormy and tasteless, so catch them for sport—and release them.

Sharks

No matter where you fish in Florida, you'll encounter sharks. Whether they're considered inshore or offshore species gets some argument, but I think most are seen and caught in shallower waters. No matter where you find them, however, they're definitely fighters, and good sport on any tackle.

There are many species of shark found throughout the Gulf, but the ones you'll likely come across are hammerheads, bonnetheads, blacktips, spinners, bulls, and an occasional big tiger shark or nurse shark.

Big hammerhead sharks are notorious for eating trophy tarpon boatside, and are ferocious. Their smaller cousins, the bonnethead sharks, are mainly found roaming the shallows and will often bite cut bait or small jigs. Rarely growing larger than ten pounds, these fish are entertaining on light tackle.

Also found on the flats and in deeper channels are blacktip sharks, which will often attack live or cut bait fished by trout anglers. They also will attack topwater plugs or flies, provided the presentation is accurate. These sharks are lots of fun and are great jumpers. Many anglers confuse blacktips with spinner sharks. Both are aggressive and acrobatic, but the spinner shark is usually narrower across the body and has less distinct black-tipped fins than the blacktip.

Bull sharks are not to be messed with. They are aggressive and rumored (with some substantial facts) to be responsible for many attacks on swimmers and wading anglers. They stay close to shore and even move into freshwater rivers in search of prey. They will strike topwater lures and eat all sorts of cut or live bait. Bulls weighing 100+ pounds are good reason not to drag a stringer of fish behind you if you're wading. If you see a bull shark, and you're wade fishing, get out of the water.

Nurse sharks are sometimes found around wrecks and rocky outcroppings by offshore anglers, and until brought close enough to identify, they are often mistaken for goliath grouper. They are fun to catch, but tiring. The same goes for tiger sharks. Big, very big, and generally found in deep water, these are caught on big tackle, with big baits, and on hooks the size of gaffs.

Just as there's an argument about whether sharks should be considered sport fish, so there's an argument about their edibility. Many veteran anglers, including the late Dick Bowles and my friend Vic Dunaway, consider shark flesh highly edible. Most shark eaters do admit that the flesh smells of uric acid (urine) unless the fish is bled, gutted, and iced immediately. That's more than I want to know. Besides, sharks have been overfished for their fins by commercial anglers, and it wouldn't hurt to practice catch-and-release to ensure their survival.

Sheepshead

Sheepshead, found all along Florida's Gulf Coast, are notorious bait stealers. During most of the year, these small-mouthed fish inhabit coastal oyster and rock bars, docks and rock jetties searching for their favorite prey: crustaceans, including small crabs, shrimp, and even barnacles. It's these smaller fish that are very difficult to catch, as their ability to crush bait, swallow the meat, and spit out the exoskeleton (with your hook) is unrivaled. Small hooks and small baits, such as fiddler crabs and cut shrimp pieces, are the key to catching sheepshead close to shore. Patience helps, too. Learning to feel the signature bite of a sheepshead takes time, and you'll likely miss a few before you get into the rhythm. And, while the size limit on sheepshead currently 12 inches, a fish that size yields very little meat upon cleaning.

It's the bigger spawning sheepshead, usually found during the late winter or spring, that excite Gulf anglers. These fish, found mostly in deeper water and around structures such as rock piles, reefs, and old navigation markers, sometime reach weights of 10 pounds or more. When their spawning ritual begins, mature sheepshead will mill around structure and seemingly eat any bait presented them. Chumming with crushed crabs, oysters, barnacles, or shrimp heads will increase the feeding frenzy. But don't over-chum. They're hungry, but they do get full. Spawning fish are mature, larger fish and their mouths are bigger. Most anglers rely on whole live shrimp as bait. To catch them, a simple knocker rig and a sturdy size 2 hook is sufficient, but many anglers simply thread a shrimp, tail first, onto a ⅜-ounce jig head. The advent of braided fishing line has certainly hurt the sheepshead population in the last few years, allowing anglers a better feel for what's going on down below. Many sheepshead experts agree that you have to set the hook on a sheepshead before it bites, or you'll miss the hookup.

Sheepshead are delicious to eat but as difficult to clean as they are to catch. Because they are big boned and heavily scaled, the meat-to-total-weight ratio of sheepshead is low, and many anglers opt to clean them with electric knives. And, no matter how good the meat, cleaning the unrealistic legal limit is a chore. Take what you can eat that night and *not* the 15-fish limit, remembering that big spawning sheepshead represent the future of that species.

Snook

Snook populations were hurt by the severe freezes during the winter of 2010, but not to the extent feared by many. It's likely the upper range of the species, northward from Pasco County, will see fewer snook for a few years; however, many of the fish were able to survive in deep rivers and residential canals, ensuring survival of one of Florida's most popular sport fish.

Snook can be found along channel edges, close to shore on beaches, under brushy mangrove roots, and around docks and snags. They are comfortable in fresh, brackish, or salt waters,

Snook are always a prized catch in Tampa Bay and southwest Florida waters.

and they eat almost any bait, including fish, crab, shrimp, and artificial look-alikes.

Snook are unparalleled fighters and jumpers. Pound for pound, they rival tarpon for action—and they're edible. Pay particular attention to Florida's bizarre closed-season schedule for snook, and don't forget to buy a snook permit for your fishing license. There's nothing worse than not being able to keep a legal snook for dinner just because you didn't spend an extra two dollars for the yearly permit!

Proper snook gear can range from light to heavy spinning rods and reels, depending on where you're fishing. If you're in open water, I suggest 10-pound class lines, but advise beefing up to 30-pound gear if you're around snags, docks, or bridges. The first thing a big snook will do is head for whatever cover is available, and you'll need to stop that run. Fly anglers should stick to 9- or 10-weight gear, unless you're fishing for smaller fish under mangrove branches. Good artificial bait choices for snook are usually light-colored or white. D.O.A. shrimp or

TerrorEyz jigs in natural or "glow" colors are effective, as are light-colored MirrOlures and Heddon Super Spooks. As for flies, big white Clouser minnows or Norm Zeigler's Schminnows are effective on snook in most situations.

Spanish Mackerel and Bluefish

Either you can target Spanish mackerel and bluefish—or they can target you. During the warmer months, finding these species is as easy as finding seagulls wheeling over bait schools in bays, off beaches, or in passes. That's seagulls—not pelicans. Gulls tend to eat scraps left behind by predators attacking baitfish, while pelicans tend to dive into schools of small fish and swallow them whole. If you see pelicans diving into bait, there may or may not be predatory fish there.

When you do find gulls scavenging near bait schools, look for fish striking the surface and get ready. Preparing for toothy Spanish mackerel and blues almost always means getting rigged with light wire leader. A 40-pound fluorocarbon might work, but toothy Spanish and blues can rough it up pretty quickly. Keeping a few store-bought Liquid Steel leaders in the bottom of your tackle box is not a bad idea. You can also make your own leaders with 12–14 inches of fine wire tied to a dark-colored swivel and a snap, using haywire twists. Many anglers enjoy tossing lures, including topwater plugs, to schools of striking mackerel or blues, but most prefer trolling the edges of a striking school of fish. Popular trolling baits for these fish are the #00 Clarkspoon or a ½-ounce Flowering Floreo jig with its fiber tail trimmed back to the end of the hook shank. The fluorescent orange Floreo jig is particularly effective, and it will work even better if you put a narrow 2-inch strip of belly meat cut from the first fish you catch on it. Strips of mullet belly meat work well too, and can be cut, heavily salted, and frozen in advance of a fishing trip for Spanish mackerel or bluefish.

Spanish mackerel and bluefish can also appear out of no-where, in water as shallow as a foot. Many a jig or topwater plug simply disappears, and it's usually the result of one of these fish foraging the edges of inshore rock piles or sandbars. However, if you're lucky, the fish will grab your bait and not your line and you'll have a bonus for that day's fishing.

Spanish mackerel and bluefish are both good to eat, but nei-ther freeze well. Blues should be eaten the same day they're caught, and Spanish mackerel will refrigerate for a day or two. Both are oily and smoke well on home smokers. You'll catch larger versions of both species in the fall, after they've had a chance to eat and fatten up all summer, but the smaller spring-time fish are good eating too.

Spotted Seatrout

Spotted seatrout are the mainstay of inshore fishing on Flor-ida's Gulf Coast. Relatively easy to catch, plentiful, and mild tasting, these fish are found in shallow coastal waters from spring until fall. On colder winter days, they can be found in river and creek channels, and in residential canals, where they seek warmth in the deeper water.

Most spotted seatrout caught are within the regulatory slot. "Gator" or trophy trout more than 20 inches long are most often caught in shallow, close-to-shore waters and don't school up like the smaller fish. Catches of spotted seatrout in the 7-pound range have become more common since Florida's gill-net ban went into force in the 1990s. Many experts reason that smaller trout are prey for larger ones. Checking the stom-ach contents of big trout at the cleaning table will sometimes reveal smaller versions of the same species there. In fact, a fa-vorite wintertime deep-water trout lure is the MirrOlure TT Series—TT stands for *tiny trout*.

Trout are voracious eaters, and bigger cold-water fish some-times eat out of sheer instinct even when they're probably not hungry. The species can resist few types of bait. Natural forage includes pinfish, pigfish, shrimp, crab, mullet, and all varieties of minnows, generically known as white bait. Based on this fish's eating habits, there are hundreds, probably thousands, of lures manufactured to attract spotted seatrout. Weighted jig heads with soft plastic tails, synthetic shrimp look-alikes, hard and soft-bodied plugs made to swim at various depths, and a variety of topwater lures crowd the shelves at marinas, tackle stores, and bait shops all along the coast. Most lures and techniques work on trout, and I suggest finding a few you like and learning to fish them in different situations. Your tackle box will thank you.

Depending on air and water temperature, sunlight or clouds, and time of year, trout will hold at specific depths. Moving water, whether rising or falling, is best. Slack or slow-moving neap tides, usually occurring between the full and the new moon phases, make trout less eager to eat. Ambush-feeders, they prefer to attack baits that wash past them in sandy holes on grass flats, or along the edges of channels or bars.

Wintertime trout in deeper water are the exception. I think many of them bite because they're simply bothered by baits hitting them in the head and attack out of sheer frustration at the attempts to hook them by the dozens of anglers above.

In general, big trout are spookier than smaller ones. Stealth becomes more important the shallower and clearer the water. No slamming of cooler lids or loud high-fiving necessary!

Many anglers assume that tactics for seatrout are the same in cold as well as warm weather. Warmer months find trout moving from the shallows during the day to cooler deeper waters. If you plan to target trout early on a warm spring, summer, or fall day, start early and fish close to shore. As the day warms, you'll notice schools of mullet and white bait moving out toward deeper water. Many trout will move with them. Big summertime high tides hold trout closer to shore in the mornings. Conversely, trout don't get too close to shore on a low tide, no matter the air or water temperature; however, sometimes rather than moving offshore, they move inside creeks or backwater holes and wait for the rising tide, becoming easy targets for anglers able to reach them with shallow-draft boats, canoes, or kayaks.

As local water temperatures reach the 70-degree mark in springtime, seatrout become generally predictable. The warm water attracts a greater number of baitfish and shrimp, and the trout move onto grass flats or areas of live bottom to chase them. To find the trout, simply make an inshore-to-offshore (or a shallower-to-deeper) drift, fishing your favorite trout bait. When the fish start biting, note the depth, toss out a marker buoy, or hit the Man Overboard button on your GPS. Typically, trout will hold at a certain depth, based on water temperature, allowing you several drifts over the area before the depth changes with the tide.

Silver, or sand, trout are also found in Gulf waters and are close relatives of spotted seatrout. These smaller fish tend to school up in sandy or shelly sloughs or holes. They are easy to catch with small jigs and very good to eat, although each fish yields very small filets. They're also great fun for kids and less-active anglers.

Tarpon

Tarpon deserve whole books. That said, I'd state that their feistiness is unparalleled and that catching one on almost any tackle is a feat worth bragging about. These "silver kings" are found all along Florida's Gulf Coast. Some run through deep passes like Boca Grande and Longboat, and then travel outside the beaches and barrier islands as part of a big springtime

Tarpon fishing can be an exercise in boatmanship as well as in angling expertise.

migration. Others simply sit out winter weather in deep rivers, canals, and backwaters and become permanent residents. And mostly they eat when they want to and not necessarily when you want them to.

And when tarpon eat, they will strike all sizes and types of lures with a passion—or they will simply pick up a live crab, white bait, pinfish, squirrelfish (sand perch), or even a chunk of cut mullet or mullet head. Like our national bird, the American bald eagle, the Silver King eats just about anything, dead or alive!

Tarpon come in all sizes and provide great angling action on all sizes of tackle. Anglers and tournament fishers who are bound and determined to land a tarpon and have a photo taken still rely on big boat rods and 4/0 to 5/0 reels. Others, in a more sporting frame of mind, tend toward smaller tackle, including fly gear. Of course there are arguments that getting a big tarpon boatside quickly doesn't tire the fish, making it a target for predators like hammerhead and bull sharks (by the way, it's not legal to "boat" a tarpon unless you have a tarpon "kill stamp" in your possession). On the other hand, many light-tackle enthusiasts enjoy the hunt, take time to make the perfect cast to tarpon, and are satisfied with just a jump or two from these magnificent fish. Tarpon are a good endorsement for CPR: *Catch, Photograph, and Release*. And if you want a trophy tarpon mount for your wall, excellent fiberglass reproductions can be made using your photo as reference.

Tripletail

Always, always, always look around floating debris, crab-trap floats, and channel markers for tripletail. These goofy-looking fish are found floating or drifting near the surface and eat a variety of baits, including live shrimp, jigs, and plugs like the MirrOlure 52M. They inhabit the entire range of Gulf shoreline. If you find one, spend the time needed to entice him to bite, and hang on. They're notorious for wrapping lines around structure, and you want to be prepared to pull the fish toward your boat. Sometimes tedious to clean, tripletail are some of the best eating fish you'll take from the Gulf.

Popular Offshore Fish Species

What exactly is offshore fishing? Personally, I consider it fishing in any water that's more than knee-deep. Many others, though, think it's silly to have a perfectly fine outboard motor aboard a boat and elect to push it along the shallows with a big stick. The National Weather Service delineates inshore- from offshore-weather forecasts at 20 nautical miles off the coastline, but I consider that unrealistic.

Depth might be a better descriptor, with any depth that regularly holds offshore species, such as grouper, considered offshore. Rules are made to be broken (by fish, of course), and plenty of keeper grouper are caught in bay channels and big king mackerel move onto shallow waters at times. So, you define offshore for yourself and I'll go with species as my guide.

Amberjack

AJs can be good and AJs can be bad. First, the bad news. If you try fishing a wreck or big rock pile anywhere in the Gulf, you're likely to find amberjack hovering somewhere between you and the grouper or snapper you're targeting—and they're always hungry. Getting live bait past them is usually an exercise in futility. Many anglers sacrifice a few baits on one side of the boat in order to let their buddies get baits to the bottom fish on the other.

The good news is that AJs are fun to catch and pound-for-pound offer a mighty struggle. They hit hard and fight up until the bitter end. They also taste pretty good, at least the smaller ones. As they grow older and larger, they tend to have more worms than in their youth, but many anglers overlook this distribution of harmless-to-humans parasites in their flesh, claiming, "They cook up just fine." Many claim that amberjack is the best fish for smoking and for dips.

While amberjack are hard fighters, a soft approach will make the task easier for anglers. Don't jerk them around; pull them up slowly and steadily, and they'll come right to the landing net or gaff.

Barracuda

Barracuda are found all along Florida's Gulf Coast. Large specimens hover over and around wrecks and reefs, seeking an easy meal, which could be the fish you're pulling into your boat.

Great fighters and suckers for bright flashy lures, big 'cudas are great fun on light tackle rigged with steel leaders, but care should be taken to release them as carefully as possible. They are not really fit to eat, as they may carry the ciguatera toxin, a poison you don't want to experience.

Cobia

Are cobia an inshore or an offshore species? I certainly don't know, as I've seen huge ones taken within sight of shore and also off of wrecks in 100 feet of water.

Structure interests cobia, as does the shade and shelter provided by big rays. Many inshore anglers make it a habit to carry a big spinning outfit rigged with an eel-like jig during the summer months, and most never miss the opportunity to check out big channel markers or passing rays for cobia. Deep offshore reefs, springs, and rock piles also interest cobia, as they're good spots to ambush passing bait, including crabs, small fish, eels (a cobia favorite), and shrimp.

Cobia can bite enthusiastically or not at all. Many anglers complain when cobia swim around their boat, nibble at chum bags, and eye the crew—but don't bite. That's just the way cobia are.

It's hard to prepare for a cobia bite, but most anglers use large spinning rods with enough backbone to pull the fish away from structure. Cobia know their neighborhoods and will wrap a line around a marker in seconds. Reels in the 30-pound class and braided lines help with the fight. If you're lucky enough to find cobia in open water or along Gulf beaches, lighter tackle is fun and practical. Ultra-clear fluorocarbon leaders help too, as cobia will back away from visible line or leader, although corks or balloons floated above free-lined pinfish or crabs don't seem to spook them. Finally, don't put a green cobia in your boat. These fish are very strong, and although you take a chance of losing one the longer you fight him, they will break cooler tops, rods, and even human limbs if brought into the cockpit of a boat too soon. Gaffing a big cobia can be dangerous too, if he's not tired and not ready to give up the fight.

Cobia are popular game fish for their sport and for their food value. Their firm clean flesh cuts nicely into steaks for the grill, and they are very good smoked. And big cobia taste as good as smaller ones, an unusual quality found in few fishes.

Dolphin

The fish, not Flipper, are also known as dorado or mahi-mahi, and are found throughout the Gulf. Offshore, they hide under weed lines or around structure, and smaller fish will travel in large schools. Great fighters, mahi can be caught on all sorts of lures and baits, live or artificial, trolled or pitched. In deep water, especially, keep a hooked-up mahi in the water and grab another rod. Mahi are schoolies and will hang around their buddies instead of disappearing on you.

Birds wheeling over the surface of the water can help you spot schools of dolphin, so try chumming to keep them nearby. Once chummed close to the boat, smaller peanut-sized fish are lots of fun on fly rods or light spinning gear. Whatever size mahi you catch at one spot is the size you can expect to catch, as these fish travel together in schools the same age and size.

The flesh of the mahi is some of the best around, and it takes well to grilling or smoking.

The Groupers

GAG GROUPER

Found Gulfwide, gags are probably the most sought-after offshore species. Delicious table fare and usually easy to catch, they are targeted by anglers at varying depths along the coast. Fish as large as 40 pounds are caught well offshore, but the bulk of gags taken are just above the legal size minimum. Frankly, these smaller fish are better eating and provide great action without having to invest in oversize tackle.

Gag grouper tend to prefer structure, including rock outcroppings, offshore springs, and artificial reefs. Juveniles, known as grass grouper, inhabit inshore flats, channels, and creeks. While they're not legal to keep, small grouper can provide fun on light tackle and surprise many an angler looking for inshore species. Remember that special care should be taken to safely release juvenile fish of all species. Avoid using gaffs or landing nets on small fish. Mechanical fish grippers and de-hookers ensure safe releases, as do circle hooks. Learn to vent the air bladders of all groupers that are suffering from decompression due to a quick trip to the surface at the end of a fishing line. Your local tackle supplier will demonstrate the use of a venting tool, an item now required on all boats fishing for reef fish. Rocky outcroppings and wrecks don't necessarily appear just in deep water. With the onset of cold weather, larger gags move closer to shore, particularly around shallow rocks north of the Anclote River, and many are taken with live bait or diving plugs in as little as 8 feet of water.

Gags are omnivorous but moody. Many successful grouper diggers begin fishing a spot with frozen baits, such as squid, Spanish sardines, or threadfin herring, and move on to live baits only when the action picks up. Pinfish, pigfish, large shrimp, menhaden, or cigar minnows are tried-and-true live baits for grouper. Large jigs and deep-jigging techniques work well over rocky live bottom, attracting strikes primarily as the lure falls toward the bottom from an upward stroke of a long rod. Imitation shrimp and mullet baits are also deadly and, like jigs, don't smell up the boat or require constant attention and baiting. While bottom fishing has its advantages in that several anglers can fish at one time, anchoring safely and accurately in rough seas can be difficult. Many grouper anglers prefer to troll large lures all day; others use them only to prospect for new fishing spots. Large diving plugs with treble hooks trolled at 4–5 knots and fished deep on modern braided line are a fun way to catch lots of nice gags, but fuel consumption can be a consideration. These big lures are sold in many size and depth configurations and can be trolled directly or used with downriggers or planers. Simply put, gags love to eat, a statement bolstered by the stories of stomachs inspected at the cleaning table containing leftover chicken bones tossed overboard by picnicking anglers.

Tides affect a gag's willingness to eat, with action falling off as the flow slackens. Even the slightest tidal change will affect not only the bite, but also the location of gags. Slow movement will hold the fish close to structure, while strong tides draw them away from cover to nearby sandy areas where they prey on bait washed toward them. Be sure to take tidal strength and direction into consideration when bottom-fishing structure, whether it be artificial reef balls, wrecks, ledges, or lone rock piles. At the time of the full moon—or just after—you will probably notice a decrease in the grouper bite. The big boys fill up with visibility of a full moon—especially in cooler weather.

RED GROUPER

Red grouper are probably served in more restaurants than any other fish from the Gulf. They roam the underwater plains and prairies in the central Gulf. Deep, live coral and grass bottom are their preferred habitat. Highly detailed structure is not necessary for the average red grouper. Notorious eating machines, undersize specimens will beat gags to anglers' baits and empty a live well or bucket of cut bait quickly. Reds also eagerly attack large plugs trolled over grassy knobby bottom. Solid advice from experienced grouper anglers is to move to another spot should nothing but short red grouper start coming to the surface.

OTHER GROUPERS

While gag grouper and red grouper make up the bulk of grouper caught by anglers along the Gulf Coast, they are not the only species in the habitat.

The most-noticed "other" grouper is certainly the goliath grouper, formerly known as Jewfish. These mammoths, some upward of 500 pounds, have fooled many anglers into thinking they've hooked Mother Earth. Adults of the species are found all over the Gulf—inside wrecks, under offshore ledges, and around artificial reef structures. Smaller juvenile fish are caught along the mangrove shorelines in southwest Florida. It is illegal to take or possess a goliath grouper, and that includes hoisting one into the boat for photos should you find yourself fortunate enough to get him to the surface. I mention the species as they seem to have become more numerous and pesky since becoming a protected species in 1990. The sight of a 15-pound gag grouper being swallowed whole at your boat's gunwales is a startling experience for any angler. Don't even try sharing a rock pile or wreck with a bunch of goliaths—just move along to another spot.

Other important, but less available, Gulf groupers are the snowy grouper, speckled hind grouper, Warsaw grouper, and the tasty scamp. Pesky at times, black sea bass can entertain

Speckled hind is a rare deepwater grouper.

frustrated anglers or kids. They're small and ferocious, and their delicate white meat is excellent. The same bottom that holds black sea bass also holds grouper, but, if you're pulling in a lot of sea bass, there probably aren't any grouper around. That means you're in a good area, but on the wrong spot. It's time to move the boat.

The Mackerels

KING MACKEREL

King mackerel, or kingfish, are found all along Florida's Gulf Coast, making an annual migration northward in spring, summering in the deep water off the panhandle, and returning south in the fall. While most of these aggressive speedsters school up, it's often the larger versions that come closer to shore in search of food. Fifty-pound fish are not unusual, and their ability to empty a reel of 400 yards or so of line and burn up a drag is legendary—hence their nickname: smokers.

Tactics for kings vary. Slow-trolling large feathers, spoons, dusters, hooded ballyhoo, or live bait is a preferred method for schoolies during the big spring and fall runs. Blue runners are a favorite bait throughout the Gulf. During the summer, anglers working the bottom for grouper and snapper will sometimes put out a free-lined live bait rigged with a stinger rig made up with a pair of 4X-strong treble hooks. The sight of a 40- or 50-pound king skyrocketing with your bait in his mouth is always exciting, but remember to keep your reel's drag set lightly and its spool filled. Stinger rig-hooked fish are mostly lightly hooked, many times snagged, and they require lots of finesse and patience to land.

There are a number of opinions about eating kingfish. Many feel only smaller ones should be eaten, and those cooked quickly after the catch—never frozen. Others enjoy the fish when smoked. Some medical experts claim the oily flesh valuable for its vitamins; others claim it a health issue due to high levels of mercury, usually in larger specimens.

Wahoo are deep-water cousins of the kingfish and members of the mackerel family. They usually are found well offshore and are generally caught while trolling at high speeds. They sometimes will attack a bait on the surface and skyrocket, like a king, but usually strike deep. Their clean, white meat makes excellent table fare.

Sailfish, Marlin, and Swordfish

Sailfish, swordfish, and blue and white marlin are collectively known as billfish, and they are game of choice for blue water anglers.

Sailfish are usually found all over the Gulf, and during the warmer months some will roam into shallow coastal waters. This species is a small billfish, rarely exceeding 100 pounds, but is a ferocious fighter and can be taken on lighter trolling tackle, including spinning gear.

White marlin are great jumpers and fighters, found in the depths of the Gulf. Like sailfish, they sometimes come inside the Continental Shelf toward shore. One-hundred-pounders are considered sizeable, and, like sails, they readily attack slow-trolled live baits or rigged ballyhoo and squid.

I don't know any angler who would object to catching a 500-pound blue marlin and having a replica mount on his family room wall. These are the fish that dreams are made of, and the opportunity to catch one is a once-in-a-lifetime experience. These deep-dwellers are found throughout the Gulf and are the targeted species of many charter-boat captains and crews. Some captains are so serious, in fact, that they subscribe to online services that predict water temperature and current flow based on real-time satellite information. Blue marlin are fond of weed lines and temperature thermoclines, as both hold baitfish. It takes big tackle and big bait to catch big blue marlin. Live bonito or whole rigged mullet or mackerel is a good bait to troll, as are artificial lures, and 80-pound-class tackle is usually considered appropriate for the fight of a lifetime.

Big and powerful, swordfish are finally making a comeback in the very deep Gulf waters. Usually caught at extreme depths off the Continental Shelf at night using squid or illuminated lures, few are taken in waters as shallow as 300 feet. Big tackle, big boats, and an experienced crew are all essential in the quest for this species.

In general, billfish have good food value, but stocks are dwindling. Special care should be taken to safely release these fish into their habitat.

The Snappers

AMERICAN RED SNAPPER

American red snapper are prime targets for Gulf anglers. Usually found in depths exceeding 60 feet, red snapper are tasty and relatively easy to catch. Because they have been fished hard commercially and recreationally and nearly destroyed by shrimp trawls, strict seasonal limits exist.

Red snapper gather over structure, and their preference seems to be ledges over which they can gather to snag passing baits. A depth finder showing an inverted Christmas-tree shape over a ledge is usually showing a school of red snapper.

More finicky about their food than grouper, red snapper prefer live baits such as pinfish, cigar minnows, and pogies (menhaden) if available. Frozen sardines and shrimp work well, but it's the live baits these fish love.

Fishing at night for red snapper in depths well below 100 feet is common practice in the Gulf. Consider extending an

Red snapper are plentiful in depths greater than 80 feet.

offshore day trip and do some night fishing for snapper. Try using underwater lights to attract various baits to the side of the boat. You'll be able to catch small live baits using a Sabiki rig and will soon replenish your live well.

GRAY OR MANGROVE SNAPPER

"Mangos" are another favorite of Gulf reef anglers—and of folks lucky enough to find legal juveniles in inshore waters. Offshore, they usually inhabit the same structure as American red snapper but are bigger and, like red snapper, provide lots of action at night. Live bait, such as cigar minnows, is the key to catching these fish, which often reach 6 or 8 pounds. Inshore, they can be found in deep river holes or in cuts through bars and are lots of fun to catch on very light tackle. All sizes of this species are excellent at the table.

A large deepwater mangrove snapper caught off Tampa Bay in the Florida Middle Grounds.

OTHER SNAPPERS

While fishing for red or mangrove snappers, you'll likely hook either Lane snappers or vermillion snappers (also called bee-liners), both of which inhabit the same waters in the Gulf. Both are smallish, and their meat is fragile, needing quick icing aboard the boat. Hogfish, or hog snapper, are also found on very deep reefs and are usually taken with shrimp rather than with baitfish. In fact, many hogfish taken seem to come up at the end of a diver's spear gun, as they're sometimes hard to entice with hook and line. Finally, I would be remiss not to include "Florida snappers" or "Cedar Key snappers," both the same fish.

There's no doubt that reef fish populations—and snapper numbers in particular—have dwindled over the years, so imagine trying to make your living as an offshore fishing captain, unable to keep fish caught during a closed season, yet having to satisfy the appetites of paying anglers. Creative marketing by guides, chambers of commerce, and marinas is the process, and the renaming of fish generally called "grunts" is the outcome. Easy to catch, generally plentiful, excellent to eat and sometimes growing to a pound or more, white grunts or Key West grunts just have unappetizing names. They range throughout the Gulf and are usually found over structure like live bottom, rocks, or wrecks.

Triggerfish

If you've ever read the menu in a fine restaurant and seen turbot listed and wondered what it was, the answer is probably triggerfish. Common in three versions (gray, queen, and ocean) throughout the Gulf, these flattish, small-mouth bait stealers are some of the best eating you'll find.

Usually not taken in great quantities on hook and line, most are byproducts of searches for grouper or snapper.

Triggerfish are extremely difficult to clean, even in comparison to sheepshead or flounder, so most anglers are happy to have only one or two of these fish to clean at the end of the day.

Tuna

Yellowfin and blackfin tuna roam the depths of the Gulf and are usually targeted from ports on Florida's panhandle, as deeper water is closer. Tuna fishing is big-boat work and good reason to hire a professional boat and crew. This is long, exhausting fishing and local knowledge is invaluable. In the northern Gulf, popular methods are trolling multiple offshore lures and/or rigged baits. Anglers from central and southwest Florida often have a tuna trip on their "bucket list."

Both yellowfin and blackfin tuna are excellent to eat—seared, grilled, or even raw. Their dark red flesh, sometimes shaved off a still-flopping specimen and splashed with tamari-style soy sauce, is a popular offshore raw lunch.

"Junk" Fish

What constitutes a junk fish? Is there such a thing?

If you're hungry enough you'll eat almost any species. Many consider mullet a baitfish, but others would rather eat mullet than grouper. Mediterranean fish markets display elaborate arrays of sardines, scad, and herring that we regularly use for bait. And, during the 1930s and the Great Depression, fried fish patties made of tarpon flesh were the highlight of many a Sunday dinner in certain areas of Florida.

Jacks, including blue runners, jack crevalle, and horse-eyes, are the great sport fish of the junk-fish category. That said, never miss an opportunity to tackle any of these fish with light tackle and flashy lures. Pound for pound, they're the best fighters you'll find and have saved the day for many fishing guides. Even little blue runners that many consider only bait for king mackerel put up a valiant struggle. The food value of these fish is suspect, and although I try to eat a smoked jack crevalle every couple of years, the news gets no better.

Bonito (Atlantic bonito, false albacore, and little tunny) are also great sport fish and always worth the effort to catch, although finicky feeders. You'll likely see schools of them offshore bashing baits and waiting for you to toss a small spoon or jig into their midst. Despite being cousins to the delicious tunas, bonito suffer the same fate as jacks when it comes to their table value: they're basically cat food.

While jacks make drag-screaming runs, ladyfish are the great jumpers. Considered by many to be "poor man's tarpon," these sleek and voracious fish rarely make it to the boat, as they're experts at head shaking and lure tossing. Many are caught by accident by inshore flats anglers, but you'll just as likely find them mixed into fast-traveling schools of Spanish mackerel, jack crevalle, and bluefish. They are terrific targets for fly rodders and will eat almost any fly tossed to them and worked rapidly. They are bony, their flesh is mushy, and they're really not fit for human consumption. They do, however, make wonderful tarpon and redfish bait.

On the subject of good tarpon bait, it's not surprising that the saltwater catfish—hardhead and gafftopsail—are a favorite of anglers fishing cut bait. The flesh is soft and smelly, and live catfish don't move all that quickly. Tarpon and cobia have no problem with the cats' sharp spines and bones. They're used to eating crabs and crushing them quickly in their jaws and consider these fish prime targets. Catfish are mostly pests, but they can provide lots of entertainment for kids on a flats fishing trip. Care should be taken in handling them, as their spines are sharp and carry a potentially infectious bacterial slime.

The list of junk fish goes on and on, as do the arguments about their sport or table value. Some are simply not fit to eat. Pufferfish are considered poisonous, and alligator gar just taste bad. But croakers, silver perch (butterfish), sand perch (squirrelfish), and the entire porgy clan all come to mind when thinking about fish with nice white meat and the willingness to fight on a hook and line. Given the right situation, any of these species can be fun to catch and will occupy easily distracted kids or adults. And, if you're hungry for fish, there's no such thing as junk fish.

Bay Scallops and Scalloping

Scallops don't really qualify as fish, but bay scalloping is the Big Bend and eastern Emerald Coast's alternative to South Florida's lobster season. It's a combination of complete madness at boat ramps and marinas, motels filled to capacity, family fun, and some of the best eating around. Unfortunately, the range of legal scalloping reaches into only one county (Hernando) covered by this book. There's a complete "scallop lesson" outlined on this book's companion website, www.saltwater anglersguide.com. A scalloping trip is an adventure everyone should put on his or her schedule—at least once!

11

~~~~~~~~

. . . And How to Catch Them

Inshore Gear and Tackle

The waters close to shore from the mouth of the Chassahowitzka River south to the northern edge of the Everglades are
an inshore angler's dream. Miles of lush, grassy flats stretch
from well north of Bayport to the mouth of the Anclote River
in northern Pinellas County, where a series of barrier islands
that protect the coastline and provide excellent backwater fishing begins. If those places don't provide you enough opportunities, consider that two of Florida's largest inlets, Tampa
Bay and Charlotte Harbor, are themselves each worthy of a
lifetime of inshore fishing. And finally, when the beaches end
at Caxambas Pass, south of glamorous Marco Island, the ap-
propriately named Ten Thousand Islands area begins—and
civilization ends.

While offshore fishing is big-boat fishing, boats are not
necessarily a requirement for the successful inshore angler.
Inshore options include wading, beach, dock, and pier fishing. There are boat options as well, including bay boats, flats
skiffs, aluminum or fiberglass johnboats, kayaks, and canoes.
No matter your budget, you have the ability to fish the Gulf
shoreline.

One of the biggest mistakes I see on inshore waters is the
use of fishing tackle that outguns an angler's prey. Yes, the occasional big jack crevalle, black drum, bull red, or tarpon may
surprise an angler, but that's an exception. Most inshore fish

~~~~~~

can be easily taken with high-quality, light to medium-class spinning, casting, or fly tackle. I think some tackle retailers recommend line, leader, and terminal tackle based on cost, not appropriateness for a particular fishing situation. Think about it. Not many fish are going to get near a shrimp pinned to the bottom by a 60-pound wire leader, two swivels, a 6/0 hook, and three ounces of lead sinker. Fish will attack a bait that swims naturally past their noses, but they're not interested in eating hardware. Heavy terminal tackle is necessary in some situations, but the lighter you can rig your tackle, the better your chance of hooking up inshore species. Inshore fishing *is* light-tackle fishing.

Your stock of good inshore tackle should include rods and reels—spinning, fly, or casting—that are comfortable to cast. Unlike offshore anglers, inshore anglers must make many more long and accurate casts on every outing. If you're throwing topwater plugs for seatrout on the flats and expect to cast as many as 500 times a day, you might consider spinning tackle rather than a baitcasting outfit. On the other hand, if you're trolling for Spanish mackerel over a reef or along a beachfront, baitcasters with quality drags are perfect. They're also good for creek fishing where short casts to banks and shorelines are needed. Fly rods should always be the lightest you can afford, as a fly rod's ability to cut through the air helps make longer, more accurate presentations to wary fish. For your first inshore spinning rod, you might consider a 6½- to 7-foot medium action graphite rod paired with a medium-light saltwater reel. If you're planning to wade- or surf-fish only, you might consider something longer, perhaps an 8-footer. A good casting rod choice would be something in the 6-foot range paired with a small saltwater reel, while 7- to 9-weight fly rods are favored by most inshore fly anglers.

Inshore Tackle Recommendations

REELS

Shimano Spheros 3000, 4000, and 6000 and Stradic 2500, 4000, and 5000 spinning reels. Shimano makes dependable light spinning reels that work well with monofilament as well as braided line. Both these reels are designed for heavy use in salt water and require little care after a day on the water. The Spheros 6000 and Stradic 5000 are adequate for tarpon, sharks, and the bigger inshore species.

Sharkfin 2000 and 4000 spinning reels. These quality German-engineered reels feature finned spools that reduce line friction when casting and eliminate tangles and loops caused during retrieves. They are designed specifically for braided lines.

Shimano Calcutta 200 and 400 baitcasting reels. These are high-quality reels with heavy-duty drag systems. The Calcutta 200 works well with 10-pound-test braided line and is lightweight enough to comfortably cast all day.

RODS

Shimano and St. Croix casting and spinning rods. These rod makers offer a complete line of inshore casting and spinning rods to suit any budget. They are available at many full-service tackle shops.

Fly Fishing Tackle

G. LOOMIS AND SAGE FLY RODS; ROSS AND TIBOR FLY
REELS; SCIENTIFIC ANGLERS AND CORTLAND FLY LINES
AND BACKING

Quality fly tackle is very expensive, but it's worth every penny
when one is casting all day or fighting a big fish. Sage, Loomis, Ross, and Tibor are simply the best when it comes to rods
and reels. Scientific Anglers and Cortland make complete selections of tropical-style lines appropriate for most Gulf fly
fishing. None are cheap. As depths can vary along any stretch
of the Florida coast, many fly anglers carry both floating and
sinking lines, usually spooled on separate reels or replacement
reel spools. I recommend anglers carry at least 8-weight fly
gear for inshore species and, if you anticipate hooking a tarpon, keep a 12-weight outfit close at hand.

Fly-fishing some-
times involves hours
of waiting, followed
by just a few minutes
of sheer panic!

Line, Leader, and Terminal Tackle

Daiichi hooks. If you're fishing live bait or replacing hooks on lures, Daiichi's super-sharp hooks are a good choice. Many inshore anglers replace the front hooks on lures with red Daiichi Bleeding Bait treble hooks to simulate the red gills of excited baitfish.

Trik Fish or Seaguar fluorocarbon leader material. Use 20-pound for trout and small inshore species and 25-pound for redfishing near oyster bars and sharp rocks. Start with 30-pound leaders for snook in passes or along beaches, but consider 40-pound if you're fishing near snags or mangroves; 80-pound is good for tarpon, and consider 40- to 50-pound test for toothy Spanish mackerel and bluefish.

PowerPro Super Braid Spectra fiber line. PowerPro typically breaks at about twice its rated strength and has a much smaller diameter than comparable strength monofilament lines. The 10-pound-test line is popular for most light-tackle applications, but 30-pound should be considered for tarpon, snook, and nearshore cobia. Also, don't overlook the informative knot diagrams and line-winding devices included with spools of PowerPro.

Popping Corks. In the spring, as the water temperatures rise in the Gulf, brightly colored Cajun Thunder popping corks rigged over live bait or jigs are popular. D.O.A. Lures also offers pre-rigged "Deadly Combo" cork-and-shrimp rigs. Easy to fish, especially for novice or young anglers, they provide lots of entertainment value as well as good catches. Expect to use lots of live shrimp if you put them below corks, as pinfish steal their fair share. However, anglers claim that by attracting pinfish to the shrimp, they attract trout to the pinfish, and the trout are caught in an attempt to steal back the shrimp. Other options to use beneath popping corks include D.O.A.'s plastic shrimp and synthetic baits such as Gulp! or FishBites. Experienced guides all along the coast also count on trapped pinfish or pigfish as trout bait. Many big warm-water trout are caught with these small fish rigged under popping corks.

To effectively use a popping cork, you must *pop* or splash the cork with your rod tip occasionally, making the trout think other fish are striking bait.

Lures

D.O.A. TerrorEyz Jigs. One of the best all-round baits, the TerrorEyz is available in many colors and several sizes. The 1/4-ounce version is most popular with inshore anglers. Use light colors, such as "chartreuse/silver glitter" (#318), in clear water and along beaches. Use dark colors, such as "root beer/ gold glitter" (#304), in muddy or stained water. Bounced slowly off the bottom near oyster and rock bars, these lures with upward-oriented hooks will produce good redfish and flounder action—and beachfront snook love the lighter colors. They also work well in deeper water when slowly dragged in a swimming motion. Their soft bodies are relatively tough but sometimes too fragile for toothy Spanish mackerel and bluefish, which attack them readily. The larger 3/8- and 1/2-ounce TerrorEyz are irresistible to tarpon.

D.O.A. Shrimp. This was the original true-to-life plastic shrimp, and it is still the best. The combination of its shape and balanced weight gives it a natural shrimp look when pulled steadily and slowly over grass tops for inshore fish. Any species that eats shrimp will eat this lure. Use light colors, such as "nite glow/fire tail" (#329) in clear water, and dark colors such as "avocado/red glitter" (#371) in dark or stained water.

Mark Nichols, D.O.A.'s chief cook and bottle washer, also developed a new method of making his shrimp easier to cast and to fish over rough bottom. After pulling out the factory hook, Mark trims off the tail fins and inserts a #3.5/0 wide gap hook (made exclusively for D.O.A.) through the tail, rigging it weedless by laying the barb along the shrimp's back. He then inserts a large glass rattle into the hole made by the original hook. This method makes the whole lure much more aerodynamic and actually more appealing in the water, like a live shrimp rigged for bonefish. The rattles and 3.5/0 hooks are available at larger tackle shops and direct from www.doalures.com.

D.O.A. Bait Buster. The Bait Buster is another lure built on an upward-oriented jig hook. Its design is very "mullet-like," with a single, very strong hook. Available in shallow running, deep-running, and trolling versions, the version with the white body and green back (#372) will catch just about any inshore species. Swim the deep runner along jetties and docks and the shallow runner on any flat where finger mullet hang out.

D.O.A. Big Fish Lures. These are probably the most lifelike soft baits on the market. They're big, at 5½ and 8 inches long, but when the big trout are hungry, they'll do the job.

Paul Brown Original Corky Mullet and Corky Devils. The Paul Brown Corkys are the lures that catch record trout all along the Gulf coast. These soft, slow, suspending or floating mullet imitations are among the best cold-water lures for trout in shallow water. The "pearl chartreuse" (#01) and "chartreuse" (#06) are both proven colors. Previously available only from Mr. Brown in Texas, these lures are now manufactured and distributed by MirrOlure.

L&S MirrOlures. Every serious angler fishing the northern Gulf should own at least one tackle box devoted solely to MirrOlures (and now, Corkys!). Period. End of statement.

This line of readily available hard baits has evolved for the last seventy years into what many anglers consider their go-to lures for all species. They are so successful that it's hard to recommend just a few of their offerings. If you're new to fishing or new to MirrOlures, try these: The 52M sinking twitchbait is the standard. The #18 color (greenback) is probably the all-time favorite of flats anglers. The spotted STTR Series III holographic lure in red is used by thousands of wintertime trout anglers. It can be trolled in creeks or fished slowly in deep river holes. The 17MR MirrOdine and the 19MR MirrOminnow are relatively new to the MirrOlure line and have become very popular in the Tampa Bay area. Fished slowly, these small slow-suspending lures are good for all species. Green or black backs are good colors with which to start. Although small in size, many are eaten by large tarpon on the flats. Finally, don't overlook the Pups and Dogs. There are Top Dogs, She Dogs, Top Pups, She Pups, and Popa Dogs in a variety of sizes and colors. Each has a specific rattle or action, and all are worth having. Many times fish will short-strike a Top Dog yet hook up on either a smaller She Dog or a Top Pup. Good basic colors include bone, hot pink, greenback, and black with a yellow head (for early mornings or after the sun goes down).

Heddon Super Spook Jr. Considered by many anglers their standard topwater lure, the Heddon Super Spook Jr. is highly effective on most inshore species. Anything that eats a wounded mullet will eat one of these. This noisy plug, walked in very shallow water, will attract trout and reds from great distances, especially in very low light. Super Spook Jr. lures come in freshwater as well as saltwater versions. The freshwater model works just fine in the salt but should be examined after catching a few big fish. Replacing the hooks may be necessary, and if so, replace them with 4X-strong #4 saltwater treble hooks, using a red Bleeding Bait Daiichi hook on the body and a more typical black hook on the tail. The science here is that the red hook emulates gill flash and attracts more strikes.

Other popular Super Spook Jr. colors are the red head, nickel bone, and chartreuse with a silver insert.

Rapala Skitterwalk. Rapala's Skitterwalk topwater lures come in two versions, both highly effective on any fish willing to hit a noisy bait on the surface. While the larger saltwater model, the SSW-11, is very effective, the freshwater model, SW-8, has been adopted by many anglers as their go-to lure for shallow-water Gulf fishing. Hook replacement is usually necessary after catching a few big fish with the smaller Skitterwalk. Both sizes are available in hot pink, silver mullet, and bone. All these colors and patterns work well on saltwater fish.

Spoons

Dragging weedless spoons slowly over oyster bars and rock piles is a successful method of fishing for redfish all along the Gulf coast. Other versions of spoons are used to fish for pelagic species such as Spanish mackerel, bluefish, and even close-to-shore king mackerel.

Johnson's Silver Minnow (which now comes in many other colors than silver) and Eppinger Rex Spoons (gold with red or yellow feathers) are good choices for inshore use. Both are weedless and can easily be used by kids and beginners, as it's simply a matter of casting them and making a slow, bottom-hugging retrieve.

The standard spoon for close-to-shore pelagics (mackerel and bluefish) is the silver Clarkspoon, available in sizes up to #7/0 (4.5 inches). It's the #00 (2 inches) that's the real inshore killer. Rigged with a short wire leader and trolled or cast near fish striking bait schools on the flats, this diamond-shaped spoon is highly effective. If you prefer casting, you might consider rigging your Clarkspoon to a weighted Clark Caster spinner head.

*   *   *

Flowering Floreos. In the 1960s, before soft-plastic tails became popular, the Flowering Floreo was the lure of choice on the flats for trout, reds, and many other species. A simple lead-head jig with a nylon skirt, the lure has taken a back seat to soft plastics in recent years, but it still holds its own when it comes to trolling for mackerel and bluefish or jigging for pompano.

The brightly colored ½-ounce version with the fluorescent orange head and yellow skirt is a popular model. Trimming the skirt back with scissors—an easy chore while the lure is still in the package—is an effective way to prevent short strikes while trolling. Leaving the skirt intact works fine when bouncing the jig along beaches or bars for pompano. Many anglers prefer to "sweeten" the hooks on Floreos, using strips of baitfish belly or FishBites when trolling, or shrimp pieces when pompano fishing.

Soft-plastics. There's no doubt that the use and development of soft-plastic baits changed the dynamic of inshore fishing. Inexpensive, easy to use, and highly adaptable to most terrains and depths, soft-plastics are probably the most popular inshore artificial bait.

Every angler seems to have their favorite soft-plastic bait and a favorite way of rigging it. Soft-plastics are available in a multitude of shapes and colors, many specific to certain manufacturers. Popular versions are shad tails, split tail, and shrimp look-alikes. Most manufacturers offer hooks and jig heads, sometimes paired with their plastic tails and "guaranteed" to catch fish. Popular soft-plastics are made by D.O.A. (www.doalures.com), Culprit/Riptide (www.culprit.com), and Bass Assassin (www.bassassassin.com). A look online will give you a good idea of each product line, its colors, and its configurations.

Rigging soft-plastics can range from simple to extreme. Anglers fishing the deeper flats, sloughs, and holes seem to prefer using ¼-ounce or ⅜-ounce lead-head jig hooks. Those fishing in extreme shallow situations prefer to rig weedless using wide-gap hooks. Some fish with soft-plastics on jig heads exclusively under popping corks, and others take their chances with snags, and there are a multitude of options in between. Exotic but successful tools for fishing soft-plastics crowd the shelves at tackle shops. Woodies Rattlers Rattl'n Hooks have rattle chambers attached, D.O.A. makes pinch weights that attach to hook shanks, and Daiichi offers ButtDragger hooks with the weights already attached.

Recently, the soft-plastics market has grown to include synthetic flavors and smells. While D.O.A. products have some flavor enhancement, they still rely on natural shape and action to attract fish. FishBites products were originally developed as simple sheets or strips and used to sweeten soft-plastic rigs by many anglers. This is still a highly effective pheromone-based product, and more lifelike versions are now in the FishBites product line. Berkley's introduction of its GULP! baits marked a departure: shape, style, and smell all became important, although a truly realistic product was clearly not a goal. Bass Assassin also makes Blurp! baits, most mirroring its popular line of shapes and colors, but with a smell ingredient included. All these smell-enhanced baits have the advantage of drawing predators from afar. They are more expensive than their less-smelly counterparts, but usually a bargain when compared to the cost of live shrimp or pinfish.

And a Couple Things Every Inshore Angler Should Have

If you're serious about your inshore fishing, I'd like to recommend a couple of essential items for your kit.

*   *   *

The Boga Grip (www.bogagrip.com) is an excellent fish-gripping tool that ensures quick release of small fish, or big ones you intend to unhook, photograph, and release. They are available in 15-, 30-, and 60-pound versions and are amazingly durable. My fifteen-year-old Boga Grip is rarely rinsed off and shows *no* signs of rust or deterioration. I do recommend attaching a large float to the lanyard, just in case you drop it overboard. In the same vein, and cheaper, is the Shakespeare/ Xtools Release Dehooker.

The Wade Aid Wading Belt (www.wadeaid.com) is a valuable asset. It holds two extra rods behind you, has a pouch for extra tackle, a D-ring for a fish gripper, and a stringer. It also offers good back support and limited (but not U.S. Coast Guard approved) flotation.

Finally, if you own an inshore powerboat and anchor frequently in shallow water, save your allowance for a **Power-Pole shallow water anchor** (www.powerpole.com). Power-Poles come in 6 and 8-foot versions and can be operated remotely from anywhere on your boat, allowing you to stop your drift immediately. This device, expensive as it is, can and will change your approach to shallow-water angling.

Offshore Gear and Tackle

Targeting offshore species in the Gulf (and even in deep spots within Tampa Bay and Charlotte Harbor) requires different equipment from that usually found at your local discount big-box store. Offshore fish are big chunks of muscle, and your tackle should match the strength of a powerful fish doing its very best to get back home, into a rocky crack, under a ledge, or just as far away from the boat as possible. Even after coming up many feet from the bottom to attack a trolled lure, grouper instinctively speed back toward their hideouts. King mackerel, billfish, cobia, and barracuda are speedsters and easily strip hundreds of yards of line from a reel just seconds after the initial strike. The snapper clan bites lightly, so it's necessary to feel them on the line, but they can also dash quickly to cover. Specific species are best caught with specific tackle.

Bottom-fishing rods and reels need not be too sophisticated if you're targeting grouper or large snapper. Stout rods in 5- to 6-foot lengths and reels capable of handling 50- to 80-pound-test lines are just fine for bottom fishing. Longer more-flexible rods paired with reels sporting sophisticated quick-to-set drags work best for trolling deep-diving plugs for grouper. Reels for table-size snapper can be lighter, while those for kings, billfish, and cobia can be small too. They need drag systems capable not only of stopping long powerful runs but also of withstanding ferocious initial strikes. A few small custom-rod makers are touting rods with spiral-guide rigging as an easier way to control fish, but depending on how deep your pockets are, less-expensive rods work just fine. Given the choice, put the bulk of your fishing budget toward a good reel. Also, spooling reels with modern braided line such as PowerPro will gain you an advantage in terms of feeling the fish bite. Unlike monofilament lines that stretch, braid has no stretch and telegraphs activity from below very well.

Many anglers who troll for king mackerel and big pelagics still prefer monofilament line, as its stretch softens hard strikes and its large diameter helps slow big fish making long runs. Braided lines are expensive, but it's not necessary to completely fill the spool of your bottom-fishing reel if you decide to use a braided line. Bottom-dwelling fish such as grouper and snapper don't make long runs or take out lots of line, so 100 yards on a reel is adequate. Spooling 400–500 yards each of PowerPro on a boatload of kingfish reels can get very expensive. To compare fishing styles, understand that seasoned deep-water grouper and snapper anglers jam the star drags on their bottom-fishing reels by hitting them with a hammer, while trollers for trophy king mackerel usually fine-tune their drags, eliminating the slip caused by the drag on the lure or bait and line in the water, and adding a little extra resistance to accommodate the run and action of a hooked "smoker."

Terminal tackle for fish on the bottom must be tough as well. Eighty- to 100-pound-test leader material, either monofilament or less-visible fluorocarbon, and big hooks are the rule for grouper. Forty- to 50-pound-test is fine for snapper, and light wire works well for trolling leaders.

Anglers argue about which hook is better for bottom fishing: circle hooks or traditional J-style hooks? Either will do, but conservation-minded anglers find that fewer undersize fish are gut-hooked with circle hooks. In fact, circle hooks are now required when fishing for reef fish in the Gulf. Learning *not* to jerk a circle hook from a fish's mouth is difficult for some anglers, but killing fewer nonlegal fish is worth the effort. A simple pull against a tugging fish is adequate to set a circle hook. Size 11/0 circle hooks are a good choice for grouper, while 4/0 hooks work for snapper. Look at the hook's gap from point to shank and assure yourself that the distance between them is sufficient to span the lips of your quarry. While sizes for J hooks are uniform among many manufacturers, sizes for circle hooks vary considerably. Use the right size for your targeted species regardless of its number. Trollers use a wide variety of hooks for live baits, but on stinger rigs, 4X strength, size 4 or 6 trebles are popular throughout the Gulf.

Terminal tackle recommendations for fishing live or cut bait are numerous. Two rigs stand out for bottom fishing: the slip-sinker rig and the dropper rig. I prefer the slip-sinker rig for live baits and the dropper rig for cut bait. The dropper rig holds chunks of bait slightly above the bottom while the slip-sinker allows live bait to swim more freely. Depth determines the weight of your sinker, but bank sinkers work best on dropper rigs, and egg sinkers are appropriate as slip-sinkers. For slow-trolling live baits, learn to make and fish a stinger rig—it's a simple, effective way to present baits to big fish.

Another method of hooking up nice grouper and snapper is

bouncing jigs off the bottom. It's a bit more work, but sometimes the action of a quickly rising and falling, brightly colored lure triggers a strike when even live bait doesn't work. Four- to 8-ounce bucktails are often used to reach extreme depths in the Gulf, and vertical deep jigging with heavy and flashy metal jigs has recently become popular. The fluttering action of the jigs seems irresistible to bottom-dwellers.

I learned to troll large plugs using planers and hand lines. Times have changed—deep-diving plugs, thinner-yet-stronger lines, and sophisticated color depth sounders have made a huge difference in both the ease and success of trolling for bottom fish. First, you don't have to guess where to find the live or rocky bottom. Not only can you see a clear image of the bottom while trolling, but also, with some training, you can actually distinguish the air bladders of fish from the structure. Bait pods even make distinctive images on modern sounders. Strikes can be predicted in many instances.

Second, after determining the depth of the fish or bait, anglers are able to pick and choose big lures designed for specific depths. Early plugs generally ran deep, but with little information from the makers as to "how deep." Finally, high-tensile-strength braided line is very thin and has little resistance in the water. Pulling 30-pound-test braid for 20-pound-class grouper will easily get a 30-foot-class lure to 55 or 60 feet with only 200 feet of line out at 5 knots of speed. Trolling live bait or smaller, shallow-running plugs for pelagics requires less speed, as slow as 1 or 2 knots. Many anglers use downriggers or spool their reels with fishing wire to fish even deeper, and others use outriggers to fish a spread of lures near the surface. In the last 20 years, modern electronic equipment, line, and lures have changed the style of offshore fishing for many anglers.

Casting live bait or medium-size plugs to rocks in water as shallow as 8 feet has become a popular pastime in recent years, especially near Bayport and Hernando Beach. Using chum to pull the fish away from their hiding spots and setting baits into the chum line are good methods of catching grouper without getting too far offshore. It's also a great way to pit your skills (and your rod) against some brutish fish. You'll need to use tackle you can cast. Big spinning outfits, spooled with 30-pound-test braid, work well here.

Offshore Tackle Recommendations

If you plan to bottom-fish, cast to, or troll for offshore species, you'll likely be confused by the selection of tackle and references available from catalogs and retail outlets. It's simpler than it seems, and what follows is a list of my recommendations.

Reels

Penn Special Senator 113H (4/0), 114H (6/0) reef reels. Penn makes these solid, hard-working, and reasonably priced reels mostly for bottom fishing.

Shimano TLD20 trolling reels (medium duty), Shimano Tekota 600 and 700 trolling reels. These reels are heavy duty like the big Penns but feature level-wind mechanisms and superior drag systems.

Shimano Trinidad trolling reels. These finely built high-end reels are manufactured to take on almost any big and fast offshore fish. Consider the TN40 and TN50 if you plan to head off to deep blue water in search of tuna, big kings, wahoo, dolphin (mahi, dorado), sailfish, or marlin.

Shimano Spheros 8000FB, 12000FB, or Baitrunner BTR 4000D, BTR6000D spinning reels. These are not everyday discount-store spinning reels, but big saltwater tackle able to withstand a wide range of offshore species, except a few bottom fish like gags and huge snapper.

Rods

Penn Slammer conventional and heavy spinning rods; Shakespeare Ugly Stik Big Water spinning and boat rods. Penn and Shakespeare each make a complete line of heavy rods, suited for all types of offshore fishing.

SpiralStiX custom spiral guide boat and trolling rods. Spiral guides on these handmade rods keep rod torque to a minimum during big fights. See www.billystix.com for complete details.

Shimano Tallus rods. Available in trolling and stand-up versions, these big-water rods cover the entire range of offshore needs. They are well built with quality components and expensive, but worth the price if a trophy fish is on the other end of the line. See www.shimano.com for more details.

Line, Leader, and Terminal Tackle

PowerPro braided Spectra fiber line. PowerPro typically breaks at about twice its rated strength and has a much smaller diameter than comparable pound-test monofilament lines. It's available in multiple strengths suited to all offshore applications. Don't overlook the informative knot diagrams included with spools of PowerPro.

Trik Fish or Seaguar fluorocarbon leader. Use 80- to 100-pound-test for grouper, 40-pound for snapper. This virtually invisible leader has excellent knot-holding strength. In addition to the basic fluorocarbon, Trik Fish makes Chum Line, a scented leader, and Red Line, a disappearing leader for blue waters.

Daiichi hooks. Use super-sharp Daiichi 10/0 to 13/0 circle hooks for grouper and 5/0 for snapper, cobia, and smaller amberjack. Make your king-mackerel stinger rigs using light fishing wire and 4X strong Daiichi Bleeding Bait treble hooks.

Mustad needle-eye J-hooks. Use 5/0 to 8/0 for stinger rigs or trolling feathers. With their forged eyes, they are made specifically for wire leaders.

Lures

Mann's Stretch trolling baits. Designed for fishing at different depths, these lures are very popular for grouper all along the Gulf coast. While the Stretch 30+ seems to be the standard, the Imitator series has proven well on king mackerel, as has the smaller Stretch 25+. Every serious offshore angler who trolls should have at least one bucket of Stretch lures aboard. Different colors and versions attract fish differently, so many anglers change lures frequently until the action starts. Different speeds change these lures' action—another means of attracting more strikes while trolling.

L&S MirrOlures. The 111MR and 113MR MirrOlures are castable lures suited for fishing shallow rocks for grouper or for casting to barracuda and amberjack over wrecks. MirrOlures such as the Top Dog and Popa Dog are also very good for any striking fish found offshore and are easy to cast with lighter tackle.

D.O.A. Lures. D.O.A.'s Swimming Mullet and larger TerrorEyz jigs are very realistic baits that are excellent for jigging over rocks or near shallow rocky channel edges for grouper. Their large plastic shrimp have proven good for grouper over shallow rocks, and for cobia and tripletail near markers or structure.

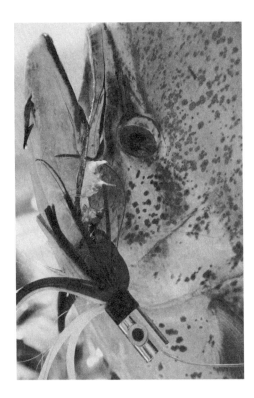

Big offshore lures and feathers catch big offshore fish.

Offshore trolling lures. If you think inshore anglers can't decide exactly which lure to fish, just take a look inside the tackle locker on an offshore boat. Deep-water trolling can involve live bait, lures, or a combination of both. Some offshore trollers pull arrays of teasers along with live bait, and others use rigged ballyhoo in combination with big noisy feathers. Bright-color feathers, some noisy and some bubbling, are often used solo, rigged through the nose with size 7/0 or 8/0 hooks and 100-pound-test monofilament leaders. There are versions for dolphin, wahoo, tuna, kings, and billfish. They are available in all colors and sizes from a number of manufacturers, including C&H (www.candhlures.com), Boone (www.boonebait.com), Williamson (www.williamsonlures.com), and Iland (www.ilandlures.com)

Just Plain Ol' Bucktail Jigs and Silver Spoons. Probably the most versatile lures any offshore angler can keep aboard his boat are heavy bucktail jigs and silver spoons. Either can be tossed at a passing cobia or school of marauding pelagics. Spoons can be trolled at various speeds and depths, using planers or downriggers. Big heavy jigs will attract grouper and snapper in 100-foot depths when even live bait won't work. And they're cheap. You can afford to keep several sizes of silver Clarkspoons aboard, rigged with a short wire leader. Even a bucketful of 6-ounce bucktails doesn't cost a whole lot more than a fancy deep-diving plug or two.

Fishing Knots

> "If you can't tie a knot, just tie a lot."

Not good advice if you're an angler. Good knots are at the core of every successful fishing trip. No matter your tackle or bait, if you can't connect the two, you're in trouble.

Good fishing knots need to be strong. Some of that strength comes from the materials involved—line, leader, or both—but following directions is important too. Recipes for knots, like those for baked bread, need to be followed to the letter. Good line material, whether monofilament or braided polyethylene fiber, is only as good as the knots used to attach it to other line or to terminal tackle. Don't skimp by purchasing the cheap stuff, and remember that most monofilament and fluorocarbon lines weaken with age and direct exposure to sunlight. It's a good habit to change these lines at least yearly and more often if you fish frequently. Braided lines cost more but hold up longer.

Knot strength is measured as a percentage of the actual breaking strength of the line or leader; 100% is excellent, but few knots approach that strength.

Many successful anglers recommend the use of a loop in the tag end of the running line when attaching leader materials.

Few anglers, except trollers, use swivels or other devices, such as snaps or swivels, in the makeup of their leaders. There is little argument that the Bimini twist is the perfect loop to make when building a rig. And although it's a matter of honor and many anglers claim to be able to tie a Bimini twist in a few seconds, I think it's hard to do in a crowded, pitching boat. For that reason, I prefer the simple surgeon's loop, an ugly but strong loop that works just fine in most conditions and with most tackle. I do use the Bimini twist for tarpon and other big-game applications, but many times I tie up several rigs in the comfort of my family room. In the same vein, the Albright knot is beautiful, but a double surgeon's knot does a pretty effective (but usually ugly!) job of attaching leaders to running lines.

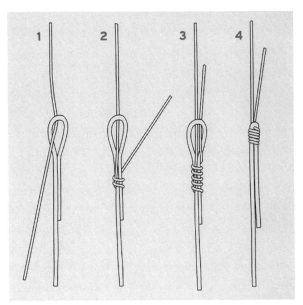

Albright Knot. Attach the backing to the fly line with an Albright knot. (1) Double up the last 2 inches of the fly line and pass the tag end of the backing through the loop. (2) Wind the backing over itself and the fly line at least five times. (3) Pass the backing through the loop as shown. (4) Tighten slowly; trim the ends closely.

All knot illustrations reproduced with the permission of Pure Fishing/Berkley.

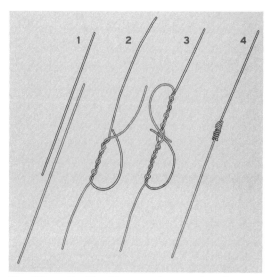

Blood Knot. The blood knot works great for splicing two lines of similar diameter. (1) Cross the two sections of line to be joined, and then wrap one tag end around the standing part of the other live five to seven times, depending on the line diameter. (2) Pass the tag end back between the two lines. (3) Wrap the other tag end in the same manner, and bring it back through the same opening. (4) Pull the stranding lines to tighten knot; trim.

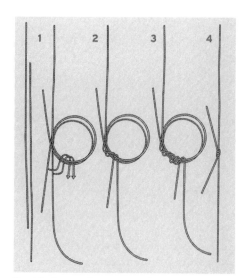

Double Surgeon's Knot. The double surgeon's knot is used for attaching tippet to leader. (1) Place the tippet next to the leader, then (2) form an overhand knot. (3) Form a double overhand knot by passing the same ends through the loop a second time. (4) Tighten by pulling all four ends slowly; trim the tags.

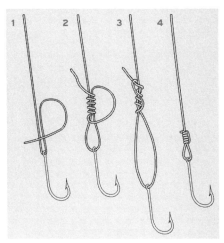

Duncan Loop. The Duncan loop allows a hook or crankbait to swing freely on a loop for maximum wobble. (1) Slide your line through the hook eye, and form a loop in the tag end as shown. (2) Pass the tag end through the loop, winding around the standing line and top section of the loop four or five times while moving away from the hook. (3) Moisten the line and pull the tag end to tighten the knot. (4) Slide the knot to the desired position by pulling on the standing line, and trim the tag end.

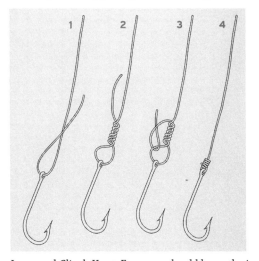

Improved Clinch Knot. Everyone should learn the improved clinch knot for attaching leaders and lines to hooks and swivels. The knot is easy to tie and retains nearly all of the line's original strength. (1) Pass the end of the line through the eye of hook or swivel. (2) Pull about 6 inches of the line through and double it back against itself. Twist the line five to seven times. (3) Pass the end of the line through the small loop formed just above the eye, then through the big loop just created. Be careful that the coils don't overlap. (4) Pull the tag end and main line so that the coiled line tightens against the eye. Again, be sure the coils haven't overlapped. Trim the excess.

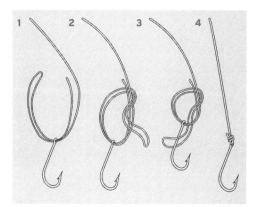

Palomar Knot. The palomar knot is easy and fast to tie, and handy for attaching hooks, swivels, and other terminal tackle to your fishing line. It is especially popular with anglers using braided fishing lines. (1) Double about 6 inches of line and pass it through the eye of the hook. (2) Tie a simple overhand knot in the doubled line, letting the hook hang loose. Avoid twisting the lines. (3) Pull the end of the loop down, passing it completely over the hook. (4) Pull both ends of the line to draw up the knot. Trim the excess.

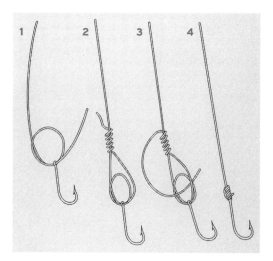

Trilene Knot. The Trilene knot is one of the easiest knots for novice anglers to learn how to tie. Experts also like the knot because it can be easily tied at night in complete darkness. (1) Slide your line through the hook eye and repeat, entering the line form the same direction and being sure to form a double loop at the hook eye, as shown. (2) Wrap the tag end around the standing line four or five times, moving away from the hook. (3) Pass the tag end back through the double loop at the hook eye, moisten, pull the knot tight against the hook eye, and trim the tag (4).

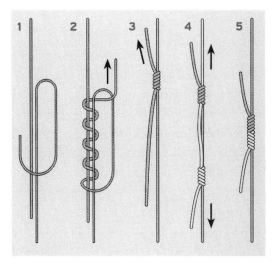

Joining Two Lines Uni-Knot. Used to join two lines of equal diameters. (1) Overlap line ends about 6 inches, forming loop in one line for Uni-knot. (2) Tie a Uni-knot with six wraps around the lines. (3) Pull the tag end to tighten the first knot around line. (4) Tie a second Uni-knot with the tag end of the other line. (5) Pull both main lines to tighten and bring the knots together. Trim the ends.

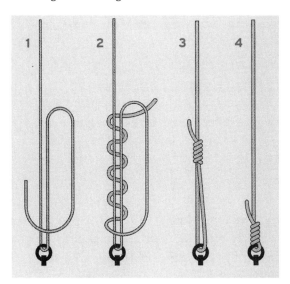

Terminal Tackle Uni-Knot. Used for attaching tackle to a line or mono leader. (1) Run the line through the eye and double it back, forming a circle. (2) Tie a Uni-knot by wrapping the tag end around the double line six turns and through the loop. Pull the tag end to tighten. (3) Pill the main line to tighten the knot. (4) Keep pulling tight in the main line and tackle until the knot slides tight against the eye.

The knots that seem to be the most popular for a wide range of anglers are the Uni-knots. These simple strong knots are easy to tie and can be used to join lines together or to attach terminal tackle. They are easier to tie than blood knots for joining lines or improved clinch knots for attaching lures, jigs, and hooks. If you wish to fish with knots that are quick and effective, learn the system of Uni-knots.

Finally, a few tips for knot construction. One, when you're tightening a knot, it's best to apply some universal lubricant, otherwise known as spit. And, it never hurts to apply a small drop of cyanoacrylate, or "super glue," to the finished knot.

Bait Your Own Hook—with Natural Bait

Fish bait comes two ways: real and fake. Natural, or real, bait can be either dead or alive, and while there's a group of anglers who proclaim that the use of artificial bait is more sporting, I don't think anyone will argue that natural bait won't catch more fish. After all, sport fish eat natural bait all their lives but seldom survive their last meal, no matter what it might be.

Anglers have several categories of natural baits to consider when fishing the Gulf Coast of Florida. There's cut bait, usually chunks of fish, a favorite of anglers willing to anchor and wait for the predators (and sometimes catfish or stingrays) to arrive. Another choice, small baitfish, can be fished live or dead and are widely distributed throughout the Gulf of Mexico. Shrimp are probably the most widely used coastal bait, either live or frozen. Even crabs, squid, miscellaneous crustaceans, and octopus have their places on the roster of baits used by Gulf anglers. Finally, using natural bait to chum or chunk is a popular method for attracting game fish, particularly when the fish are scattered. Chum can be homemade or purchased commercially and is generally used to attract small baitfish, which in turn attract larger predators. Chunks are typically used to create a feeding frenzy and to confuse larger fish. Almost any natural bait is suitable for chumming or chunking.

Cut bait can range from mullet heads to almost surgically "butterflied" pinfish. In the overall scheme of things, it's really pretty basic. Using cut bait is easy. Simply attach it to a circle hook, and either get it to the bottom or suspend it under a float. Its fish-attracting value is its smell, and many cut-bait anglers are not so concerned with what species they cut as with the smell. Oily fish tend to smell fishier, and do make the most effective cut bait. Mullet are almost always considered the universal choice for cut bait, but pinfish, squid, sardines, shrimp, ladyfish, and even lizardfish work well too. Cut bait is also easy to obtain. Frozen mullet, squid, and shrimp can almost always be purchased at bait shops, or the by-catch from a previous day's fishing can be used. A supply of dead pinfish or ladyfish can speed up a hot afternoon of flats fishing when you're just looking for action, even if it's in the form of small sharks or rays.

Bottom and grass dwellers such as pinfish and pigfish, as well as other porgies, are excellent inshore and offshore live baits. The sight of any of these small baitfish struggling against a cork on the flats or a sinker on a rock pile is enough to attract ferocious strikes from trout, redfish, grouper, and snapper. Hooked through the nose or tail and free-lined, they do the same for cobia, snook, tarpon, and king mackerel. They are generally hardy and survive in aerated live wells so long as the water is not too hot. There are a number of ways of catching these baits. Most can be caught on grass flats or over live bottom. Size 16 hooks baited with cut shrimp, FishBites, or leftover Gulp! bait work well, giving the kids something to do while the grownups fish. Live-bait anglers wishing to quickly fill their live wells often use pinfish traps baited with fish scraps, set on the grass flats the night before the big day. Others use cast nets after chumming baitfish close to the boat. I recommend

The best way to catch a bait well full of white bait is to chum and cast net.

½-inch mesh for a pinfish cast net, and a mixture of canned cat food or jack and mackerel mixed with whole wheat bread as chum. Chum slowly, and the little guys will come steadily to the boat.

The schooling-baitfish group, generally classified as white bait, includes scaled sardines (pilchards), Atlantic thread herring, Gulf menhaden (pogies or alewives), cigar minnows (round scad), and bay anchovies (glass minnows). Usually seen in huge numbers boiling the water's surface, they can also be found in lesser numbers around structure such as channel markers and small inshore rock piles and bars. They can be used either live or dead, and many of these small fish are available frozen from bait shops. All can be chummed-up and cast-netted for live bait, but care should be taken to choose the right net mesh size. A mesh that is too fine can result in gilled fish, making a mess of dead baits. I recommend a ⅜-inch mesh cast net for most species of white bait. Also, as you'll likely be chumming in water more than 10 feet deep, use the largest diameter net you can comfortably throw. As well as being chummed up and used as live bait, dead white bait can also make darn good chum for larger species, either ground up or "chunked."

Bigger white baits can also be caught on hooks. The Sabiki rig has become a popular method of catching baitfish all over the Gulf. It features an array of natural-looking tiny jigs and is weighted and dropped into schools of baitfish. Some anglers sweeten the small hooks with live or synthetic baits for more hookups. These rigs are highly effective for cigar minnows around markers and at night under lights when fishing offshore.

All the white baits make excellent offshore baits but are sometimes difficult to keep lively. Considerable aeration is needed in live wells, and special care should be taken not to overcrowd the baits.

I've been told that the most prevalent fish species anywhere is the bay anchovy, or glass minnow, but it represents only one of many species of white bait in the Gulf. White bait, on the basis of numbers alone, is a significant part of the Gulf's food chain and an always-excellent bait.

While on the subject of offshore fishing with live bait, I'd be remiss not to mention the blue runner, a member of the jack family, and the ballyhoo. Blue runners are often found in schools or over flats in the warmer months. These feisty "hardtails" make excellent bait for most offshore species, in particular grouper and pelagic species. They are easily caught with Sabiki rigs or small jigs and keep well with good aeration. A popular method of preparing blue runners as bait is to trim

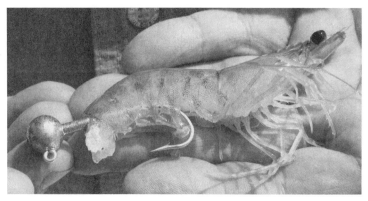

Live shrimp are always a popular bait. Rig them tail-first when you're fishing them deep.

the tips off their tails, making them more active than usual, and more attractive to predators. Stinger rigs, made using two hooks and a short piece of wire, are popular with king-mackerel anglers who use large baits such as blue runners. One hook, usually a J-hook, is put through the bait's lips and the other, a treble, is inserted near the bait's tail. Short-striking predators have little chance.

Ballyhoo are a version of needlefish and usually found in bait stores, sometimes pre-rigged for offshore trolling. They, along with big mackerel, are the natural bait of choice for big-game anglers fishing the deep canyons of the upper Gulf of Mexico.

Shrimp is as close to a universal saltwater bait as exists. Found over grassy bottom in various sizes, shrimp are the candy of the Gulf. Many anglers will attest to game fish eating shrimp and paying no attention to hordes of small bait-fish or mullet. Try it sometime. If you see fish striking mullet or white bait, throw a live shrimp or a shrimp imitation, into the melee. Shrimp will turn heads and mouths. Most anglers prefer to buy live shrimp from bait houses, and depending on location and supply, shrimp are sold by the dozen or hundred-count. Some anglers prefer to keep their shrimp frisky in a live well, but others simply put them in plastic bags and lay them in their coolers, insulated from the ice itself by a piece of newspaper. Amazingly, shrimp keep fresh for many hours using this method, and fresh-dead shrimp work fine for many applications, particularly inshore under popping corks or for spawning sheepshead. Shrimp are also effective offshore when bottom fishing but tend to attract small fish such as Key West grunts and black sea bass. These smaller snappers and grouper are also perfectly happy to eat frozen shrimp—a good thing, as their larger cousins are usually not quick enough to get to the hook.

Another almost-universal bait is the lowly mullet. Found everywhere along the Gulf Coast and in varying sizes, mullet work well dead or alive. Juvenile finger mullet are excellent live baits for any species, offshore and inshore, and are easily cast-netted. Larger mullet, cut into chunks, are highly fragrant and make very good cut bait for tarpon, redfish, trout, and even grouper. Avoid freshwater mullet caught up coastal rivers, though. While they are the same species as coastal mullet, their diet of algae affects their appeal to predators.

And speaking of appeal, many native Floridians (like me) prefer a fried freshly caught coastal mullet over fried grouper any day.

Other baits are by no means lesser baits. Fiddler crabs make excellent sheepshead bait, and sand fleas are certainly much more tasty to beachside pompano than nylon jigs. Sand fleas are also effective snook baits in rolling surf along beaches. Both are available at bait shops Gulf-wide, especially when the sheepshead are spawning in late winter and the pompano are active from spring through fall. Small blue crabs (or chunks of larger ones) will stop tarpon and cobia in their tracks and are always in demand during the warmer months. Try a small blue crab the next time you go grouper fishing too. Fiddlers, sand fleas, and blue crabs all keep well in a covered bucket with a bed of wet seaweed. Mud minnows, or killifish, are those small

Removing the pinchers of a crab makes it more appealing to game fish like tarpon and cobia.

minnows you see swimming along Gulf shores, usually in very shallow water and in small schools. When nothing else is working for redfish or trout, many inshore anglers will free-line mud minnows. They are hardy and easy to catch with either cast nets or small hooks baited with scraps of shrimp.

Finally, resist the urge to pickle the next octopus you bring aboard. They do make a great meal when doused with olive oil, lime juice, salt, and pepper, but they make even better grouper and snapper bait. It's a tough choice: whether to eat octopus ceviche or broiled grouper? I usually can't decide whether to fish or cut bait.

Hire Your Very Own Captain

Why hire a guide? Why not?

You've trailered your boat a zillion miles to a destination you don't know, expecting to fish every day. Hiring a professional who regularly fishes the area for the first day of your visit makes good sense. He likely fished there yesterday, and the day before, and the day before that. He knows what's biting and where. Most guides don't mind showing visiting anglers around and giving them tips, so long as the information isn't abused. If you hire a guide for a scouting trip, be sure to let him know your intentions. He may not show you his honey holes, but I can assure you that you'll take home more knowledge from one day with him than you would from a month on your own.

Another reason to hire a guide may be that you're not equipped to do the type of fishing he offers. Inshore anglers can enjoy a day offshore in a boat that's safer offshore. And many avowed beach and shore anglers hire guides for boat trips, fully understanding the amortized cost of owning an infrequently used, yet expensive, boat. A perfect example is tarpon fishing. Great sport, but not necessarily something you want to do every day. Hiring a professional guide for a tarpon trip makes perfect sense. He has the right tackle, boat, baits,

Professional fishing guides, like Chokoloskee's Capt. Charles Wright, offer anglers many fishing options.

and skills for the job, allowing you to concentrate on landing what could be the fish of a lifetime.

Professional fishing guides are professional people, and they should run professional businesses. Be sure to hire a guide who holds at least a U.S. Coast Guard 6-Pack or Operator of Uninspected Vessels license. Holders of this license have passed USCG scrutiny and tests and are also trained in First Aid and CPR. He or she should also have liability insurance and hold a Florida fishing license covering all the anglers on his boat. If a guide asks you to purchase your own fishing license—start asking questions. I've listed many local guides in this book and all have claimed to be insured and licensed, but ask them individually and directly to be sure. Other good sources of information about professional guides are the Florida Guides Association (www.florida-guides.com) and the Coastal Conservation Association (www.ccaflorida.org) websites.

Expect to pay your guide a fee, which will likely include use of his or her skills and his boat, tackle, ice, and bait. It may or may not include soft drinks, a shore lunch, a bag lunch, or fish cleaning. Offshore boats typically have at least one mate aboard who works mostly for tips, so be generous if he works hard. Inshore guides and offshore captains also deserve tips, based not necessarily on the number of fish caught, but on the effort they put into the day. Fifteen to twenty percent of the basic charter fee is reasonable, with a higher percentage in order for a big boat with a crew.

There's nothing worse than coming home with no fish or tales of no action. Hiring a guide can improve your chances of catching, and you'll likely have a good time. But remember that even guides are subject to the foibles of bad weather, muddy water, and moody fish.

To quote the cliché, "I'm a fishing guide, not a catching guide."

Party Boats, Head Boats, and Pukers

An alternative to chartering an individual boat and captain for you and a few friends or family members is to sign on to a fishing boat outfitted to fish offshore with as many as 100 anglers aboard. And, much like Ishmael coming aboard the *Pequod*, captained by Captain Ahab in the novel *Moby Dick*, you might find yourself fishing alongside a modern-day version of Queequeg, with tattoos, scars, and an ugly sneer.

This sort of fishing is not for everyone, but it's perfect if you enjoy catching potluck and the camaraderie of a big crowd.

Essentially, you pay a fee to fish, and the fee usually includes tackle and bait. Tackle isn't great, but it's sturdy, and bait can range from frozen fish to squid. You can take your own gear, but why buck the system? And, besides, free is good. This is

Not every fish that comes aboard a head boat is huge, but even the smallest ones bring smiles to happy anglers.

very basic bottom-fishing. Some boats fish half-days, usually in winter, but many fleets offer full-day trips. Some offer multiday and overnight excursions too. Expect to spend about 25 percent of your time in transit to the fishing if you're leaving from one of our Gulf ports for a day trip.

A typical day aboard a head boat involves a ride to a fishing area selected by the captain. On the trip offshore, the mates stay busy rigging rods and preparing bait, while the galley doles out coffee and breakfast. Galley food, though good and reasonably priced, is not included in the cost of the trip, and many anglers bring coolers with their own supplies, if the boat allows them. Call ahead or check the operator's website for boat rules.

On arrival at the fishing spot, there's usually no anchoring involved; anchoring one of these big boats is not easy. Party boats usually fish in water that's fairly deep; with engines running, the captain simply holds the boat over the selected spot and orders, "Lines in, folks."

Standard fishing gear is big, simple reels on very short rods, rigged with 80-pound-test monofilament line, double-hook dropper rigs, 3/0 hooks, and as much as 12 ounces of lead. There's a lot of hard reeling involved in bottom fishing, even with no fish on the end of the line, and lots of anglers whine toward day's end. Once you're hooked up, don't worry about playing the fish. The main goal is to get your catch to the surface without getting tangled in the other anglers' lines. Mates are standing by and will help you get your fish aboard, tagged, and iced.

Most of the catch aboard party boats is grouper, snapper (American red, vermillion, Lane), and a variety of bottom fish. Amberjacks, Spanish and king mackerel, cobia, and even a few wahoo appear during the summer months, depending on the depth and bottom structure—and there's always a buzz when a big shark is hooked or a trophy grouper or snapper comes aboard.

An 80-foot boat can handle big, wallowing seas, but can you? Jokingly called "pukers" by captains, crew, and regular customers, these big boats can pitch and roll in even the calmest seas, causing seasickness among even experienced passengers. Preparing yourself with over-the-counter remedies (Dramamine, Bonine) or prescriptions (transdermal patches) is a good idea. Avoid going below to cure queasiness; stay on deck, breathe fresh air, stay away from the engine's exhaust, and keep your eyes focused on the horizon. Watch what you eat too. If you're prone to seasickness, keep your food intake light, and for sure avoid a hearty, greasy breakfast or a late night of drinking before the trip. But if you get sick, go ahead and get it over with. No one will make fun of you, as most have been in your shoes before.

If you're lucky enough to go fishing on a head boat on a slow business day, you'll probably have plenty of room to stretch out; however, most of the party or head boats fishing from Gulf ports are crowded much of the year. Actually, some cancel trips if the number of reservations is low, finding it not profitable to take just a few anglers. With anglers shoulder-to-shoulder along the gunnels, lines can tangle easily, so it's best to pay attention to what you're doing and the location of your own line. Certain fish, bonito and cobia in particular, are famous for tangling line. Snapper and grouper just get tugged to the surface, but these speedsters can really make a mess. Should you tangle with your neighbor, ask a mate to help, and keep your cool.

Finally, a word about money, specifically tips. At the end of the day, a tip jar will be passed around, and its take is usually distributed among the mates and the galley crew. These folks, sometimes students, count on your gratuities to supplement their wages. A $20 donation to the tip jar is not much to pay for the crew's putting up with you. And, if there's a crewmember who was especially helpful or cheerful, slip him a fiver at the end of the day.

Party Boat Operators

HERNANDO BEACH

Thunder Party Boat, (352) 597-3900, www.thunderpartyboat.com

TARPON SPRINGS

Viking Fleet, (888) 358-7477, www.vikingfleet.com

CLEARWATER

Double Eagle Deep Sea Fishing, (877) 446-1653, www.doubleeagledeepseafishing.com

ST. PETERSBURG

Hubbard's Marina (Johns Pass), (800) 755-0677, www.hubbardsmarina.com

Miss Pass-a-Grille (South St. Pete Beach), (727) 367-9833, www.misspassagrille.com

SARASOTA

Flying Fish Fleet, (941) 366-3373, www.flyingfishfleet.com

CHARLOTTE HARBOR

Kingfisher Fleet (Punta Gorda), (941) 639-2628, www.kingfisherfleet.com

FORT MYERS

Capt. Tony's, (239) 415-0515, www.capttonys.com

Cruise Naples/Double Sunshine, (239) 263-4949, www.cruise
naplesflorida.com

Don't Have a Boat? Take a Walk!

Having access to a fishing boat certainly is an advantage, but
it's not an absolute necessity in many areas along Florida's
Gulf Coast. In fact, *not* having a boat is an advantage in many
situations.

There are places you just can't fish easily with a boat. Beaches
with rough-breaking surf are sometimes perfect habitat for
pompano and snook, but boaters must avoid getting too close
to the shore. Some shallow shorelines within bays and estuaries are too shallow to approach by boat, or even by kayak or
canoe, yet they offer excellent shallow-water trout and redfish
action. Public fishing piers offer structure and habitat for game
fish underneath, sometimes along busy beaches, accessible
only to the anglers on the pier. And, even if you have a boat,
you'll probably find areas, such as oyster and shell bars, that
you'll just want to fish quietly and efficiently by wading.

Surf and shoreline wade fishing is very democratic. Anyone
can walk along a public beach and throw jigs, sand fleas, or
flies into the trough behind the first set of breakers. Pompano
and snook feed in these troughs as sand fleas and other crustaceans wash away with receding waves. Other options for surf
fishing are live shrimp under corks fished outside the breaking waves for mackerel, trout, and even reds along the shoreline. Artificial lures such as noisy topwater plugs work well but
usually when there's a run of baitfish and predators along the
beaches. There are many public landings and parks all along
Florida's Gulf Coast that allow anglers to get their feet wet.
And you'll often see folks stopped along stretches of coastal
roads getting their wading gear ready or just loading a stringer
of nice fish into their cooler.

Wade-fishing is a popular pastime along the edges of Gulf passes.

There are two types of public piers along the Gulf Coast. One is the pier that juts into the Gulf; the other is the pier that runs alongside big bridges, typically the byproduct of an older demolished bridge. Both are natural traps for bait and predators, including offshore species such as grouper and pelagics such as king mackerel. Long Gulf piers are usually constructed along a beach and offer refuge to fish from the miles and miles of white-sand bottom. Bridge piers are usually in the flowing stream of waterways, and the natural tidal action provides a constant flow of bait beneath the structure. Both are fun places to fish, but there may be rules restricting certain types of tackle. Otherwise, it's usually a free-for-all when the schools of striking fish start to hit or someone hooks up a trophy-size cobia, tangling lines and heating tempers.

All along the Gulf Coast, you'll find areas in bays and coves where you could easily edge your boat up to a bar or deep shoreline, clatter around, splash an anchor, and generally run all the fish off to Mexico. Stalking fish, particularly redfish and big seatrout, by foot is akin to turkey hunting. It's just you and the fish, but they know their habitat better than you and can sense you coming toward them at great distances. After you've learned how to shuffle along a bar top and make long casts to attentive game fish, you'll be hooked. Fishing by foot takes a different skill set than boat fishing. It also takes special and sometimes specialized gear.

Beach fishing can be as simple as using a single rod and reel and a pocketful of bait—or it can involve a modified wheelbarrow with rod holders, a tackle box, a cooler, chest waders, and a supply of snacks for the day. Most surf anglers use longer rods capable of getting the lure or bait well offshore, but that's not necessary all the time. Remember that many game-fish species run so close to the shore that they are pitched, rolled, and confused by the wave action. Don't buy a special rod and reel for your first trip to the surf; just bring one of your medium-sized spinning outfits.

Pier and bridge fishing usually involve tackle heavy enough to handle the weighty rigs needed to get the baits to the bottom and to pull fish away from pilings. Many anglers use gear carts, as there's usually a fair walk from the pier's entrance to the end, where all the pros congregate. Remember to try the close-to-shore trough, and you may not have to walk all the way out to the end of the pier. And fish landing nets or hooks are always a good idea on these higher structures, as fishing line is not really ideal for hoisting flopping fish once they're out of the water.

In general, wade fishing on flats and bars is easier if you have some specialized gear. Longer rods, even those of light to medium action, are helpful to make long casts. Wading belts offer the convenience of extra rods, tackle storage, and stringers at close hand. The Wade Aid Belt (www.wadeaid.com) is excellent, and despite not being able to claim the feature, it offers some flotation should you trip and fall. High-top wading shoes are also good, as oysters, sharp rocks, and stingrays are not easy on the feet or ankles. Stringers with breakaway features are also popular with many wade anglers, but I'm not among that crowd. I'm 6 feet tall, and if I'm wading to my armpits in 5 feet of water towing a stringer of trout, I'm an easy target for a cruising bull shark. Nope. No stringers for me!

Pier, bridge, beach, and wade fishing all deserve attention from anglers wishing to experience the full range of Gulf fishing in Florida. They're generally less expensive, and in many instances, more productive, than boat fishing. And, for the landlubbers—or those prone to seasickness—who want to fish, it's the only way to go.

Artificial Reefs and Wrecks, Tampa Bay and Southwest Florida

I obtained this information from the Florida Fish and Wildlife Conservation Commission (FWC). I cannot guarantee accuracy, as some reef materials can be displaced or completely removed by storms or other natural causes; however, this is probably the best list available.

The latitude–longitude format is shown in decimal–minute (DDMM.MMM) format.

Reef information is listed alphabetically by county and has been abbreviated to the most recently deployed reef materials.

Information is listed for Charlotte County (Punta Gorda and the Gulf Islands), Collier County (Naples, Marco Island), Hernando County (Bayport, Hernando Beach), Hillsborough County (Tampa Bay to Egmont Key), Lee County (Fort Myers, Sanibel Island, Captiva Island), Manatee County (Bradenton, Southern Tampa Bay), Pasco County (Port Richey, Hudson), Pinellas County (St. Petersburg, Clearwater, Tarpon Springs), and Sarasota County (Sarasota, Venice).

Table 1. Reefs of Charlotte County

Deploy Date	Reef Name	Material	Latitude	Longitude	Depth	Relief
7/2/2009	Captain Jeff Steele Reef-#09-1	Concrete culverts	2655.674	8235.832	60	8
9/3/2008	Captain Jeff Steele Reef N-5	Concrete culverts (58)	2655.830	8235.897	55	12
9/2/2008	Captain Jeff Steele Reef N-4	Concrete culverts (72)	2655.823	8235.890	55	12
9/2/2008	Captain Jeff Steele Reef N-3	Concrete culverts (83)	2655.826	8235.915	55	12
8/30/2008	Captain Jeff Steele Reef N-2	Concrete culverts (49)	2655.820	8235.910	55	12
8/30/2008	Captain Jeff Steele Reef N-1	Concrete culverts (87)	2655.819	8235.893	55	12
1/6/2005	Tremblay Reef Barge	Barge steel 90'	2648.415	8222.651	42	8
7/16/2004	Novak Reef 04-Buoy #3	Concrete culverts (398) three drops	2648.644	8219.539	30	13
7/14/2004	Novak Reef 04-Buoy #3	Concrete culverts (266) two drops	2648.604	8219.654	30	13
7/12/2004	Novak Reef 04-Buoy #1	Concrete culverts (88)	2648.680	8219.604	30	13
7/9/2004	Novak Reef 04-Buoy #1	Concrete culverts (81)	2648.671	8219.620	30	13
7/8/2004	Novak Reef 04-Buoy #1	Concrete culverts (140)	2648.500	8219.541	30	13
5/28/2003	Tremblay Reef	Concrete bridge rubble (60)	2648.350	8222.700	41	11
4/21/2003	Novak Reef #4	Concrete bridge sections (24)	2648.573	8219.703	30	10
4/18/2003	Novak Reef #3	Concrete bridge sections (22)	2648.572	8219.702	30	7

(continued)

Table 1—*Continued*

Deploy Date	Reef Name	Material	Latitude	Longitude	Depth	Relief
4/16/2003	Novak Reef #2	Concrete bridge sections (24)	2648.571	8219.701	30	6
4/14/2003	Novak Reef #1	Concrete bridge sections (18)	2648.570	8219.700	29	7
6/19/2000	Marys Reef Site #3	Concrete culverts three drops	2646.235	8218.430	29	5
12/2/1999	Charlotte Harbor Site B (Bay)	Modules concrete reefballs (52)	2651.502	8205.296	12	3
12/2/1999	Charlotte Harbor Site A (Bay)	Modules concre te reefballs (53)	2651.502	8205.318	12	3
5/21/1999	Palm Island Barge Reef	Barge steel 70'	2649.221	8231.879	56	8
5/7/1999	Charlotte Harbor Site B (Bay)	Modules concrete reefballs (52)	2650.989	8205.296	12	3
5/7/1999	Charlotte Harbor Site A (Bay)	Modules concrete reefballs (53)	2650.989	8205.317	12	3
3/12/1999	Palm Island Ferry Reef	Ship steel ferry 60'	2649.236	8231.951	55	5
5/10/1995	Cape Haze Reef (Bay)	Steel units	2645.769	8209.446	18	4
5/21/1992	Stump Pass 3 Mile Reef	Concrete culverts	2652.256	8226.434	42	5
5/1/1992	M-14	Concrete culverts	2652.269	8226.430	45	8
3/1/1991	Charlotte Harbour #1 (Bay)	Concrete culverts	2650.650	8205.317	12	3
12/31/1988	Danger Reef	Ship steel crewboat	2645.554	8211.167	12	6
6/15/1987	Charlotte Harbor Site (Bay)	Concrete culverts	2650.600	8205.317	12	3
12/31/1983	Charlotte Harbor Reef (Bay)	Bridge concrete	2650.500	8205.317	12	
7/3/1981	Boca Grande Reef	Concrete pilings	2638.200	8217.083		
12/31/1960	Englewood Fish Haven	Bridge rubble	2654.700	8221.800	22	

Table 2. Reefs of Collier County

Deploy Date	Reef Name	Material 1	Latitude	Longitude	Depth	Relief
7/2/2009	Dr Pass 4.5 Mile Site-#09–4	Concrete pilings (200)	2610.241	8154.043	30	10
6/12/2007	Marco 9 Mile Reef, #3	Concrete culverts	2552.844	8154.206	40	10
6/7/2007	Marco 9 Mile Reef, #2	Concrete culverts	2552.875	8154.186	40	10
5/22/2005	Marco Island 12 Mile, M12cd05	Concrete rubble	2554.526	8159.037	46	8
11/23/2004	Amt Reef	Concrete rubble (400)	2554.607	8159.088	45	10
6/9/2004	Rock Reef 2	Rock limestone (130)	2618.286	8152.376	24	5
10/1/2003	Wiggins Pass 3 Mile C & D	Concrete rubble (600)	2618.324	8152.426	27	10
9/26/2003	Clam Pass 3 Mile –C & D	Concrete rubble (500)	2613.445	8152.229		
6/24/2003	Keewaydin 3 Mile, C & D Reef 02	Concrete rubble (150)	2602.184	8149.859	28	10
6/14/2003	Marco 9 Mile, Cp1- M9c	Concrete culverts & boxes (40)	2552.972	8154.057	39	8
6/14/2003	Marco 12 Mile, Site M12c	Concrete culverts & boxes (720)	2554.695	8159.038	45	8
6/14/2003	Marco 12 Mile, Site M12b	Limestone boulders (50)	2554.674	8159.198	45	10
6/9/2003	Marco 12 Mile, Cp2 (Site M12c)	Concrete railroad ties (180)	2554.692	8159.027	45	6
8/6/2002	Davey Jones Reef -Memorial Reef Balls	Modules concrete reefballs (15)	2552.784	8154.080	39	5
6/6/2002	Keewaydin 3 Mile #1	Rock limestone boulders	2602.034	8149.787	27	8
6/6/2002	Keewaydin 3 Mile #3	Rock limestone boulders	2602.169	8149.899	27	12
6/5/2001	Marco Island 9 Mile-Sport Fishing Club Reef-2	Bridge concrete decking (11)	2552.849	8154.143	39	5

(continued)

Table 2—*Continued*

Deploy Date	Reef Name	Material 1	Latitude	Longitude	Depth	Relief
6/1/2001	Clam Pass 3 Mile - Pile	Concrete railroad ties (1800)	2613.574	8152.074	26	11
5/24/2001	Eca Reef	Concrete rubble (200)	2618.369	8152.354	24	10
5/22/2000	Clam Pass 3 Mile -02	Concrete rubble (100)	2613.390	8152.051	25	8
6/1/1999	Marco Island 5 Mile Site	Concrete culverts	2551.898	8147.788	32	4
5/30/1997	Marco Island 2 Mile	Concrete culverts	2555.436	8146.236	22	5
5/28/1997	Caxambas Pass 2.5 Mile	Concrete pilings	2555.920	8145.200	24	
4/30/1997	Santa Lucia	Ship cement	2605.388	8150.626	24	
6/5/1996	Gordon Pass 5 Mile	Concrete pilings	2605.150	8153.333	26	3
6/17/1995	Naples Pier Reef	Concrete culverts	2607.815	8150.703	22	3
5/27/1994	Doctor's Pass 5 Mile	Concrete culverts	2610.215	8154.375	34	4
12/31/1993	Gordon Pass 14 Mile Reef	Concrete culverts	2614.190	8207.579	42	
5/4/1993	Wiggins Pass 9 Mile	Concrete culverts	2614.010	8207.736	42	
3/1/1993	Gordon Pass 5 Mile Reef	Bridge rubble concrete	2605.794	8153.320	35	4
6/29/1992	Gordon Pass 9 Mile	Modules concrete	2603.770	8159.350	23	
12/31/1991	Wiggins Pass 14 Mile Reef	Concrete culverts	2614.860	8205.830	48	
5/18/1991	Caxambas Pass 14 Miles Reef	Concrete culverts	2547.520	8157.245	46	
12/31/1989	Pavilion Key 6 Mile Reef	Concrete culverts	2541.180	8128.000	16	

Date	Reef	Material	Coord 1	Coord 2	Depth	No.
7/22/1989	Gordon Pass 5 Mile Reef	Concrete culverts	2604.888	8153.131	28	3
4/28/1989	Pavilion Key 6 Mile Reef	Concrete culverts	2541.300	8128.000	18	
12/7/1987	Gordon Pass 5 Mile Reef	Airplane dc3	2605.434	8153.698	25	5
2/4/1987	Wiggins Pass 4.5 Mile Reef	Barge steel	2617.469	8155.165	31	7
12/31/1986	Marco Island 5 Mile Reef	Barge steel	2551.884	8147.971	30	4
12/31/1986	Marco Island 5 Mile Reef	Steel pipe	2551.931	8147.819	31	5
9/1/1986	Wiggins Pass 5 Mile	Steel school buses	2617.474	8155.808	30	
12/30/1983	Marco Pass Reef Site	Concrete culverts	2555.400	8146.250	22	3
11/8/1980	Collier 5 Mile Reef	Concrete pilings	2551.826	8147.633	31	6
10/29/1980	Collier 5 Mile Reef	Barge steel 72'	2551.896	8147.788	31	
12/31/1972	Caxambas Pass 5.0 Mile	Concrete culverts	2551.788	8147.664	30	4
12/31/1972	Marco Island 2 Mile Reef	Concrete rubble	2555.434	8146.236	23	8
	Pavilion Key 6 Mile Reef	Barge steel	2540.962	8127.810	17	5
	Gordon Pass 5 Mile Reef	Bridge rubble concrete	2605.804	8153.302	35	

Table 3. Reefs of Hernando County

Deploy Date	Reef Name	Material 1	Latitude	Longitude	Depth	Relief
5/17/1997	Bendickson Reef	Concrete culverts	2831.770	8258.650	25	
5/15/1997	Bendickson Reef	Concrete culverts	2831.774	8258.640	25	
5/8/1997	Bendickson Reef	Concrete culverts	2831.700	8258.630	25	
5/5/1997	Bendickson Reef	Concrete culverts	2831.730	8258.710	25	
11/21/1995	Reef Ball Reef #2	Modules concrete reefballs (107)	2830.033	8258.700	25	6
11/20/1995	Reef Ball Reef #1	Modules concrete reefballs (107)	2830.035	8258.700	25	5
4/21/1995	Bendickson Reef - Tanks	Army tanks m-60	2831.710	8258.690	26	12
4/21/1995	Bendickson Reef - Tanks	Army tanks m-60	2831.660	8258.730	26	12
4/21/1995	Bendickson Reef - Tanks	Army tanks m-60	2831.790	8258.770	26	12
4/21/1995	Bendickson Reef - Tanks	Army tanks m-60	2831.660	8258.620	26	12
4/21/1995	Bendickson Reef - Tanks	Army tanks m-60	2831.620	8258.620	26	12
4/21/1995	Bendickson Reef - Tanks	Army tanks m-60	2831.750	8258.630	26	12
4/21/1995	Bendickson Reef - Tanks	Army tanks m-60	2831.660	8258.720	26	12
4/21/1995	Bendickson Reef - Tanks	Army tanks m-60	2831.750	8258.670		
4/21/1995	Bendickson Reef - Tanks	Army tanks m-60	2831.740	8258.750	26	12
4/21/1995	Bendickson Reef - Tanks	Army tanks m-60	2831.730	8258.750	26	12
4/28/1994	Jim Champion Reef	Concrete culverts	2836.441	8256.469	20	
6/23/1993	Jim Champion Reef	Concrete culverts	2836.443	8256.469	20	

Date	Name	Type			
6/25/1992	Jim Champion Reef	Concrete culverts	2836.445	8256.469	20	8
6/14/1991	Jim Champion Reef	Concrete culverts	2836.438	8256.521	20	
12/31/1989	Richardson Reef	Bridge spans	2830.500	8255.800	20	
6/19/1989	Ah Richardson	Concrete culverts	2831.489	8255.067	18	

Table 4. Reefs of Hillsborough County

Deploy Date	Reef Name	Material 1	Latitude	Longitude	Depth	Relief
1/23/2009	Egmont Key Reef (Bay) #25	Modules concrete reefballs (19)	2734.970	8244.680	18	3
4/4/2006	Bahia Beach Reef (Bay) #5	Bridge rubble	2744.950	8230.900	19	8
3/7/2006	Bahia Beach Reef (Bay) #4	Bridge rubble	2744.930	8230.900	19	8
2/15/2006	Bahia Beach Reef (Bay) #2	Bridge rubble	2744.900	8230.960	19	8
6/22/2005	Bahia Beach Reef (Bay)	Bridge pilings	2744.940	8230.950	19	8
4/23/2005	Whiskey Stump Key	Fossilized locally mined shell bags (1,265)	2748.888	8224.117	3	1
4/13/2005	Bahia Beach Reef (Bay)	Bridge pilings	2744.800	8230.880	19	8
3/25/2005	Bahia Beach Reef (Bay)	Bridge pilings	2744.810	8230.880	19	8
3/4/2005	Bahia Beach Reef (Bay)	Bridge pilings	2744.850	8230.920	19	8
3/2/2004	Port Manatee Reef (Bay)	Bridge spans	2739.730	8234.680	21	8
2/19/2004	Port Manatee Reef (Bay)	Bridge spans	2739.770	8234.800	21	8
2/1/2004	Port Manatee Reef (Bay)	Bridge spans	2739.850	8234.820	21	8
1/23/2004	Port Manatee Reef (Bay)	Bridge spans	2739.860	8234.800	21	8
9/25/2003	Port Tampa Reef (Bay)	Limestone imbedded in concrete	2751.710	8233.800	24	1
7/1/2003	Port Manatee Reef (Bay)	Bridge spans	2739.840	8234.710	19	8

Date	Site	Description				
6/3/2003	Port Manatee Reef (Bay)	Bridge spans	2739.890	8234.800	19	8
10/17/2002	Port Tampa Reef (Bay)	Modules limestone in concrete (17)	2751.700	8233.800	21	1
5/28/2002	Port Tampa Reef (Bay) #6	Concrete pile cutoffs	2751.730	8233.790	21	10
5/17/2002	Egmont Key Reef (Bay) #26	Concrete pile cutoffs	2734.980	8244.630	18	8
5/16/2002	Bahia Beach Reef (Bay) #5	Bridge spans	2744.850	8230.940		
12/21/2001	Egmont Key Reef (Bay) #25	Bridge spans	2735.010	8244.520	18	8
12/4/2001	Egmont Key Reef (Bay) #23	Bridge spans	2735.080	8244.540	18	8
11/27/2001	Egmont Key Reef (Bay) #22	Bridge spans	2735.070	8244.680	18	8
11/6/2001	Port Manatee Reef (Bay)	Bridge spans	2739.750	8234.820	19	8
11/2/2001	Bahia Beach Reef (Bay) #2	Bridge spans	2744.930	8230.960	19	8
10/19/2001	Port Manatee Reef (Bay)	Bridge spans	2739.830	8234.800	19	8
10/16/2001	Egmont Key Reef (Bay) #16	Bridge spans	2735.070	8244.550	18	8
10/8/2001	Egmont Key Reef (Bay) #14	Bridge spans	2735.040	8244.600	18	8
9/25/2001	Egmont Key Reef (Bay) #10	Bridge spans	2734.910	8244.670	18	6
9/12/2001	Egmont Key Reef (Bay) #8	Bridge spans	2735.050	8244.680	18	6
8/29/2001	Bahia Beach Reef (Bay) #1	Bridge spans	2744.840	8230.890	19	8
8/24/2001	Egmont Key Reef (Bay) #5	Bridge spans	2735.030	8244.620	18	6
8/9/2001	Egmont Key Reef (Bay) #2	Bridge spans	2735.060	8244.540	18	6

(continued)

Table 4—*Continued*

Deploy Date	Reef Name	Material 1	Latitude	Longitude	Depth	Relief
10/19/2000	Port Tampa Reef (Bay)	Concrete rubble	2751.628	8233.790	24	2
12/8/1999	Bahia Beach Reef (Bay)	Bridge slabs concrete	2744.910	8230.890	24	6
6/26/1999	Egmont Key Reef	Modules concrete pyramids (22)	2735.000	8244.600	18	8
9/11/1997	Chief Reef (Bay)	Concrete blocks (50)	2751.632	8233.790	24	12
8/16/1997	Port Manatee Reef (Bay)	Concrete blocks	2739.708	8234.794	20	1
10/10/1996	Chamberlain High School (Bay)	Concrete blocks (75)	2751.650	8233.800	19	
6/29/1993	Bahia Beach Reef(Bay)	Concrete rubble	2744.881	8230.961	21	
12/31/1991	Howard Franklin Site (Bay)	Bridge rubble	2754.630	8233.230	16	8
12/31/1991	Courtney Campbell Site (Bay)	Concrete pilings	2757.750	8236.860	16	8
9/10/1991	Port Manatee Site (Bay)	Concrete culverts	2739.738	8234.743	17	
7/15/1991	Picnic Island Pier Reef (Bay)	Modules concrete pyramids	2751.390	8233.200		
5/17/1989	Bahia Beach Reef (Bay)	Modules concrete pyramids	2744.933	8230.978	20	
12/31/1987	Ballast Point Pier (Bay)	Concrete pilings	2753.273	8228.749	8	5
5/28/1987	Picnic Island Reef (Bay)	Concrete culverts	2749.967	8233.606	26	
3/21/1987	Port Tampa Site (Bay)	Barges steel (4)	2751.650	8233.840	24	12

Table 5. Reefs of Lee County

Deploy Date	Reef Name	Material 1	Latitude	Longitude	Depth	Relief
10/11/2010	Dh3	Modules concrete blocks (14)	2622.358	8217.337	45	3
3/1/2010	Poseidons Garden	Modules concrete blocks (14)	2622.347	8217.383	45	3
11/21/2008	Gasparilla Mitgation Reef South	Rock limestone	2645.265	8216.015	12	5
11/21/2008	Gasparilla Mitgation Reef Center	Rock limestone	2645.325	8216.025	12	5
11/21/2008	Gasparilla Mitgation Reef North	Rock limestone	2645.375	8216.035	12	5
8/26/2008	Dean Hicks	Rock limestone	2622.173	8217.297	45	6
2/5/2008	Blanda's Reef -Bl4	Modules concrete reefballs (5)	2625.363	8218.940	38	3
1/7/2008	Causeway Reef #29	Concrete pilings - pile caps (50)	2622.976	8201.203	26	6
12/10/2007	Causeway Reef #27	Concrete pilings - (75)	2623.990	8201.240	26	8
11/27/2007	Causeway Reef #23	Concrete pilings - cutoffs (50)	2622.934	8201.219	26	8
9/24/2007	Causeway Reef #18	Concrete guard rails (50)	2622.912	8201.250	26	8
4/17/2007	Eternal Reefs -Bl4	Modules concrete reefballs (6)	2625.360	8218.940	38	3
3/8/2007	Charlotte's Reef-Rock (N2)	Rock limestone	2645.836	8227.434	50	7
9/11/2006	Causeway Reef #9	Concrete pilings - cutoffs (70)	2622.980	8201.082	26	6
5/9/2006	Causeway Reef #5	Concrete pilings - cutoffs (70)	2622.930	8201.142	26	7
5/5/2006	Pace #10	Concrete culverts (78)	2631.215	8216.986	35	8

(continued)

Table 5—*Continued*

Deploy Date	Reef Name	Material 1	Latitude	Longitude	Depth	Relief
9/16/2005	Causeway Reef #1	Concrete pilings - cutoffs (135)	2622.949	8201.147	26	7
6/28/2005	Pace's Place Reef-Juvenile Habitats	Concrete juvenile fish refuge habitats (28)	2631.171	8216.968	34	5
6/24/2005	Blanda's Reef Rock	Rock-limestone boulders (200)	2625.313	8219.086	44	5
10/20/2004	Wildmans Reef	Ship concrete sailboat 50'	2631.177	8217.046	36	16
6/11/2004	Arc-Reefballs	Modules concrete reefballs (84)	2624.898	8224.672	57	5
7/29/2003	Blanda's Reef	Ship steel sailboat 45'	2625.185	8219.100	45	8
2/26/2002	Cape Haze Reef(B)	Concrete culverts (125)	2645.761	8209.494	18	6
6/21/2001	Helens Barges	Barge steel (60')	2637.933	8217.161	30	6
5/29/2001	Pace Rub 2	Concrete precast materials (100)	2631.249	8216.940	36	17
5/18/2001	Arc Rubble	Concrete precast materials (110)	2624.830	8224.684	58	10
5/9/2001	Arc Tet	Modules concrete tetrahedrons (150)	2624.865	8224.640	58	10
9/5/2000	Doc Kline Lincolin Logs	Concrete pilings	2620.349	8205.392	30	8
6/19/2000	Mary's Reef	Concrete culverts	2646.239	8218.430	30	13
6/15/2000	Pace's Place Barge Reef	Barge steel deck	2631.169	8216.952	34	12
5/25/2000	Evan Thompson Reef Units	Concrete module lincoln logs	2620.282	8205.123	32	12
5/24/2000	Arc '00 Reef	Concrete precast materials	2624.941	8224.816	58	15

Date	Reef	Material				
7/9/1999	Pegasus Tugboat	Ship steel tugboat (110')	2633.130	8243.415	85	36
6/9/1999	Arc Barge Site	Concrete culverts (24 sets)	2624.785	8224.826	56	8
3/19/1999	May Reef	Concrete boxes	2622.377	8155.112	22	10
5/10/1997	Belton Johnson Reef	Concrete slabs	2625.400	8211.783	32	5
2/1/1997	Vixen Wreck	Ship wood 57'	2632.838	8224.793	60	20
5/24/1995	G-H Reef	Concrete culverts	2620.743	8157.190	28	
5/10/1995	Cape Haze (B)	Modules steel units	2645.729	8209.466	18	4
5/7/1994	G-H Reef	Rock limestone	2620.656	8157.518	28	6
1/25/1994	Charlie's Reef	Boxcars steel/hopper	2633.373	8243.367	90	24
12/8/1993	Arcoa Reef	Modules pvc concrete	2632.487	8225.080	60	6
6/30/1993	E-F (Jaycees) Reef	Concrete culverts	2620.149	8205.556	31	8
3/1/1993	Edison Bridge	Bridge rubble	2618.407	8213.474	40	
8/31/1992	Power Pole Reef	Barge steel	2640.957	8222.470	45	
6/7/1991	E-F (Jaycees) Reef	Concrete culverts	2620.148	8205.352	31	8
6/17/1989	Redfish Pass Reef	Barge steel	2633.653	8214.199	26	10
6/30/1988	Sanibel Reef	Concrete rubble	2624.943	8203.160	20	
12/31/1984	Bokeelia Reef (B)	Concrete culverts	2643.038	8209.642	10	4
8/1/1984	G-H Reef	Barge steel	2620.591	8157.239	30	4

Table 6. Reefs of Manatee County

Deploy Date	Reef Name	Material 1	Latitude	Longitude	Depth	Relief
7/15/2009	7 Mile North Reef, Site "09–01–07"	Rock limestone boulders (300)	2732.340	8252.673	40	18
12/6/2006	7 Mile North Reef, Site "06–02–04"	Concrete light poles (150)	2732.378	8252.729	42	10
6/27/2005	1 Mile Reef, Site 05–7	Modules concrete reefballs (48)	2729.370	8244.080	22	6
6/27/2005	1 Mile Reef, Site 05–3	Modules concrete reefballs (48)	2729.315	8244.090	22	6
6/27/2005	1 Mile Reef, Site 05–1	Modules concrete reefballs (48)	2729.336	8244.160	22	6
2/6/2004	Southeast Tampa, 04–12	Modules concrete reefballs (81)	2732.917	8240.291	14	3
2/6/2004	Manatee River-Emerson Point, 04–18	Modules concrete reefballs (81)	2731.836	8238.767	10	3
2/6/2004	The Bulkhead Reef, 04–12	Modules concrete reefballs (85)	2733.207	8242.368	15	3
2/5/2004	Bayshore-North Reefballs, 04–10	Modules concrete reefballs (81)	2724.491	8236.095	10	3
7/2/2003	1 Mile Reef, Site 03–2	Modules concrete reefballs (44)	2729.394	8244.118	22	5
6/26/2003	1 Mile Reef, Site 3–12	Modules concrete reefballs (44)	2729.387	8244.038	22	5
6/26/2003	1 Mile Reef, Site 3–10	Modules concrete reefballs (45)	2729.387	8244.077	22	5
6/27/2002	7 Mile South Reef, Site 'P'-02–05	Concrete culverts (18)	2726.579	8249.254	40	3
6/26/2002	7 Mile South Reef, Site 'P'-02–06	Concrete culverts (20)	2726.593	8249.215	40	3
6/13/2002	7 Mile South Reef, Site 'P'-02–04	Modules concrete reefballs (20)	2726.526	8249.211	40	3
6/7/2002	7 Mile South Reef, Site 'P'-02–02	Modules concrete reefballs (42)	2726.552	8249.135	40	3

Date	Location	Material				
6/5/2002	7 Mile South Reef, Site Er-9	Modules concrete reefballs (30)	2726.509	8249.231	40	3
10/4/2001	Southeast Tampa Bay, Site 01-07 Reefballs	Modules concrete reefballs (175)	2732.900	8240.342	15	3
6/22/2001	3 Mile South Reef, Site 'D'-01-10	Modules concrete reefballs (20)	2726.650	8244.850	31	2
6/22/2001	3 Mile South Reef, Site 'D'-01-13	Modules concrete reefballs (40)	2726.506	8244.858	31	2
6/21/2001	3 Mile South Reef, Site 'D'-01-4	Modules concrete reefballs (20)	2726.470	8244.876	31	2
6/21/2001	3 Mile South Reef, Site 'D'-01-6	Modules concrete reefballs (20)	2726.551	8244.908	31	2
6/21/2001	3 Mile South Reef, Site 'D'-01-7	Modules concrete reefballs (20)	2726.589	8244.912	31	2
6/21/2001	3 Mile South Reef, Site 'D'-01-11	Modules concrete reefballs (36)	2726.624	8244.847	31	2
7/7/2000	7 Mile South Reef, Site 'C'-00-06	Concrete light poles (20)	2726.646	8249.206	41	6
7/5/2000	7 Mile South Reef, Site 'C'-00-04A	Modules concrete reefballs (25)	2726.550	8249.197	41	2
6/29/2000	7 Mile South Reef, Site 'C'-00-04	Concrete light poles (24)	2726.494	8249.126	41	10
6/23/2000	7 Mile South Reef, Site 'C'-00-03	Concrete culverts (30)	2726.593	8249.132	41	8
6/14/2000	7 Mile South Reef, Site 'C'-00-01	Bridge beams concrete (40)	2726.687	8249.265	41	10
11/19/1999	3 Mile South Reef, Site D	Concrete light poles	2726.510	8244.890	30	
6/10/1999	3 Mile South Reef, Site D	Concrete culverts (120)	2726.600	8244.880	30	10
6/8/1999	3 Mile South Reef, Site D	Concrete culverts (100)	2726.480	8244.900	30	10
6/22/1998	3 Mile South Reef, Site D	Concrete culverts	2726.490	8244.840	30	6

(continued)

Table 6—*Continued*

Deploy Date	Reef Name	Material 1	Latitude	Longitude	Depth	Relief
6/19/1998	3 Mile South Reef, Site D	Concrete culverts	2726.510	8244.810	30	6
4/3/1997	South 3 Mile Reef	Concrete pilings	2726.530	8244.860	30	
3/27/1997	South 3 Mile Reef	Concrete pilings	2726.590	8244.860	30	
3/19/1997	South 3 Mile Reef	Concrete pilings	2726.530	8244.863	30	
3/17/1997	South 3 Mile Reef	Concrete pilings	2726.610	8244.800	30	
12/31/1993	Near Shore Reef	Bridge spans	2726.981	8241.816	16	5
11/12/1992	1 Mile Reef	Concrete culverts	2729.500	8244.000	27	10
12/22/1990	3 Mile Reef South	Concrete culverts	2726.753	8244.785	30	
6/20/1989	3 Mile Reef South (D Reef)	Concrete culverts	2726.750	8244.785	25	
3/20/1987	3 Mile Reef -North (B Reef)	Fiberglass boat molds	2729.960	8247.040	30	10
12/19/1985	Misener Barge	Barge steel 100	2732.678	8250.706	25	8
12/31/1976	1 Mile Reef	Bridge material	2729.059	8244.119	21	
12/31/1976	3 Mile Reef North	Tires	2729.570	8247.000	30	
12/31/1976	7 Mile Reef South	Tires	2726.703	8249.165	40	

Table 7. Reefs of Pasco County

Deploy Date	Reef Name	Material 1	Latitude	Longitude	Depth	Relief
6/9/2008	Pasco Reef #4-Hudson, Addition 1E	Ship concrete sailboat 45'	2822.300	8257.005	27	10
5/30/2007	Pasco Reef #4-Hudson 1-F & 2-F	Concrete culverts (216) + (60)	2822.438	8256.980	27	10
5/28/2007	Pasco Reef #4- Hudson 1-E & 2-E	Concrete culverts (174) + (60)	2822.298	8256.980	27	10
6/12/2003	Pasco Reef #4-Hudson #2	Concrete culverts (264)	2822.380	8257.000	27	9
6/9/2003	Pasco Reef #4-Hudson #1	Concrete culverts (59)	2822.458	8256.999	27	9
6/9/1998	Pasco Reef #4	Concrete culverts	2822.355	8256.970	27	8
6/3/1998	Pasco Reef #4	Concrete culverts	2822.258	8256.999	27	8
4/30/1997	Pasco #2	Concrete culverts	2817.640	8301.101	36	8
4/24/1997	Pasco #2	Concrete culverts	2817.641	8301.031	36	8
4/21/1997	Pasco #2	Concrete culverts	2817.655	8301.101	36	8
4/17/1997	Pasco #2	Concrete culverts	2817.637	8301.123	39	7
4/21/1995	County Site #2	Army tanks m-60	2817.641	8301.086	39	12
4/21/1995	County Site #2	Army tanks m-60	2817.735	8301.123	39	12
4/21/1995	County Site #2	Army tanks m-60	2817.000	8301.000	39	12
4/21/1995	County Site #2	Army tanks m-60	2817.632	8301.089	39	12
4/21/1995	County Site #2	Army tanks m-60	2817.766	8301.093	39	12
4/21/1995	County Site #2	Army tanks m-60	2817.768	8301.086	39	12
4/21/1995	County Site #2	Army tanks m-60	2817.010	8301.000	39	12

(continued)

Table 7—*Continued*

Deploy Date	Reef Name	Material1	Latitude	Longitude	Depth	Relief
4/21/1995	County Site #2	Army tanks m-60	2817.637	8301.083	39	12
4/21/1995	County Site #2	Army tanks m-60	2817.709	8301.053	39	12
4/21/1995	County Site #2	Army tanks m-60	2817.641	8301.059	39	12
12/31/1994	County Site #3	Modules pvc	2811.500	8303.560	40	8
11/27/1993	Reef Site #1	Concrete pilings	2815.413	8257.019	40	
10/22/1993	Reef #2, Buoy "O"–"C"	Concrete culverts	2817.542	8301.186	40	
10/26/1990	Reef Site #1	Concrete culverts	2815.148	8257.394	30	
10/26/1990	Reef Site #2	Concrete culverts	2817.148	8257.394	30	
7/11/1990	Reef Site #2	Concrete culverts	2817.544	8301.186	40	
6/1/1989	Reef Site #2	Concrete culverts	2817.546	8301.186	40	
6/15/1988	Reef Site #2	Concrete culverts	2818.067	8301.928	30	
3/15/1987	Reef Site #2	Concrete culverts	2817.631	8301.362	30	
11/27/1985	Reef Site #2, "O"–"C"	Concrete culverts	2817.540	8301.186	40	
1/29/1982	Reef Site #1	Barge steel (3)	2815.316	8257.235	28	6
1/29/1982	County Site #2	Barge steel 195'	2817.535	8301.100	35	8
1/18/1982	County Site #1 - Buoy S	Barge steel 130'	2815.318	8257.452	25	7
10/13/1981	County Site #1 - Buoy P	Barge steel 130'	2815.070	8257.452	25	7
12/31/1980	County Site #2	Barge steel	2817.630	8301.090	40	18
12/31/1980	County Site #1	Barges steel (4)	2816.750	8257.450	25	8

Table 8. Reefs of Pinellas County

Deploy Date	Reef Name	Material 1	Latitude	Longitude	Depth	Relief
7/14/2009	Wj Shrimpboat	Vessel steel shrimp boat 45'	2741.686	8317.547	100	25
12/16/2008	Pinellas South Site #7	Concrete bridge rubble	2743.457	8258.420	45	4
11/14/2008	Pinellas South Site #7	Concrete bridge pilings (14)	2743.457	8258.418	45	2
9/14/2007	Rube Allyn Reef Site 8(2)-Load #16	Concrete culverts (18)	2755.846	8301.477	48	12
9/11/2007	Pinellas South Site 5 (13)-Load #29	Concrete poles, slabs & manholes (18)	2743.447	8258.610	48	12
9/7/2007	Rube Allyn Reef Site 8(2)-Load #15	Concrete culverts (35)	2755.838	8301.485	48	12
9/6/2007	Rube Allyn Reef Site 8(2)-Load #14	Concrete culverts (19)	2755.838	8301.490	48	11
9/4/2007	Pinellas South Site 7 (2)-Load #1	Concrete sinkers (17)	2743.457	8258.418	48	9
8/30/2007	Rube Allyn Reef Site 8(2)-Load #12	Concrete culverts (21)	2755.839	8301.472	48	10
8/28/2007	Pinellas South Site 5 (13)-Load #27	Concrete poles & slabs (18)	2743.446	8258.610	50	17
8/17/2007	Rube Allyn Reef Site 8(2)-Load #11	Concrete culverts (22)	2755.847	8301.479	48	7
8/15/2007	Pinellas South Site 5 (13)-Load #26	Concrete anchors (20)	2743.444	8258.606	50	15
8/10/2007	Rube Allyn Reef Site 8(2)-Load #8	Concrete culverts (22)	2755.831	8301.483	48	7
8/8/2007	Pinellas South Site 5 (13)-Load #24	Concrete culverts (9)	2743.436	8258.617	49	10
8/1/2007	Pinellas South Site 5 (13)-Load #23	Concrete culverts (19)	2743.444	8258.605	49	10
7/23/2007	Rube Allyn Reef Site 8(2)-Load #6	Concrete culverts (34)	2755.837	8301.499	48	7

(continued)

Table 8—Continued

Deploy Date	Reef Name	Material 1	Latitude	Longitude	Depth	Relief
7/9/2007	Rube Allyn Reef Site 8(1)-Load #4	Concrete culverts (36)	2755.834	8301.483	48	7
6/28/2007	Rube Allyn Reef Site 8(1)-Load #2	Concrete culverts (20)	2755.848	8301.746	48	7
6/27/2007	Pinellas South Site 5 (12)-Load #22	Concrete culverts (26)	2743.448	8258.586	49	10
6/26/2007	Pinellas South Site 5 (11)-Load #21	Concrete culverts (20)	2743.453	8258.593	48	7
6/25/2007	Rube Allyn Reef Site 8(1)-Load #1	Concrete culverts (13)	2755.828	8301.494	47	9
6/19/2007	Pinellas South Site 5-(11)-Load #19	Concrete junction boxes (15)	2743.456	8258.589	49	9
6/13/2007	Pinellas South Site 5-(11)-Load #17	Concrete bridge rubble (13)	2743.464	8258.594	47	6
6/12/2007	Pinellas South Site 5-(11)-Load #16	Concrete bridge rubble (30)	2743.464	8258.592	47	14
5/3/2007	Johns Pass Bridge Load #27	Concrete bridge rubble	2751.757	8301.742	43	12
4/12/2007	Pinellas South Site 5(9)-Load #10	Concrete bridge rubble (19)	2743.474	8258.607	48	9
4/10/2007	Pinellas South Site 5(9)-Load #9	Concrete rubble (58)	2743.474	8258.606	47	8
2/27/2007	Johns Pass Bridge Load #26	Concrete bridge rubble	2751.760	8301.742	43	12
11/14/2006	Johns Pass Bridge Load #22	Concrete culverts (28)	2751.794	8301.742	43	12
11/2/2006	Johns Pass Bridge 10 Loads Total	Concrete slabs and pieces	2751.774	8301.725	44	19
10/10/2006	Johns Pass Bridge Load #18	Concrete culverts (20)	2751.808	8301.725	45	20
8/16/2006	Indian Shores Reef Site #6(18)-Load 30-Fwc	Concrete culverts (20)	2751.799	8301.878	42	13
8/16/2006	Indian Shores Reef Site #6(18)-Load 29-Fwc	Concrete culverts (21)	2751.809	8301.879	42	13

5/22/2006	Indian Shores Reef Site #6(16)-Load 20-Fwc	Concrete slabs (16)	2751.785	8301.940	40	5
5/15/2006	Indian Shores Reef Site #6(15)-Load 19-Fwc	Concrete culverts (24)	2751.796	8301.897	40	4
5/9/2006	Indian Shores Reef Site #6(15)-Load 17-Fwc	Concrete culverts (29)	2751.796	8301.908	40	4
5/2/2006	Indian Shores Reef Site #6(15)-Load 16-Fwc	Concrete bridge pieces (23)	2751.808	8301.906	40	10
4/25/2006	Indian Shores Reef Bridge Site	Concrete bridge pieces (85)	2751.777	8301.743	44	10
11/7/2005	Sand Key Nourishment Reef, Imr#16	Concrete cut-offs (32)	2753.489	8251.222	17	5
10/18/2005	Indian Shores Reef Site #6(9)	Concrete culverts (18)	2751.791	8301.923	40	5
9/14/2005	Indian Shores Reef Site #6(8)	Concrete culverts (30)	2751.771	8301.915	35	4
8/23/2005	Sand Key Nourishment Reef, Imr#15	Concrete bridge materials	2757.330	8250.245	16	8
8/22/2005	Indian Shores Reef Site #6(8)	Concrete culverts (36)	2751.800	8301.904	40	4
3/14/2005	Indian Shores Reef Site #6(3)	Concrete culverts (24)	2751.798	8301.899	35	5
3/11/2005	Indian Shores Reef Site #6(2)	Concrete culverts (30)	2751.797	8301.901	35	5
3/5/2005	Tarpon Key Oyster Reef #1	Fossilized locally mined shell bags (535)	2740.065	8241.396	1	2
2/24/2005	Indian Shores Reef Site #6(2)	Concrete culverts (26)	2751.803	8301.900	35	5
2/18/2005	Tarpon Key Oyster Reef #1	Fossilized locally mined shell bags (980)	2739.941	8241.710	1	2

(continued)

Table 8—*Continued*

Deploy Date	Reef Name	Material 1	Latitude	Longitude	Depth	Relief
2/17/2005	Indian Shores Reef	Concrete culverts (21)	2751.796	8301.921	35	5
2/15/2005	Indian Shores Reef	Concrete culverts (29)	2751.793	8301.911	35	5
2/10/2005	Sand Key Nourishment Reef, Imr#1–10	Concrete culverts (31)	2753.405	8251.239	16	4
2/9/2005	Sand Key Nourishment Reef, Imr#1–9	Concrete culverts (30)	2753.413	8251.230	16	4
2/7/2005	Sand Key Nourishment Reef, Imr#1–7	Concrete culverts (34)	2753.404	8251.244	16	5
2/3/2005	Indian Shores Reef	Concrete culverts (25)	2751.810	8301.912	35	5
2/2/2005	Sand Key Nourishment Reef, Imr#1–6	Concrete culverts (33)	2753.423	8251.240	16	3
1/28/2005	Little Bird Key Oyster Reef #1	Fossilized locally mined shell bags (350)	2741.134	8243.022	1	2
1/27/2005	Indian Shores Reef	Concrete culverts (24)	2751.807	8301.901	35	5
1/12/2005	Sand Key Nourishment Reef, Imr#1–4	Concrete culverts (22)	2753.418	8251.246	16	4
1/5/2005	Sand Key Nourishment Reef, Imr#1–2	Concrete culverts (25)	2753.427	8251.249	16	4
1/4/2005	Sand Key Nourishment Reef, Imr#1–1	Concrete culverts (35)	2753.419	8251.254	16	4
12/8/2004	Shrimp Boat Reef	Ship steel shrimpboat 80'	2741.751	8317.557	97	39
11/30/2004	Veterans Reef	Barge steel 60'	2802.969	8300.843	40	14
11/8/2004	Sand Key Nourishment Reef, Imr#1	Concrete culverts (65)	2753.415	8251.241	15	5
11/2/2004	Pinellas South Reef, Site-5	Concrete culverts (35)	2743.490	8258.586	47	11

Date	Site	Material				
10/29/2004	Sand Key Nourishment Reef, Imr#1	Concrete culverts (12)	2753.417	8251.225	15	5
10/26/2004	Pinellas South Reef, Site-5	Concrete culverts (9)	2743.493	8258.583	48	9
10/21/2004	Sand Key Nourishment Reef, Imr#1	Concrete culverts (13)	2753.413	8251.233	18	5
9/1/2004	Pinellas South Reef	Concrete culverts (30)	2743.492	8258.604	46	20
8/30/2004	Sand Key Nourishment Reef, Imr#1	Concrete culverts (40)	2753.403	8251.242	18	4
8/26/2004	Pinellas South Reef	Concrete culverts (41)	2743.490	8258.605	46	20
8/25/2004	Sand Key Nourishment Reef, Imr#1	Concrete power poles (105)	2753.420	8251.239	20	4
6/17/2004	Pinellas South Reef	Barge steel 110'	2743.388	8258.622	50	10
6/17/2004	Pinellas South Reef	Barge steel 75'	2743.335	8258.485	50	9
6/14/2004	Sand Key Nourishment Reef, #2	Concrete boxes (4)	2753.418	8251.239	18	5
6/10/2004	Veterans Reef	Concrete culverts (29)	2802.914	8300.826	45	6
6/3/2004	Veterans Reef	Concrete culverts (28)	2802.945	8300.821	45	8
5/30/2004	Sand Key Nourishment Reef, #2	Concrete culverts (34)	2753.467	8251.223	14	5
5/5/2004	Veterans Reef	Concrete boxes (17)	2802.930	8300.847	44	6
4/29/2004	Sand Key Nourishment Reef, #2	Concrete culverts (18)	2753.489	8251.221	15	5
4/19/2004	Veterans Reef	Concrete pilings (32)	2802.914	8300.810	44	6
4/8/2004	Veterans Reef	Concrete culverts (29)	2802.916	8300.802	44	9
3/17/2004	Sand Key Nourishment Reef, #2	Concrete culverts (50)	2753.458	8251.225	15	5

(continued)

Table 8—*Continued*

Deploy Date	Reef Name	Material 1	Latitude	Longitude	Depth	Relief
3/1/2004	Sand Key Nourishment Reef, #2	Concrete culverts (42)	2753.477	8251.222	15	6
2/11/2004	Veterans Reef	Concrete pilings (16)	2802.924	8300.805	43	7
10/14/2003	Veterans Reef	Concrete cutoffs (41)	2802.927	8300.814	44	6
10/8/2003	Sand Key Nourishment Reef, #3	Concrete culverts (28)	2753.507	8251.212	17	5
9/22/2003	Veterans Reef	Concrete cutoffs (18)	2802.932	8300.820	44	5
9/17/2003	Sand Key Nourishment Reef, #3	Concrete cutoffs (34)	2753.500	8251.232	16	4
9/15/2003	Veterans Reef	Concrete cutoffs (31)	2802.934	8300.826	44	4
9/10/2003	Veterans Reef	Concrete manholes (27)	2802.918	8300.821	44	5
9/9/2003	Veterans Reef	Concrete culverts (28)	2802.928	8300.825	44	6
9/2/2003	Sand Key Nourishment Reef, #3	Concrete culverts (30)	2753.514	8251.224	16	4
8/26/2003	Sand Key Nourishment Reef, #3	Concrete culverts (26)	2753.525	8251.225	18	4
8/13/2003	Sand Key Nourishment Reef, #3	Concrete culverts (30)	2753.518	8251.222	16	6
8/11/2003	Sand Key Nourishment Reef, #3	Concrete culverts (29)	2753.526	8251.208	18	5
7/21/2003	Indian Shores Reef	Concrete culverts (64)	2751.690	8301.859	40	15
5/27/2003	Indian Shores Reef	Concrete culverts (33)	2751.689	8301.866	40	15
5/22/2003	Sand Key Nourishment Reef, #5	Concrete culverts (22)	2753.515	8251.201	16	5
4/24/2003	Indian Shores Reef	Concrete culverts (15)	2751.695	8301.881	39	10

Date	Location	Material				
4/21/2003	Rube Allyn Reef	Concrete culverts (9)	2755.924	8301.416	43	12
4/16/2003	Indian Shores Reef	Concrete culverts (17)	2751.693	8301.874	41	10
4/8/2003	Pinellas South Reef	Ship steel tugboat 80'	2743.375	8258.450	45	20
4/2/2003	Pinellas South Reef	Concrete sinkers (16)	2743.375	8258.452	42	5
3/25/2003	Pinellas South Reef	Concrete junction boxes (8)	2743.375	8258.449	41	6
3/19/2003	Indian Shores Reef	Concrete culverts (24)	2751.696	8301.860	40	10
3/10/2003	Indian Shores Reef	Concrete culverts (22)	2751.681	8301.869	40	8
8/1/2002	Sand Key Nourishment Reef, #5	Concrete culverts (19)	2753.686	8251.198	17	6
7/29/2002	Indian Shores Reef	Concrete culverts (21)	2751.703	8301.859	40	17
7/24/2002	Indian Shores Reef	Concrete culverts (17)	2751.701	8301.856	41	12
7/23/2002	Sand Key Nourishment Reef, #5	Concrete culverts (25)	2753.678	8251.186	20	6
7/18/2002	Indian Shores Reef	Concrete culverts (27)	2751.882	8301.871	38	15
7/11/2002	Sand Key Nourishment Reef, #5	Concrete culverts (24)	2753.695	8251.184	20	5
7/10/2002	Sand Key Nourishment Reef, #5	Steel boxes (15)	2753.697	8251.193	20	4
7/8/2002	Indian Shores Reef	Concrete culverts (16)	2751.703	8301.871	40	10
7/1/2002	Sand Key Nourishment Reef, #5	Concrete culverts (26)	2753.695	8251.179	20	6
6/20/2002	Pinellas South Reef, Site1	Concrete culverts (24)	2743.379	8258.524	47	12
6/13/2002	Sand Key Nourishment Reef, #5	Concrete culverts (34)	2753.695	8251.203	20	6
6/12/2002	Pinellas South Reef, Site1	Concrete culverts (26)	2743.389	8258.555	50	15

(continued)

Table 8—*Continued*

Deploy Date	Reef Name	Material 1	Latitude	Longitude	Depth	Relief
6/11/2002	Sand Key Nourishment Reef, #5	Concrete culverts (34)	2753.696	8251.202	19	6
6/4/2002	Rube Allyn Reef	Concrete culverts (27)	2755.926	8301.429	45	13
4/4/2002	Rube Allyn Reef	Concrete culverts (25)	2755.924	8301.422	47	6
4/1/2002	Rube Allyn Reef	Concrete culverts (21)	2755.943	8301.428	46	
3/28/2002	Rube Allyn Reef	Concrete culverts (26)	2755.943	8301.427	46	10
3/21/2002	Pinellas South Reef, Site1	Concrete culverts (36)	2743.373	8258.547	48	9
3/19/2002	Rube Allyn Reef	Concrete cutoffs	2755.940	8301.409	48	5
12/17/2001	Sand Key Nourishment Reef, #5	Concrete culverts (24)	2753.694	8251.177	17	5
12/13/2001	Pinellas South Reef, Site1	Concrete culverts (39)	2743.380	8258.537	48	16
12/11/2001	Sand Key Nourishment Reef, #5	Concrete culverts (28)	2753.692	8251.174	17	6
12/5/2001	Pinellas South Reef, Site1	Concrete culverts (17)	2743.371	8258.545	47	16
11/30/2001	Sand Key Nourishment Reef, #5	Concrete culverts (12)	2753.709	8251.180	20	4
11/29/2001	Sand Key Nourishment Reef, #5	Concrete culverts (12)	2753.705	8251.174	20	6
11/28/2001	Pinellas South Reef, Site1	Concrete culverts (22)	2743.382	8258.537	48	16
11/21/2001	Sand Key Nourishment Reef, #5	Concrete culverts (21)	2753.696	8251.191	18	5
11/20/2001	Pinellas South Reef, Site1	Concrete culverts (24)	2743.378	8258.543	47	13
11/19/2001	Pinellas South Reef, Site1	Concrete culverts (26)	2743.368	8258.545	47	13
11/7/2001	Pinellas South Reef, Site1	Concrete culverts (23)	2743.374	8258.538	47	13

Date	Location	Material			
11/1/2001	Sand Key Nourishment Reef, #5	Concrete culverts (37)	2753.705	8251.186	20	5
10/8/2001	Sand Key Nourishment Reef, Ne	Concrete culverts (25)	2753.701	8251.180	18	6
10/4/2001	Pinellas South Reef, Site1	Concrete culverts (23)	2743.376	8258.535	48	10
9/26/2001	Sand Key Nourishment Reef, 1Mr6	Concrete culverts (24)	2753.800	8251.181	18	5
1/29/2001	Veterans Reef	Steel containers	2802.664	8300.739	44	8
9/21/2000	Veterans Reef	Concrete culvert	2803.028	8300.744	44	12
9/11/2000	Veterans Reef	Concrete culvert	2803.025	8300.733	44	5
7/2/2000	Veterans Reef	Barge	2802.848	8300.713	44	
1/27/2000	North County Reef (Center)	Concrete culverts (9)	2800.023	8300.774	47	8
1/17/2000	Veterans Reef	Steel containers	2802.636	8300.754	44	
1/10/2000	North County Reef (Ne)-A	Concrete slabs (27)	2803.580	8300.607	48	15
12/22/1999	North County Reef (Ne)-A	Concrete culverts (29)	2803.494	8300.606	47	10
12/21/1999	North County Reef (Ne)-A	Concrete slabs (24)	2803.506	8300.600	48	17
12/20/1999	North County Reef (Ne)-A	Concrete slabs (23)	2803.505	8300.606	47	17
12/10/1999	North County Reef (Ne)-A	Concrete culverts (20)	2803.491	8300.617	48	16
12/6/1999	North County Reef (Ne)-A	Concrete culverts (21)	2803.505	8300.591	48	12
12/3/1999	North County Reef (Ne)-A	Concrete culverts (19)	2803.465	8300.479	49	11
11/30/1999	North County Reef (Ne)-A	Concrete culverts (18)	2803.490	8300.618	47	8
11/29/1999	North County Reef (Ne)-A	Concrete culverts (27)	2803.485	8300.606	46	5

(continued)

Table 8—*Continued*

Deploy Date	Reef Name	Material 1	Latitude	Longitude	Depth	Relief
11/24/1999	North County Reef (Ne)-A	Concrete culverts (19)	2803.497	8300.617	48	5
9/3/1999	North County Reef (South)	Rock limestone	2802.938	8300.757	45	
9/1/1999	North County Reef (Ne)-A	Modules concrete tetrahedrons	2803.013	8300.714	45	18
8/31/1999	North County Reef (Center)	Barge steel 150'	2802.976	8300.732	42	10
8/17/1999	North County Reef (Nw)	Concrete polygonals (100)	2803.013	8300.759	42	6
8/4/1999	Veterans Reef (Center)	Barge steel	2802.980	8300.741	42	7
8/2/1999	North County Reef (Center)	Barge steel 120'	2802.980	8300.753	45	7
7/30/1999	Clearwater C Site	Concrete culverts	2800.854	8253.588	30	14
7/23/1999	Rube Allyn North	Concrete culverts	2756.133	8301.333	48	14
7/7/1999	Clearwater C Site	Concrete culverts	2800.858	8253.569	30	12
7/6/1999	North County Reef (Nw-Corner)	Concrete junction box anchor	2803.497	8300.875	44	4
7/6/1999	North County Reef (Ne-Corner)	Concrete junction box anchor	2803.500	8300.625	44	4
7/6/1999	North County Reef (Se-Corner)	Concrete junction box anchor	2802.499	8300.621	44	4
6/29/1999	Clearwater C Site	Concrete culverts	2800.859	8253.569	33	13

Table 9. Reefs of Sarasota County

Deploy Date	Reef Name	Material 1	Latitude	Longitude	Depth	Relief
4/2/2010	I-1, Lynn Silvertooth, #25	Modules concrete reefballs (17)	2717.160	8235.961	30	5
10/5/2009	I-1, Lynn Silvertooth, #34	Concrete anchors (12)	2717.115	8235.870	30	4
7/13/2009	I-1, Lynn Silvertooth, #25–3	Modules concrete reefballs (11)	2717.163	8235.944	30	4
2/23/2009	I-1, Lynn Silvertooth, #25–2	Modules concrete reefballs (11)	2717.156	8235.966	30	4
8/28/2008	W2 Kyle Jackson Trail, Landingcraft	Modules concrete reefballs (17)	2712.538	8248.109	58	4
8/28/2008	W2 Kyle Jackson Trail, Tanks #4 & #5	Modules concrete reefballs (17)	2712.675	8248.218	58	4
8/28/2008	W2 Kyle Jackson Trail, Tanks #2 & #3	Modules concrete reefballs (17)	2712.639	8248.187	58	4
8/18/2008	I-1, Lynn Silvertooth, #12	Rock rubble	2717.221	8235.918	30	3
6/18/2008	I-1, Lynn Silvertooth, Site #34	Concrete blocks and sinkers (18)	2717.115	8235.868	30	5
2/28/2008	I-1, Lynn Silvertooth, Er1–08	Modules concrete reefballs (16)	2717.126	8235.983	30	5
7/4/2007	I-1, Lynn Silvertooth, Nep1–07	Modules concrete reefballs (135)	2717.254	8235.920	30	5
6/5/2006	I-1, Lynn Silvertooth, 38–06	Modules concrete reefballs (50)	2717.089	8235.992	25	5
6/5/2006	I-1, Lynn Silvertooth, 31–06	Modules concrete reefballs (50)	2717.122	8235.992	25	5
6/5/2006	I-1, Lynn Silvertooth, 30–06	Modules concrete reefballs (50)	2717.122	8236.029	25	5
2/28/2006	I-1, Lynn Silvertooth, Mji-06	Concrete rubble	2717.254	8235.884	30	7
2/27/2006	I-1, Lynn Silvertooth, Eri-06	Modules concrete reefballs (10)	2717.157	8235.955	30	5

(continued)

Table 9—*Continued*

Deploy Date	Reef Name	Material 1	Latitude	Longitude	Depth	Relief
9/13/2005	I-1, Lynn Silvertooth,	Concrete deck slabs (22)	2717.199	8235.853	30	5
6/17/2005	I-1, Lynn Silvertooth, Reefball Site#9	Modules concrete reefballs (54)	2717.223	8236.029	30	3
6/17/2005	I-1, Lynn Silvertooth, Reefball Site#2	Modules concrete reefballs (54)	2717.254	8236.030	30	3
6/17/2005	I-1, Lynn Silvertooth, Reefball Site#1	Modules concrete reefballs (54)	2717.254	8236.069	30	3
5/4/2005	I-1, Lynn Silvertooth, Site #28	Concrete rubble	2717.155	8235.844	30	10
9/29/2004	I-1, Lynn Silvertooth, Site #27	Concrete pilings (63)	2717.155	8235.890	30	10
6/2/2004	I-1, Lynn Silvertooth, Site #39	Concrete pilings (40)	2717.155	8235.881	30	10
3/29/2004	I-1, Lynn Silvertooth Reefballs	Modules concrete reefballs (18)	2717.155	8235.953	30	5
11/4/2003	I-1, Lynn Silvertooth, Site #17	Bridge decking with rails (7)	2717.188	8235.992	30	10
11/1/2003	I-1, Lynn Silvertooth, Site #16	Bridge pilings (34)	2717.188	8236.029	30	10
10/31/2003	I-1, Lynn Silvertooth, Site #39	Bridge rubble	2717.089	8255.954	30	5
10/29/2003	I-1, Lynn Silvertooth, Site #13	Bridge pilings (26)	2717.221	8235.881	30	10
10/24/2003	I-1, Lynn Silvertooth, Site #10	Bridge pilings (40)	2717.221	8235.992	30	15
10/20/2003	I-1, Lynn Silvertooth, Site #8	Bridge decking with rails (5)	2717.221	8236.066	30	15
10/18/2003	I-1, Lynn Silvertooth, Site #7	Bridge decking with rails (4)	2717.254	8235.845	30	15
10/18/2003	I-1, Lynn Silvertooth, Site #6	Bridge pilings (20)	2717.254	8235.882	30	15
10/16/2003	I-1, Lynn Silvertooth, Site #4	Bridge pilings (24)	2717.254	8235.956	30	15
10/13/2003	I-1, Lynn Silvertooth, Site #3	Bridge decking with rails (5)	2717.254	8235.992	30	10

Date	Site	Material				
9/23/2003	I-1, Lynn Silvertooth	Bridge rubble-stressing blocks (120)	2717.151	8235.955	30	5
8/13/2002	Walker Reef (Bay)	Modules concrete reefballs (235)	2722.504	8235.691	12	4
7/3/2001	Walker Reef -Nep Site (Bay)	Modules concrete reefballs (154)	2722.894	8235.876	12	2
6/19/2001	Walker Reef-Center Site (Bay)	Modules concrete reefballs (230)	2722.671	8235.717	12	2
4/6/2000	Mote Reef (Bay)	Pvc modules (3)	2720.420	8233.273	15	4
2/2/2000	Mote Reef (Bay)	Pvc modules (2)	2720.418	8233.328	14	3
11/13/1999	Mote Reef (Bay)	Modules concrete reefballs (40)	2720.409	8233.316	15	5
10/10/1999	Walker Reef (Bay)	Modules concrete reefballs (140)	2722.994	8235.938	11	2
10/10/1999	Walker Reef (Bay)	Modules concrete reefballs (35)	2722.291	8235.500	12	3
10/10/1999	Walker Reef (Bay)	Modules concrete reefballs (35)	2722.678	8236.013	12	3
7/30/1999	Gerkin (Bay)	Modules concrete reefballs (9)	2720.429	8233.288	12	3
9/29/1998	Saprito Pier (Bay)	Modules concrete reefballs (150)	2720.030	8233.372	10	2
6/25/1998	Sportfish Anglers Reef (Bay)	Modules concrete reefballs (150)	2721.080	8235.883	13	2
6/24/1998	M-4 Site	Modules concrete reefballs (106)	2715.160	8243.190	43	3
9/29/1997	Channel Marker Reefs (Bay)	Modules concrete reefballs (7)	2719.909	8234.356	10	2
9/26/1997	Jantzen #5 (Bay)	Modules concrete reefballs (70)	2719.709	8233.849	10	2
9/24/1997	Hart Family Reef #2 (Bay)	Modules concrete reefballs (75)	2722.075	8234.477	12	2
6/28/1997	M-13 Site	Concrete culverts	2655.099	8227.882	42	4
6/26/1997	M-13 Site	Concrete culverts	2655.134	8227.900	42	2

(continued)

Table 9—*Continued*

Deploy Date	Reef Name	Material 1	Latitude	Longitude	Depth	Relief
6/26/1997	M-13 Site	Concrete culverts	2655.121	8227.898	42	2
11/21/1996	Lido Channel Markers (Bay)	Modules concrete reefballs	2719.793	8234.431	6	3
11/30/1995	Sarasota Sportsman Reef, M-17	Modules concrete reefballs (60)	2702.470	8238.810	60	4
11/28/1995	Sarasota Sportsman Reef, M-17	Modules concrete reefballs (60)	2702.674	8238.791	60	4
6/21/1995	Johnson Reef, M-7 Site	Concrete culverts	2716.283	8248.043	50	
4/26/1995	Miller (#3) (Bay)	Concrete blocks	2720.195	8234.550	21	3
4/22/1995	Fallen Heroes Reef, Tank#3, Reefex #6	Army tank m-60	2712.654	8248.166	63	12
4/22/1995	Fallen Heroes Reef, Tank #2, Reefex #7	Army tank m-60	2712.626	8248.204	63	12
4/22/1995	M-9 Site, Reefex #1	Army tank m-60	2704.354	8242.033	63	12
4/22/1995	M-9 Site, Reefex #3	Army tank m-60	2704.354	8242.036	63	12
4/22/1995	M-9 Site, Reefex #2	Army tank m-60	2704.338	8241.980	65	12
12/16/1994	M-5	Concrete culverts	2713.422	8243.131	40	8
5/27/1993	Gary Service Reef, M-1	Concrete culverts	2719.172	8243.164	42	5
4/8/1993	Hart Family Reef (#2) (Bay)	Concrete blocks	2722.015	8234.574	10	
4/7/1993	Powers (#7) (Bay)	Concrete blocks	2718.869	8234.292	13	2
2/27/1992	Hart Family Reef (#2) (Bay)	Concrete blocks	2722.017	8234.574	10	
1/31/1992	Jantzen (#5) (Bay)	Concrete blocks	2719.785	8233.829	10	2
11/14/1991	M-4	Concrete rubble	2715.170	8243.162	42	5

Date	Name	Material				
10/1/1991	M-15	Concrete culverts	2705.001	8232.524	42	5
7/12/1991	M-9	Concrete rubble	2704.176	8242.101	63	7
3/27/1991	Jantzen (#5) (Bay)	Concrete blocks	2719.586	8233.934	10	2
3/12/1991	Evans (#6) (Bay)	Concrete blocks	2719.710	8233.464	10	
3/7/1991	Hart Family Reef (#2) (Bay)	Concrete blocks	2722.013	8234.574	10	4
8/6/1990	Tom Wallin Reef M-2	Concrete culverts	2718.745	8243.001	41	4
2/8/1990	D-6	Boat molds steel	2706.190	8303.192	110	5
7/6/1989	M-6	Concrete culverts	2711.301	8243.595	52	
5/22/1989	Jantzen (#5) (Bay)	Concrete blocks	2719.584	8233.934	14	2
5/12/1989	Hart Family Reef (#2) (Bay)	Concrete blocks	2722.113	8234.498	10	14
5/11/1988	D-3	Boxcars steel	2715.931	8307.207	105	15
5/11/1988	D-4	Boxcars steel	2715.440	8307.136	105	12
5/11/1988	Bob Johnson	Boxcars steel	2716.134	8248.125	65	5
5/11/1988	Fallen Heroes Reef, M-8	Boxcars steel	2712.506	8248.104	63	8
6/30/1987	Gary Service Reef, M-1	Barge steel	2719.176	8243.209	40	2
6/25/1987	Coker (#8) (Bay)	Concrete blocks	2718.698	8232.537	9	2
6/25/1987	Hart Family Reef (#2) (Bay)	Concrete blocks	2722.015	8234.576	10	
12/10/1985	Fallen Heroes Reef, M-8	Ship steel landing	2712.570	8248.110	63	10
7/28/1981	Venice Reef Site, I-4	Concrete culverts	2704.587	8227.509	28	3

(continued)

Table 9—*Continued*

Deploy Date	Reef Name	Material1	Latitude	Longitude	Depth	Relief
6/23/1981	I-1, Lynn Silvertooth	Concrete rubble	2717.017	8236.000	30	2
6/21/1981	Donald Roeher-Lido Key Reef	Concrete rubble	2718.203	8235.516	23	3
6/21/1981	Donald Roeher-Lido Key Reef	Concrete rubble	2718.218	8235.544	23	3
10/27/1980	Venice Reef Site	Concrete rubble	2706.296	8228.910	28	5
9/16/1980	Alan Fisher, I-2	Concrete rubble	2718.111	8237.125	31	2
8/15/1980	Venice Reef Site	Concrete rubble	2706.042	8227.999	28	3
5/12/1980	I-1, Lynn Silvertooth	Concrete blocks	2717.182	8235.897	30	2
	Md-1	Barge steel	2709.691	8253.062	78	7
	M-10	Barge steel	2701.887	8242.583	70	9
	D-9	Barge steel	2654.719	8255.893	105	10
	Md-1	Barge steel hopper	2709.436	8253.207	78	10
	Johnson Reef, M-7 Site	Boxcars steel (10)	2716.281	8248.043	50	6
	M-3	Concrete culverts	2716.713	8243.247	43	4
	M-3	Concrete culverts	2716.717	8243.261	43	4
	M-14	Concrete culverts	2652.236	8226.441	43	5

On-the-Water Etiquette

What does etiquette have to do with a successful fishing trip? I'm not talking about your mom making you remove your fishing cap at the dinner table, but about good-sense, on-the-water fishing manners. Knowing the rules of the road, understanding proper radio procedures, and using common courtesies may not put more fish in the boat, but it will certainly make the trip safer and more stress-free for you and for others.

Rules of the Road

Many boat captains licensed by the U.S. Coast Guard (USCG) will agree that the most difficult questions on the Captain's Examination deal with *Rules of the Road*. Not unlike highway rules, these boating rules are complicated but can be distilled to a few basic components.

First, motor on the right side of *any* channel or navigable waterway, and always pass oncoming traffic with them on your port (left) side, just as in your car. You may pass a boat ahead of you on either side, provided there is ample channel width to do it safely without impeding the other boat's travel. Remember, too, in channels marked "Intracoastal Waterway" in western Florida, red channel markers will be on your starboard (right) side when you're traveling north. Also, in most cases, red markers will be on your starboard side when you're coming toward port, or shore—*Red, Right, Returning*. It's also important to pay attention to local signs and informational markers pointing out shoals, manatee zones, no-motor, and idle-speed zones. When the sign says "Slow Down" or "Be Careful," obey it.

Second, always assume that any boat approaching you is under the command of an operator who neither knows the rules nor has read the previous paragraph. Be cautious, slow down if necessary, make your intentions clear, and then proceed. When it comes down to the bottom line, only you are responsible for the safety of your passengers and your vessel. If you have time, I recommend you take a look at either *Chapman's Piloting, Seamanship & Small Boat Handling* (ISBN 0-688-14892-1) or *Boater's Bowditch* (ISBN 0-071-36136-7), both excellent references. Florida also requires residents born after September 30, 1980, to take a boater education course before operating a vessel powered by a motor of 10 horsepower or more. The Florida Fish and Wildlife Conservation Commission (FWC) publishes *How to Boat Smart*, a book containing the course information and test materials. Whether you need to take the course or not, I highly recommend you read the book. It's available at many marinas and tackle shops, or by calling the FWC's Boater Safety Section at (850) 488-5600.

Communications Etiquette

Depending on your style of fishing and the size of your boat, you should have at least one marine-band VHF radio aboard. It should also be turned on, monitoring at least channel 16, while you're under way. Many marinas monitor other channels (channel 9, for example), and local boaters sometime monitor specific channels (68 or 73 are good ones) for boat-to-boat communications. Channel 16 is for hailing only. Once you contact your party, switch to another channel to complete the conversation. Channel 22A is the USCG's private channel—use it only in case of an emergency and only if they instruct you to do so. Always hail the USCG on Channel 16.

Handheld VHF radios are fine for close-to-shore use or for emergency backups to larger permanently mounted units, but their transmitting power is limited. VHF radios are more public, in that everyone on the channel you're working is listening, but that can be good in times of peril. And don't encourage children (or childlike adults) to play with VHF radios while aboard your boat. There are serious safety considerations that require the channels be kept free of idle chatter.

Finally, cell phones are good, but coverage can be limited in some offshore areas of the Gulf and nonexistent in some areas in the Ten Thousand Islands. They're also no use in areas where you don't have local phone numbers aboard the boat.

Boat-Ramp Etiquette

Just the thought of a busy Saturday at a boat ramp is enough to raise any boater's blood pressure. A little bit of planning can go a long way toward making the experience of launching your boat a smooth seamless operation.

First, stop a good distance from the ramp and remove your tie-downs, put in your drain plug, prime your engine, turn on your batteries, unhook your trailer-light connections, and load the cooler and tackle. Then, attach enough line to your boat's front cleat so your boat will be under control of your assistant standing alongside the launch ramp or on the dock. Or, if you're launching solo, tie the line to the winch post of your trailer.

Then, slowly and without becoming flustered, wait your turn and back down the ramp. It's okay to stop part of the way down the ramp to remove your safety chain and winch snap. *Don't* try backing on a busy weekend day if you've never done it before. Bring a friend who knows how to back a trailer, or even better, practice backing at home during the week.

Third, get the boat into the water and float it away from the ramp so that the next person in line can quickly launch. If you're powering the boat off the trailer, be sure to let whoever is driving the trailer know exactly where to park your rig.

Finally, on your return, keep your boat as far from the ramp as possible to unload your crew. Your gear can wait to be unloaded into the car until the boat is up on the trailer. Get your trailer and get in line. Be sure to attach your safety chain and winch strap before coming up the incline. Then, pull to a not-so-busy area to finish readying the boat for travel.

No Wake and Idle Zones

"No Wake" means no wake and "Idle Speed" means idle speed. They're plain and simple.

Both are slow-speed zones with the interest of docks, moored boats, and sea life in mind. There are usually good reasons these zones exist along Florida's Gulf Coast, and most are strictly enforced.

Keeping your wake to a minimum generally means running slow enough to keep your bow down and your wake flat behind your boat. Idle speed usually means running at 1,000 rpm or less, or at the speed your motor typically runs when out of gear. Idle speed is sometimes much slower than no wake. Pay close attention to regulatory signage, as many of these zones apply to areas outside of marked channels only.

Fishing Etiquette

This is a fishing book, and it would be unfair not to mention a couple of pet peeves passed along to me by several experienced Gulf anglers. All involve good common sense, good manners, and the Golden Rule.

Never, never motor over to another boat that's fishing an area and ask, "How's the fishin'?" This is the ultimate sin. In certain areas, the unwritten rule is that if you can tell the color of the angler's shirt, you're too close. Also, don't run close to a boat that's on an obvious drift. You can easily tell which way a person is fishing by paying attention to the wind, tide phase, or just the direction he or she is casting. One thousand feet or one-quarter mile is a reasonable distance on the flats, and as much as a mile between offshore boats is common.

On the same subject, don't creep toward another boat that's fishing a particular spot—even if it's your favorite spot. It's first-come, first-served on the water. You'll just have to wait for the other boat to leave—or come back another time. Don't even think about fishing *next* to it.

The same general concept applies to trolling. Experienced trollers understand that trolling involves making overlapping courses and wide turns. If another boat is trolling, be aware that it might be working an area as big as a square mile and needs several hundred yards to make a turn. The exception to this rule might be trolling for Spanish mackerel nearshore or within bays, where boats tend to troll on parallel courses close together. Still, you should never crowd another boat, particularly when trolling.

Fishing near and around residential docks is popular all over the more-populated areas of the state. Docks with boats generally have deeper water than residential docks, and sunlit pilings hold heat—both good bait and fish attractors. In addition, electric lights on docks make them great spots for night fishing. If you plan to fish residential docks, take time to practice your casting so you can accurately cast your lure under a dock. There's nothing that riles a homeowner more than hearing a heavy lure slap the side of his or her boat, safely hung on the dock from davits. And if the homeowner asks you to leave, be courteous, and move on down the shoreline.

Finally, certain areas along the Gulf Coast are home to commercial fishermen, trying their best to eke a living from oyster beds and crab traps. Take care not to run through lease areas or over active oyster beds. And *never* pull a crab trap just to see what's inside—it's illegal to interfere with traps—and besides: crabs pinch.

ACKNOWLEDGMENTS

While I'd love to take credit for every bit of information in this guide, I just can't. I have the good fortune of knowing a group of fishing guides and serious fishermen who were more than willing to give their opinions on various subjects.

I thank them all:

John K. and Townsend Tarapani, Tarpon Springs
Capt. Mark Gore, Tampa
Capt. Rick Grassett, Sarasota
Rusty Chinnis, Sarasota
Capt. Geoffrey Paige, Sarasota
Capt. Ralph Allen, King Fisher Fleet, Punta Gorda
Byron Stout, Fort Myers
Capt. Rob Modys, Fort Myers and Estero
Capt. Mark Ward, Naples
Capt. Bill Baldus, Port of the Islands
Capt. Jack Lloyd, Port of the Islands
Capt. Charles Wright, Chokoloskee

Also, for their help with logistics, I'd like to thank the following:

Tammy Heon, Hernando County Convention and Visitors Bureau
Bill AuCoin, St. Petersburg
The Bungalows Island Retreat, Treasure Island
Jennifer Huber, Charlotte Harbor Visitor's Bureau
Best Western Waterfront Hotel, Punta Gorda
Banana Bay Waterfront Motel, Charlotte Harbor
Nancy Hamilton, Lee County Visitors and Convention Bureau
Rob Wells, The Tarpon Lodge, Pineland
JoNell Modys, Naples, Marco Island, Everglades CVB
The Lemon Tree Inn, Naples
Port of the Islands Resort, Ten Thousand Islands

RECOMMENDED READING

Sport Fish of the Gulf of Mexico, Vic Dunaway, ISBN 0-936240-18-0, www.floridasportsman.com.

Sportsman's Best Book and DVD Series, Snapper & Grouper, ISBN 0-936240-31-8, www.floridasportsman.com.

The Cobia Bible, Joe Richard, ISBN 0-9649317-2-9, available from the author at rich2735@bellsouth.net.

Maptech Chartkit, Region 8 (Florida West Coast and the Keys), Maptech Chart Navigator Software, www.maptech.com.

DeLorme Florida Atlas and Gazetteer, www.delorme.com.

Waterproof Charts, www.waterproofcharts.com.

Florida Sportsman Fishing Charts, www.floridasportsman.com.

Florida Boating and Angling Guides, Florida Fish and Wildlife Conservation Commission (FWC), Florida Marine Research Institute. Available at tackle shops and visitors' bureaus.

How to Boat Smart, Florida Boating Safety Course, FWC, www.myfwc.com, (850) 488-5600.

The Florida Boater's Guide, A Handbook of Boating Laws and Responsibilities, FWC, www.myfwc.com, (850) 488-5600.

Federal Requirements & Safety Tips for Recreational Boats. Available at tackle shops and marine dealers, or from the U.S. Coast Guard at uscgboating.org.

Back to the Basics, DVD Series, Omega Media Group, www.nutsandboltsfishing.com.

Redfish on the Fly, A Comprehensive Guide, Capt. John Kumiski, www.spottedtail.com.

Catching Made Easy, Capt. Rodney Smith, www.catchingmadeeasy.com.

Chapman Piloting: Seamanship & Small Boat Handling, Hearst Marine Books, ISBN 0-688-14892-1.

Boater's Bowditch, The Small-Craft American Practical Navigator, Richard K. Hubbard, International Marine/McGraw-Hill, ISBN 0-07-136136-7.

Practical Fishing Knots II, Mark Sosin and Lefty Kreh, The Lyons Press, ISBN 1-55821-102-0. This is a well-illustrated, complete guide to many popular fishing knots.

Know Your Knots, Pure Fishing, Inc. A pocket-size guide to popular knots. Reproduced in this book with the permission of Pure Fishing/Berkley.

Knots to Know, Innovative Textiles/PowerPro. Included with every PowerPro line purchase. Knots shown work well with braided fiber lines.

Animated Knots by Grog, Grog LLC, www.animatedknots.com. Helpful website featuring animated instructions for tying fishing and boating knots.

South Australia's Ultimate Fishing Resource Guide, www.fishsa.com/kntesbi.php.

Hatteras Outfitters, www.hatterasoutfitters.com/bimini.htm. Illustrated and animated instructions for tying a Bimini twist.

INDEX

Tommy L. Thompson is a licensed USCG charter boat captain and fishing guide on Florida's Gulf Coast and executive director of the Florida Outdoor Writers Association. He is the author of *The Saltwater Angler's Guide to Florida's Big Bend and Emerald Coast*. As a journalist specializing in saltwater fishing, he has frequently contributed to such magazines as *Florida Sportsman* and *Shallow Water Angler*.

Wild Florida

Edited by M. Timothy O'Keefe

Books in this series are written for the many people who visit or move to Florida to participate in our remarkable outdoors, an environment rich in birds, animals, and activities, many exclusive to this state. Books in the series will offer readers a variety of formats: natural history guides, historical outdoor guides, guides to some of Florida's most popular pastimes and activities, and memoirs of outdoors folk and their unique lifestyles.

30 Eco-Trips in Florida: The Best Nature Excursions (and How to Leave Only Your Footprints), by Holly Ambrose (2005)

Hiker's Guide to the Sunshine State, by Sandra Friend (2005)

Fishing Florida's Flats: A Guide to Bonefish, Tarpon, Permit, and Much More, by Jan S. Maizler (2007)

50 Great Walks in Florida, by Lucy Beebe Tobias (2008)

Hiking the Florida Trail: 1,100 Miles, 78 Days, Two Pairs of Boots, and One Heck of an Adventure, by Johnny Molloy (2008)

The Complete Florida Beach Guide, by Mary and Bill Burnham (2008)

The Saltwater Angler's Guide to Florida's Big Bend and Emerald Coast, by Tommy L. Thompson (2009)

Secrets from Florida's Master Anglers, by Ron Presley (2009)

Exploring Florida's Botanical Wonders: A Guide to Ancient Trees, Unique Flora, and Wildflower Walks, by Sandra Friend (2010)

Florida's Fishing Legends and Pioneers, by Doug Kelly (2011)

Fishing Secrets from Florida's East Coast, by Ron Presley (2012)

The Saltwater Angler's Guide to Tampa Bay and Southwest Florida, by Tommy L. Thompson (2012)